CONSTRUCTIVISM AND COMPARATIVE POLITICS

DANIEL M. GREEN
EDITOR

M.E.Sharpe
Armonk, New York
London, England

The quote by Jim Morrison on p. 230 is from "The End," words and music by
The Doors, Copyright © 1967 by Doors Music Company, copyright renewed,
all rights reserved, used by permission.

Library of Congress Cataloging-in-Publication Data

Constructivism and comparative politics / by Daniel M. Green, editor.
 p. cm. — (International relations in a constructed world)
Includes bibliographical references and index.
 ISBN 0-7656-0860-X (cloth: alk. paper) — ISBN 0-7656-0861-8 (pbk.: alk. paper)
 1. International relations—Philosophy. 2. Constructivism (Philosophy)
3. Comparative government. I. Green, Daniel M., 1961- II. Series

JZ1253.C664 2001   2001049049
320.3—dc21   CIP

Printed in the United States of America

The paper used in this publication meets the minimum requirements of
American National Standard for Information Sciences
Permanence of Paper for Printed Library Materials,
ANSI Z 39.48-1984.

BM (c)   10   9   8   7   6   5   4   3   2   1
BM (p)   10   9   8   7   6   5   4   3   2   1

Table of Contents

About the Editor and Contributors

Kurt Burch is an associate professor in the Department of Political Science at St. Olaf College, Northfield, Minnesota. He is the author of *"Property" and the Making of the International System: Constituting Sovereignty, Political Economy, and Modernity* and many articles on international political economy and social theory.

Patricia M. Goff is an assistant professor in the Department of Political Science at the University of Utah. Her primary interest is in constructivist approaches to international political economy issues. Her most recent publication appeared in *International Studies Quarterly*.

Daniel M. Green is an associate professor in the Department of Political Science and International Relations at the University of Delaware. He is the author of several articles on the politics of neoliberal economic reform in Africa and on global waves of democratization in the twentieth century. His current project is a constructivist analysis of global order-building in World War I.

Rodney Bruce Hall is an assistant professor in the Department of Political Science at the University of Iowa. He is the author of *National Collective Identity: Social Constructs and International Systems* and coeditor of a forthcoming book on international private authority.

Patrick Thaddeus Jackson is an assistant professor of international relations in the School of International Service at American University. He is presently developing his dissertation, titled "Occidentalism: Rhetoric, Process, and Postwar German Reconstruction," into a book.

Bruce A. Magnusson is an assistant professor in the Department of Politics at Whitman College. He has published several articles on politics in Benin, most recently in *Comparative Politics*. His current book project concerns the construction of democratic legitimacy in contemporary Benin.

Daniel Nexon is a doctoral candidate in the Department of Political Science at Columbia University and is currently a MacArthur Consortium Fellow at the Center for International Security and Cooperation, Stanford University. His dissertation examines international political change in the context of the rise and decline of dynastic empires in early modern Europe.

Virginia Q. Tilley is an assistant professor in the Department of Political Science at Hobart and William Smith Colleges. She is author of a number of articles on ethnicity, indigenous peoples, politics, and ethnic dimensions of the international system. Her current research focuses on the political economy of indigenous ethnicity and the politics of ethnotourism in Latin America and East Asia.

Acknowledgments

This project began as two panels at a conference in Boston in November 1998. Since that time, we have all learned a great deal—about constructivism, about the interfaces between comparative politics and international relations, about our disciplinary strengths and weaknesses. We have especially learned from each other, in what has been a fruitful and stimulating cross-pollenization of e-mail exchanges, sharing of citations, and loud conversations in noisy restaurants. We would like to thank Vendulka Kubálková, Ralph Pettman, Patricia Kolb, and Bob Denemark for their help in bringing this project to fruition. And we thank Nick Onuf for his insightful comments on all our chapters. We hope this volume is a useful resource for comparativists rethinking their research perspectives, and for all political scientists contemplating transgressing the boundaries of their fields, their received categories, and their conventional wisdoms.

Part I
Theoretical Issues and Overview

1

Constructivist Comparative Politics: Foundations and Framework

Daniel M. Green

A whirlwind of unanticipated global changes and new analytical and metatheoretical developments in the social sciences have brought intellectual crisis and a soul-searching review of approaches, methods, and research questions to comparative politics (CP). These problems have left comparativists in a kind of internal impasse that threatens our identity as a field, its purpose and direction: "[c]omparative politics ... has lost its way."[1] Divisions, in a field that has always been spread thin to cover the world's regions and national political systems, may be deeper than ever before. On the one hand, comparativists are proud of their boundless eclecticism in topic and method, and their pragmatic habit of letting daily events dictate their research—a big tent that holds many (Kohli et al.1995). Yet conversely, this lack of a common ontology and of concern for broader social theoretic debates is also newly criticized, as theoretical infertility and stagnation (Lichbach and Zuckerman 1997). A significant portion of what many comparativists do, often counted as deeply historical and culturally adept "area studies" research, is under attack as both unscientific and unworthy of funding as government and university budgets tighten (Bates 1997; Johnson 1997). This in turn reflects a larger division between context-rich "idiopaths" and generalizing "nomothets." In this schism a rising "culturalist" trend has given qualitatively-oriented scholars new ammunition against other approaches. Yet others find that the threat from "postie" culturalism equals that of rational choice reductionism, trapping mainstream comparativists in the middle (e.g., Kohli et al. 1995).

The subject matter of mainstream comparative politics is quite familiar, and can be gleaned from the topics in comparative politics texts or from article titles in such leading journals as *Comparative Politics*, *Comparative Political Studies*, *Government and Opposition*, and *World Politics*: formal government institutions and their workings, elections, political parties, public policies and policy processes, group political conflict, impacts of economic change and political transformation. Much of comparative political analysis has always been problem-driven, tuned to the topic of the day: in the 1990s, concerned with the two major political phenomena of this decade, regime change as democratic transitions/consolidation and the political economy of liberalizing economic reform, in developed (decline of the welfare state) and developing (impact of International Monetary Fund/World Bank neoliberal reforms) countries. These topics are not somehow inappropriate or wrong-headed. But, while articles in the above journals rarely give indication of it, the traditional approaches and assumptions in the study of these topics are under profound challenge today. It is no longer advisable for comparativists to think and write within their tried and true analytic frames. Three challenges to traditional comparative politics are, if not completely novel, more evident and pressing than ever before, creating the opportunity for a new "constructivist" comparative politics.

Challenges to Traditional Comparative Politics

A Globalized World

First, the pace of global economic and sociocultural integration has greatly increased since 1945, and especially in the last two decades, such that the classic unit of comparativist analysis, the insular sovereign state, is no more. Political and economic globalization increasingly challenge the state on several grounds. International market forces have grown stronger than ever, challenging states in policy areas from exchange rates to taxation and fiscal expenditure policies (Cerny 1995). A tremendous expansion in the number and influence of nonstate actors has reduced state privilege and power in international fora. While the state retains a considerable degree of agency in many areas, and is in no danger of disappearing completely, these changes diminish the state's capacity for autonomous policy making and invalidate old conceptualizations of the insular national polity and the domestic-international boundary (Armstrong 1998; Axford 1995; Jarvis and Paolini 1995; Lyons and Mastanduno 1995; McGrew and Lewis et al. 1992). These changes have also affected "domestic" political identities, patterns of contestation and policy debates, away from left-right class politics to a new identity politics and a new set of issues on national agendas, concerning free trade, protectionism, immigration, minority rights, religious identities, and political decentralization (Cable 1995).

Secondly, one is struck by the increasing synchronicity of political and economic change across polities. Events clustered around 1989 alone are extraordinary, with a wave of countries newly created, dozens of democratic transitions, the sputtering to life of numerous ethnic conflicts and breakdown of several multiethnic states. These are ever more powerful evidence of a global sociopolitical system which, regularly and throughout history, ripples with pulses of change affecting many or all countries at once; as if national polities are in fact cells of a larger entity with a life all its own.[2]

Both the above realizations have led many international relations scholars to the conclusion that there has been a fundamental system change at the global level, a transition from an *international* system of interactions between insular states to a world best viewed as a *global social system*. This social system is ordered and governed by the interactions of states, international organizations, international nongovernmental organizations and numerous networks of communication between them. Order is also provided by the special collectively held principles and standards that guide, prohibit, and render actions appropriate, *norms*.

For comparativists trying to conduct their research and analysis in this new world, broader systemic processes appear just as significant and relevant to comparativist concerns, if not more so, than the details of national events. What should comparativists do in response? Some suggest a need to rethink the entire "metageography" of comparative politics (Jackson and Nexon, chapter 3 of this volume). Social relations have so transcended local and national spaces that a new paradigm for comparative politics is needed. This book argues that two steps need to be taken. First, comparativists need to take seriously the global environment of supposedly "national" processes, and develop a theorized understanding of it as, for example, one with state-centered polities that are relatively boundless, deeply integrated into many circles of power with authority and political processes at several layers of interaction.[3] Second, once they have a grasp of the dynamics of the global sociopolitical system, comparativists need to incorporate it into all their analyses at all points, not as single external shocks but as an ongoing social influence.

An Interpretivist Revolution

Further, there have been very important theoretical developments in the social sciences in recent years, which, for convenience, can be lumped together as *interpretivism* (a category that includes postmodern, culturalist, and "constructionist" approaches). Interpretivism challenges rationalist methodology and neopositivist epistemology—that is, what we need to look at and what we can find out in analysis. It restates the challenge to positivist notions of an objective, natural world, perhaps appropriate in the natural sciences, but not in the human sciences. Instead, interpretivism insists on the centrality of human interpretation, perception, and cognition to explain any action, and therefore to all analysis in the social sciences, and certainly in mainstream CP.[4]

Interpretivism/culturalism is especially valuable as it offers an improved means of answering one of the quintessential social sciences questions: Where do the reasons, preferences, and interests that inspire action come from? This is problematic for many political scientists, who typically hold preferences to be exogenous, fixed, and probably material (Wildavsky 1987), as in most materialist (political economy, Marxist approaches) and utilitarian (rational choice) accounts of action: Actors always seek material wealth; actors always seek political power. After interpretivism, many argue that rationalism is trumped by the need to first determine preferences and goals, which are contextual and socially constructed (Grenstad and Selle 1995; Wildavsky 1987, 1994).[5]

Interpretivism implies an essential methodological shift in that, to aid in understanding action when we cannot assume interests, new factors or "variables" must be brought in, and assumptions about the nature of old elements questioned. Actors have *identities*, worldviews, and cognitive frames, informed by *culture*, that shape perception and interests. While culturalist approaches are not particularly popular in comparative politics today (Ross 1997), there is a growing sense that we must explore the construction of interests, motives, and intentions within complex contexts of cultural codes and norms. The argument is not that rationalist, materialist, and utilitarian motivations are not possible, only that they must not be assumed.

To many, the turn to culture and identity is also a timely and necessary reflection of daily events. Especially since the end of the cold war, polities new and old have suffered through what were once hoped to be bygone atavisms—extreme nationalism, the horrific neologism of "ethnic cleansing," and genocide (Tilley, chapter 5 of this volume). These are conflicts based not especially on material interests (and suitable to a purely political-economy analysis, perhaps), but a new "identity" politics, challenging analysts to explore the worldviews and mindsets of these actors, to understand action. While attention has centered on ethnic identities, nationalism, and conflict processes, it is also clear that identity in all its senses, given its inherent connection to interests and action, is an essential dimension to any analysis. This also implies that whole swathes of analyses based on assumed "natural" interests must be called into question, revisited, and revised.[6]

A companion of interpretivism's problematization and contextualization is the notion of "constructionism," the idea that most sociopolitical phenomena are constructed by human social interaction and the resultant shared understandings of their value and meaning, as opposed to being naturally occurring. Constructionism has cropped up in a variety of areas of study and disciplines (Hacking 1999), and is not necessarily revolutionary to comparativist work, since most things political scientists study—law, money, power, political office, social structures—are socially constructed. The more useful, even liberating, implication of constructionism is that social categories and kinds are not natural or obvious, and need to be questioned (hence constructionism's critical element).

Finally, within the broad rubric of constructionism lies the specific approach of *constructivism* that this book is devoted to. Constructivism as defined here combines the "social construction of everything" with a metatheoretical device for understanding the process of construction and theorizing about it, the agent-structure relation. This variety of constructionism has appeared in a new sociological institutionalism, in some of political science's historical institutionalism, and in constructivist international relations (CIR). While this distinction between constructionism and constructivism does not hold across all disciplines, it communicates the way many constructivists in political science use the term, as incorporating a deliberate sensitivity to the agent-structure problem and debates about the construction process, the co-constitution of agent and structure, more broadly.[7]

New Metatheoretical Sophistication

The challenge posed by interpretivist insights, social constructionism, and other factors has also shaken up many social scientists in terms of what they think and how they think. At an extreme, traditional Enlightenment epistemology is questioned by a new postmodern antifoundationalism, in which truth claims cannot be judged, all theories are stories about an unknowable world, the world of texts, to be deconstructed to reveal the inequities of power and domination. From more centrist positions as well, scholars in many disciplines of the newly reflexive academy have become more familiar with the issues and vocabulary of ontology, epistemology, and philosophy of science and adept at attacking the underlying suppositions of rival perspectives. The move to metatheory may not be an enthusiastic one for many, but is increasingly unavoidable, as attacks upon metatheoretical presuppositions can be fatally convincing. (Indeed it has largely been the devastating metatheoretical challenges of constructivism in international relations, for example, that explains the perspective's overnight ascent in that field [Dessler 1999: 123].)

Comparativists as a whole have dealt with epistemological and metatheoretical debates with caution and a measure of disdain, preferring a pragmatic, problem-driven style (Kohli et al. 1995). We tend to aim for issue-specific "middle-range theory," based on materialist, instrumentalist logics of action and neopositivist scientific goals that go unexamined. To be sure, comparativists have not shied entirely away from controversies among their core research programs, described as structuralist, culturalist, and rationalist by Lichbach and Zuckerman (1997). These confrontations can be seen in many places in the literature (e.g., Hall 1986; Koelble 1995; Kohli et al. 1995; Pontusson 1995; Taylor 1989; Wildavsky 1987, 1994). But these rarely go deeper. Most comparativists do not bring metatheory, epistemology and ontology into their writing on given topics; hence Lichbach's anguished "[c]an a discipline mature if no one specializes in its ideas?" (1997: 240, fn2). It is even more accurate to say that when comparativists do venture into such areas, their bibliographies are full largely of noncomparativist citations. Comparative debates on these issues mostly revolve around methods within a neopositivist epistemology, in controversies over, for example, qualitative versus cross-national quantitative approaches, fights against the simplifications of rational choice and formal modeling, and others. These fights assume that the big epistemological questions are answered, when they are not. Above all, there remains little in the way of "CP theory," in the way that there is such a wealth of "IR theory."

This situation has prevented comparativists from benefiting from developments such as the agent-structure debate mentioned above. Only very recently and tentatively has CP begun to link itself to this analytic device (Hall and Taylor 1998; Hay and Wincott 1998; Katznelson 1997; Lichbach 1997; Rothstein 1992), one which casts the world in terms of actors and their structured environments and is commonly identified as the central problem in social and political theory. The agent-structure metaphor points to the problem of how actors and their environments affect each other, and to the famous resolution of this issue in the "structurationist" notion of Anthony Giddens that agents and structure must be given equal ontological status, as co-constituted or co-determined, in an interactive process. This metaphor can inform comparativist theorizing and act as a guidepost to theory building, on the proper balance between structure and individual action in explanation, theories of agency, the status of intermediaries between agent and structure such as norms and rules, culture as context and the constitution of identities, and so forth.

The time is ripe for comparative politics to renew and invigorate its links to core debates in the rest of the social sciences. Given where others outside comparative politics in parts of sociology and international relations have gone with these challenges, comparative political scientists are well advised to engage more fully with metatheory and the fundamentals of social theory that underlay all our work, to ask and answer tough questions.[8] The present *agenda* conjuncture suggests that to improve explanation and understanding of political processes, comparativists need to: (a) adopt a research perspective amenable to the boundary-crossing flux of the late modern world, which incorporates the extra-national fully into comparativist work; (b) engage with social theory and the agent-structure debate as a path to improved theorizing; and (c) incorporate interpretivist concerns as a means of problematizing old assumptions about actors and political action. These lead us to constructivist comparative politics (CCP).

Toward a "Constructivist" Comparative Politics

What should a "constructivist comparative politics" look like? The goal is an analytic framework, incorporating the interpretivist revolution, that is adept at examining sociopolitical change in the late modern world and that places the state/polity/society in a larger, and theorized, global-systemic and historical context. To better understand and appreciate a CCP approach, the rest of this chapter first lays out CCP's basics by discussing some appropriate positions on theory and methodology, ontology, and epistemology, taking care to accommodate a range of perspectives. The chapter then reviews some of the literature in comparative politics in the last two decades that shows the development of constructivist tendencies in the field.

Theoretical and Methodological Basics

From the outset, CCP can be distinguished from much of comparativist work by its differing theoretical and methodological positions, about the way research should be conducted and the relevant elements to be incorporated into analysis. For CCP, these are along interpretivist and transnational themes, plus a sensitivity to the agent-structure relation. As *interpretivist*, CCP is convinced of the value of intersubjectivisms for understanding actors and action and fully incorporates many such elements, including identity, culture, worldviews and cognitive frames, norms, principles, and ideas. Depending on the individual scholar's ontological positions, full interpretivism may mean that political life is "ideas all the way down." More proximately, culture variables may be mediated by contestation and structures of greater fixity, including formal political and economic institutions.

As *transnationalist*, CCP drops the "internal/external" barrier between state and international system that is often assumed in comparative analysis; CCP transnationalizes all comparativist inquiry.[9] It adopts a view of the world of countries as a global social system, of overlapping webs of social interaction and politics. It in particular seizes on the constructivist international relations notion of systemic *norms* as a means of mapping the cultural structure of the global system and the context of "domestic" politics.

Finally, CCP seeks to encourage comparativists to engage with social theory and metatheory and use the agent-structure debate as an analytic tool when appropriate. Sensitivity to the agent-structure duality and the proper balance between the two in explanation also allows one to anticipate a host of theoretical and methodological problems and pitfalls, and avoid them (Wendt 1987). For example, it has become very difficult to sustain a purely structuralist position, as the storm around Skocpol's 1979 book on social revolutions or a lesser controversy over the world polity school (Finnemore 1996a) demonstrate.[10] In addition, some comparativists have simply sought to use the agent-structure relation as an analytic diagnostic tool (Lichbach 1997, Mahoney and Snyder 1999), and to good effect. Mahoney and Snyder (1999) use it to categorize and dissect theories of democratic transition; Mark Lichbach (1998), to discuss the strengths and weaknesses of rationalist and political opportunity structure approaches to protest movements. Lichbach (1997) has also used agent-structure language to create the "socially embedded unit act," which offers a common meta-framework for uniting structuralist, culturalist, and rationalist comparative politics. Others are focused on the agent-structure relation itself. Hay and Wincott (1998) suggest, for example, that comparativist historical institutionalists have, unwittingly, formulated an improved perspective on the agent-structure problem that captures the enabling and constraining effects of structure and the bounded-strategic nature of agency.

Ontology

Any discussion of a new constructivist comparative politics must also discuss ontology and epistemology. It is sometimes argued to take up ontology first, since our positions here will considerably determine epistemology (Wendt 1999; Patomäki and Wight 2000). Ontological claims are statements about what the world is made of; what are the entities that populate our analytic world and what is their nature?[11] Ontological positions can range from the real and natural to "extreme ontological skepticism." The realist, natural position common to the natural sciences holds that the world is composed of facts that exist regardless of human apprehension. Things in the natural world have linear and determined relationships among variables, even mechanistic "clocklike patterns" (Almond and Genco 1977; Zuckerman 1997). By contrast, the skeptic position is a social ontology and at the extreme is pure subjectivism: Nothing exists unless humans are there to perceive it. Choice of ontology has strong implications for the kind of science one can do, and for methods.

Presently, comparativist positions on ontology are multiple and somewhat confused (see Hall 2001). It is generally agreed, on the other hand, that constructivists embrace what has been termed an idealist "ontology of becoming," of emergence, of entities in flux rather than the substantialist natural position. Comparativists and CCP must take this path, that the world is socially constructed by actors creating intersubjective meanings (culture, norms, common understandings) through interaction in a community. In this sense, the "structure" of the social world is ideas. Constructed social practices shape cognition, judgment, and action. Beliefs and expectations largely determine the character of social life. They provide the meaning with which actors understand the so-called material world and develop material interests. (This ontology also cohabits nicely with concern for agent-structure relations, co-constitution, and the details of how co-constitution occurs.)

What is often described as the midpoint alternative between a radical skepticism and natural science objectivism is the popular position taken by Alexander Wendt and others, of scientific realism. Indeed, this is one of the reasons Wendt takes this position, since it allows any epistemological position to be taken subsequently, though it favors neopositivism (1999). If social kinds are made real, then we can be more positivist in epistemology. This is probably the more comfortable position for mainstream comparativists, but, as discussed below and in the chapters by Jackson and Nexon in this book, an ontology of becoming does not necessarily sit well with neopositivism.

Epistemology

Several epistemological labels are available to us: positivist, neopositivist, postpositivist, scientific realist, interpretivist, intersubjectivist, postmodern. All are different statements about the scientific goals of analysis and the kind of knowledge and level of "truth" that can result. At issue are our theory-building goals and whether we take a highly positivist, deductive-nomological path. Or is general theory and causal explanation impossible in the open-ended systems of human affairs? From a naturalist ontology one would logically adopt a positivist epistemology that mimics expectations in the natural sciences, seeking general laws of the human world, causal understanding of relationships between variables, and "explanations" of events and outcomes.

But what are the implications of our social "ontology of becoming"? Several epistemological positions are found among scholars who consider themselves constructivists. Some argue that a culturalist-constructivist perspective requires an "interpretative epistemology" (Hollis and Smith 1994). Others are more noncommittal on the issue: "[c]onstructivism effectively leaves epistemology to the philosophers" (Kubálková, Onuf, and Kowert 1998: 19). Yet a constructivist ontology of becoming should not be adopted without repercussions for mainstream comparativists' neopositivist epistemological goals. Most comparativists currently take a position of mild positivism. Even if we don't avowedly seek broad general laws, we do our case study work with an eye to contributing to such efforts. There are some important interior positions. Dessler (1999), for example, reminds us that positivists need not all be searching for general laws, but can simply seek "reconstructive" explanations that explain a single outcome. Wendt's own scientific realist position is a median one as well.

I examine these issues in greater detail later. For now, it can be said that epistemological positioning is a major issue dividing constructivists, and it would be impolitic to insist upon one position here. Nonetheless, a bare core of statements constructivist comparativists might agree upon include, first, that the goal of investigation is causal *and* constitutive explanation *and* understanding,[12] through thick description and analytic dissection of processes. Second, CCP, true to its comparativist roots, should also seek to produce compelling concepts that can be applied to and illuminate phenomena across cases. Third, CCP is sensitive to the possibility of more generalizable conclusions, beyond the specificities of case studies.

The above positions constitute first steps into constructivism, ones which all the essays in this book take. The path beyond them is open, and some alternatives are discussed in the next section.

Further Comments on Ontology and Epistemology

The merging of standard comparativist work with culturalist methods and constructivism must be done carefully, as the modifications and additions could easily send mainstream comparativists and the important questions they address into fruitless confusion. Caution necessitates some further elaboration of CCP's relation to the above points, to debates over epistemology and ontology that preoccupy much constructivist writing—born of metatheory to a newly reflexive academy, constructivists may never get the lid back on this Pandora's box. I address some of these issues here, but cannot resolve them. Indeed, the emerging conclusion to these debates appears to be a tense pluralism. No position can honestly claim unchallenged superiority, leading some to advocate tolerance of epistemological and ontological diversity. But many deny that all positions are equal, so the fighting between them continues. What we can say is that work that is ignorant and oblivious of its ontological and epistemological assumptions and the tensions between them is vulnerable; these issues are no longer easily dismissed.[13]

Though several labels and perspectives are available, our epistemological choices are usually presented as a set of binary opposites: the natural world versus the social world, regularities and universal laws versus context and specificity, explanation versus understanding, linear versus nonlinear relationships, causal versus constitutive relationships, outsider versus insider perspectives, "why" questions versus "how possible" questions, expectability versus intelligibility, substantialism versus flux, emergence, and a process orientation. Positivist social science is nomothetic, seeking general explanations and asking "why" questions of simple causality, much as do the natural sciences. It assumes exteriority; "outsiders" examine the social world as a natural world, seeking to explain its workings with lawlike generalizations. Interpretivist or culturalist inquiry, conversely, does not seek general explanation, but rather takes an "insider's" interest in understanding the meanings of events. Generalizing is almost impossible, since each "case" is inherently different. It asks "how" or "how-possible" questions about how systems are constituted, how the properties of something can be. By this account, interpretivists, convinced of the uniqueness of perceptions, can only find difference and particularity.

When described as polar opposites, the choice of an epistemological position is not an easy one. Neopositivists typically attack interpretivism for its baggage of extreme relativism, antifoundationalism, and rejection of the possibility of a social science. One of its dangers is the "hermeneutic circle" of continuous interpretation and deconstruction of everything. From this perspective there is no reality at all, only texts to be analyzed. Conversely, opponents of neopositivism find huge problems in its application to the social world. Many argue that neopositivist expectations of discreteness and linear relationships between variables makes neopositivism impossible for all comparativists (Almond and Genco 1977; Hall 2001; Jackson and Nexon, chapter 3 of this volume; Zuckerman 1997). Getting to even midrange causal generalizations is probably going to be done only at the sacrifice of the contextual details many comparativists care deeply about.

A way out of the dilemma of epistemological absolutisms is offered by the variety of median, compromise positions on various points that try to "square the circle," hopefully without sacrificing integrity and internal consistency. Max Weber, for example, long ago made the case for allowing explanation *and* understanding in the social world (Crotty 1998). Among comparativists, King, Keohane, and Verba have lent their weight to this position as well in, for example, their discussion of descriptive inference (1994).

Constructivists in IR have been articulating median positions as well. Wendt is emblematic here, confessing that in ontology he is an interpretivist, and in epistemology he leans positivist (1999). Wendt does this by embracing scientific realism as his ontology, which makes social kinds "real" and therefore allows normal science in epistemology. He also echoes Weber, arguing that any social scientist is actually interested in arriving at both explanation and understanding of a given phenomenon and needs both, that constitutive stories are also in part causal and explanatory. David Dessler points out that there are at least two kinds of "explanation" within positivism—predictive and reconstructive—and the latter is a variety much more in accordance with the limited scientific goals of interpretivists (1999). A further argument for synthesis is the point some critics of postpositivism make, that a postpositivist epistemology cannot really be said to exist, in full form at least, since almost all postmodern analyses make arguments that deploy evidence to convince the reader of the veracity of a set of arguments (Wendt 1998, 1999; Wight 1999; Patomäki and Wight 2000).[14] Patomäki and Wight argue for epistemological pluralism (2000).

The overarching question is how tight must the fit between ontology and epistemology (and methodology) be? On this there is little real agreement, but a growing sense of do's and don'ts. For some, median positions completely unravel around the argument to combine both explanation and understanding (Hollis and Smith 1990; Smith 2000). Recently, Peter Hall has advanced an argument about these incompatibilities, addressed specifically at comparativists (Hall 2001). He argues that innovations in comparativist ontologies in the past twenty years have gone well beyond and become incompatible with currently popular methodologies, which are increasingly rationalist and/or quantitative and employ regression analysis. Instead, current ontologies and their concomitant conceptualizations of possible causal relations are more compatible with small-N structured comparisons and "systematic process analysis," which better unlocks understandings of causality. In short, a sense of ontological developments must cause us to revisit our methods. Though it hearkens back to the old quantitative-qualitative split, Hall's discussion is a model for comparativists to follow, engaging as it does with broader metatheoretical precepts to clarify contradictions that hamper comparativist work. A new sensitivity to tensions between ontology and method would be useful across the field. Lichbach and Zuckerman's (1997) concluding chapters, for example, look to ways for "creative confrontation" between their three paradigms, but fail to elaborate on the epistemological and ontological tensions and incompatibilities this might entail, and how these can be resolved. Admittedly this is a very difficult task, but we need to progress further through these issues.

Another objectionable element to CCP might be the argument to adopt constructionism and culturalism but temper them with a somewhat positivistic dissection of processes, to uncover causal and constitutive mechanisms. In effect, this would mean engaging comparative work with social theory, but on comparativists' traditional neopositivist terms. This may prove popular. Debates about structure and agency are mind numbing to some, and seemingly distant from politics itself (Hall and Taylor 1998). Therefore, for some comparativists, pulling back to what might be called a "late modern" science position is important. For example, Jepperson, Wendt, and Katzenstein assert that all work in their *The Culture of National Security* (1996) is within "modern science." They argue that their coauthors simply seek to identify and investigate new factors and processes that others had overlooked, to improve explanation.

We have seen that some would object to analytic pragmatisms as fundamentally contradictory and impossible, and there is reason for caution. But constructivism itself is a delicate compromise in the middle on these issues. As Emanuel Adler (1997) asserts, "the true middle ground between rationalist and relativist interpretive approaches is occupied neither by an interpretive version of rationalism, nor by some variety of 'reflectivism' . . . but by constructivism" (322). Similarly, constructivism is said to save us from epistemological excess: "[C]onstructivism is a constructive response to the challenge of the 'post' movement. It rejects the 'slash-and-burn' extremism of some post-modern thinkers. . . . While constructivists join the 'post' movement in calling into question much of the orthodoxy of postwar IR scholarship, they reject neither empirical research nor social science as such. Instead, constructivism maintains that the sociopolitical world is constructed by human practice, and seeks to explain how this construction takes place" (Kubálková, Onuf, and Kowert 1998: 20).

If we think of positivist and interpretive epistemologies as opposite ends of a spectrum, there is space in the middle for a necessary dialogue about their component positions, combinations, and compromises. This is a logical position for CCP to take, for both explanation and understanding, as it would be difficult to fully incorporate the global social system into analysis (and be attentive to sociological institutionalism's puzzle of isomorphism) and not also be tempted by the possibility of generalization. Advancing beyond caricatures of neopositivism and interpretivism to median positions may smooth ruffled feathers, but opens us up to simply constructing whatever set of precepts validates what we do already. At this stage the writing on these issues tends toward casual eclecticism and makes only the grossest incompatibilities among epistemological, ontological, and methodological positions evident. If CCP's positions are at present contradictory, they are representative of the compromises made in constructivism today.

Other, "later" modern and postmodern constructivisms offer alternative routes beyond "modern" interpretivist social science. Postmodern constructivists, for example, have taken their interpretivism closer to the relativistic, antifoundational side of the spectrum, adding a semiotic, linguistic turn and a critical Foucauldian bent, concentrating on "the sociohistorical conditions under which language, meaning and social power interact" (Price and Reus-Smit 1998: 269). Their substantive subjects include the construction of meanings of sovereignty, of the cold war, the Gulf War, and so forth.

Another "later" modern alternative is the relational, processual approach discussed at length in chapters by Jackson and Nexon in this volume. Relationalism's target is "substantialism." It insists upon a fundamental shift from analysis of neatly bounded entities and their essentialized properties, to the relations and ties between actors which constitute these actors and their many dimensions. The things social scientists focus upon, such as character and interests of actors and their actions, are the product of ongoing social interactions. Relationalists emphasize the relational production of multiple identities, the ways in which actors hold multiple identities depending on the interaction in question, and the various structural and discursive contexts that provide the frames for judging and understanding action. Everything is context specific. From a relationalist perspective, the oddity is not change, but apparent fixity or "arrestation" of entities in perpetual flux. (The appearance of arrestation is what deceives us into assuming that stable entities with stable identities exist.)

Though highly complex in its contextualization and purist problematization of entitivity, relationalism's ontology and accompanying epistemology are more neopositivist than postpositivist and certainly pull back from full postmodern interpretivism. There is causality and empirics. Once analysts adopt a new focus—on positionality, causal mechanisms, path dependence, discourse—a vaguely more positivistic normal science investigation can proceed. Indeed, the break with substantialism is especially useful and interesting to mainstream social scientists *because* it is a way of avoiding the things about postmodernism that scare many of them. The postie "abyss" as some have termed it, is avoided by this move beyond holism—agency, structure, constitutive processes are analytically broken up instead.

It should be said that there are scholars doing very much the kind of work proposed here. There are, for example, approaches to studying political change and individual analyses which fully incorporate external influences as cultural scripts, near structural *diktats*, to explain "isomorphism" across polities (the Stanford School of sociological institutionalism of John Boli, John Meyer, Francisco Ramirez, and George Thomas; Finnemore 1996b). Some go a step further, treating their cases in terms of clashing, mutating politico-cultural scripts, external and internal (Mamdani 1996; Rueschmeyer and Skocpol 1996; Skocpol 1992; Sohrabi 1999). But two caveats. First, few of these scholars are comparative political scientists—comparativists are too unaf-fected by the important insights mentioned above. Second, proto-CCP writings are rarely systematized within a larger conceptual and theoretical frame. They are unaware of debates in social theory that demand increasing episte-mological and ontological specificity and exposition, and metatheoretical testing. Bringing a transnational constructivism into comparative politics, CCP seeks to address these concerns.

The rest of this chapter deals (of necessity, far too briefly) with substantive areas any new comparativist framework must come to grips with—culture, identity, order in a global social system, and concepts and general processes from social theory. This draws from the following literatures: culturalist comparative politics, the new institutionalisms in sociology and political science, the new social movements literature, the "world polity" school of sociological institutionalism, and constructivist international relations. More specifically, I examine first a broadly drawn literature on approaches to *culture* and its effects on political behavior, processes, and outcomes, including a policies-as-culture perspective; group and organizational cultures, drawn from the new institutionalisms in sociology and political science; new social movements; and constructivist IR theory. Second, I review a literature on the *identities* of political actors—individual and collective—as represented in work on national and state identity, new social movements, and other identity groups. Third, I look at work on the national/international world as one *global social system*, the transnational propagation of policy, culture, and order through systemic norms, from the "world polity" perspective as well as constructivist IR. Finally, themes and issues in epistemology and metatheory will appear throughout, including reference to issues of causality, standards and strategies of explanation, concerns about agency, structure, their interrelations and co-constitution, and so forth.

Four Sources of Constructivist Comparative Politics

This section examines those topical literatures and analytic approaches within or about comparative political topics whose insights bring us to it. From structuralisms, our interest is in understandings of structure and co-constitution; from culture literatures, I discuss how cultural elements are integrated and the uses of cultural explanations; from the identity literatures, I am interested in how notions of identity are used in analyses and how they are integrated with other elements; and from transnational literatures, I seek approaches to transnationalizing comparative politics. In none of the four areas discussed below will I begin at the beginning—not with Weber, Marx, Durkheim, Montesqieu, or others. Rather, the attempt is to skim the surface of several recent literatures along four themes central to CCP, to better understand some of the current positions of comparativists on each.

Structuralisms: Historical Institutionalism and Beyond

Ira Katznelson (1997) has described structuralism as macroanalytic grand theory, noting that it was especially hallowed in the 1960s and 1970s, stretching from Barrington Moore (1966) to Theda Skocpol (1979). As it developed in the 1970s, comparative's structuralism became state-centric, and the state theory of the 1980s appeared a contrast to previous society-centered analysis and interest group approaches. The new insight was that policy processes and outcomes were shaped by the state and bureaucrats, by administrative preferences, the existence and creation of particular government agencies, and so forth (Skocpol and Finegold 1982). Thus bureaucracies were newly treated as actors with interests. This also meant that, as explored by sociological institutionalists, policy making should now be seen as subject to bounded rationality and organizational-cultural influences (Meyer and Rowan 1977; March and Olsen 1984).

Comparative's structuralism has become more complex and inclusive over the years, transmuting into historical institutionalism and also a relatively nondeterminist macrostructuralism—"configurationalism"—that combines the precision of historical institutionalists with attention to large-scale processes (Katznelson 1997). From three structure-oriented schools, one can discern three developments that contribute to a constructivist comparative politics: co-constitution of actors and structures in historical institutionalism; a complex, multidimensional rendering of structure in configurationalism; and an advanced transnational notion of structure in the new social movement literature on "opportunity structures."

Structure and Co-Constitution in Historical Institutionalism

At their most cautious, analysts in comparative's historical institutionalism allow that institutional structures of the state affect preexisting actors. This insight was significant mainly as an addition to standard interest-group approaches—institutional structure matters, refracting interests through channels of access to power, for example.

The next logical step in analysis was to suggest the potential for institutions to actually create or constitute actors, a line of argument that would eventually lead historical institutionalism to address agent-structure issues on abstract theoretical grounds, and to dabble in co-constitution analysis. For example, Weir and Skocpol (1985) point out how different agricultural policy regimes in Sweden and the United States in the 1930s mobilized some farmers and not others. Haggard (1988: 93) notes how the shifting of American trade policy toward the executive branch in the 1930s weakened the power of protectionists and provided a spur to export-oriented industries to organize more fully and form associations. Similarly, Skocpol (1992) finds that, in general, policies restructure subsequent political processes. In other words, policies are not simply maintained by an existing array of forces and interests: They may have generated those forces and interests in the first place.

Beyond the notion of institutions constituting actors is a still further step, to limited structurationism and co-constitution: formal institutions, informal institutions, and ideas mobilize social groups and create actors, their interests, and their goals, but actors also create their institutional and ideational environments. This work amounts to a "limited" structurationism in that it does not embrace full interpretivism and the "social construction of everything." Nonetheless, it is an important midstep, one most mainstream comparativists are likely to feel comfortable with and should certainly be attentive to, for application in their own work.

Comparativists who embrace this co-constitution dynamic are few. An early example is the work of Philip Cerny, a specialist in French politics who in 1990 authored a breakthrough book of comparative political theory, *The Changing Architecture of Politics.* Cerny is heavily influenced by Anthony Giddens and uses agent-structure language and structurationism from the outset. As a structurationist, Cerny acknowledges that structure is both enabling and constraining, and has constitutive effects. He provides elaborate explanations of structure and the ways in which structure shapes actions, a discussion that allows him to incorporate comparativist work on pluralism, corporatism, and markets. Cerny also spends much time on the state, as a special, privileged structure with positional advantages—at the juncture between the domestic and the external—which have reinforced its power.

Other work in historical institutionalism and comparative labor politics began to take the next step into limited co-constitution of agents and structures. For example, Kathleen Thelen's study of Germany's system of labor relations describes this system as featuring "dynamic constraints": Actors are constrained by institutions and policies, but also act to manipulate the function and impacts of institutions and thus reshape structure (1991: 23). She emphasizes that the meaning and utility or function of institutions can change over time, and that politics is not just within institutions, but also about them.

A landmark in comparativist historical institutionalism, Steinmo, Thelen, and Longstreth's *Structuring Politics* (1992), is among the first treatments of co-constitution as well, and employs the agent-structure lens to some utility. Thelen and Steinmo highlight a limited co-constitution in the observation that institutions "can shape and constrain political strategies in important ways, but they are themselves also the outcome (conscious or unintended) of deliberate political strategies, of political conflict, and of choice" (1992: 10). And in Rothstein's chapter (1992) we find explicit use of agent-structure language, focusing on the agent-to-structure vector and what he argues is the crucial moment of institutional creation. His case discusses how actors (labor unions and movements) design institutions to give them advantage in future power games, as well as dealing with the impact of political institutions and public policy on the subsequent actions of agents.

Historical institutionalism (HI) has become fairly sophisticated in its treatment of agent, structure, and co-constitution. In fact, HI recently has been praised as a significant advancement upon rationalist and sociological institutionalist approaches in its handling of the agent-structure relationship, offering a solution to the question of balance between the two in analysis and explanation (Hay and Wincott 1998). Hay and Wincott find it has a workable approach to the agent-structure problem in that in HI actors are strategic; they seek to achieve contingent and changing goals, but within a context that favors some strategies over others, which they navigate based upon perceptions.

Configurationalism and Relationalist Sociology

Another important development from structure-oriented political science and elsewhere is the advanced structuralism of "configurationalism," which comments upon issues of co-constitution, accounts of agency, critiques of standard social science method, and the incorporation of cultural variables. Ira Katznelson (1997) has described recent, advanced historical institutionalism, beginning perhaps with Theda Skocpol's book of 1992, as a qualitatively different "configurationalist macroanalysis" that is more expansively historical and less finely focused than institutionalisms. Skocpol provides a wonderfully elaborate representation of agent-structure dynamics, plus interpretivist concerns with cultural elements such as policy cultures, worldviews, and identities which are used to flesh out context and illuminate reasons for action. Configurationalists avoid structural determinism with the "how possible" line of argumentation and an epistemological shift. In fact, configurationalism has greatly reduced ambitions for any kind of structural arguments, claims to causality, or sweeping narratives, offering instead a deeply inductive approach that can "reconstruct and plot over time and space the ontological narratives and relationships of historical actors, the public and cultural narratives that inform their lives, and the crucial intersection of these narratives with other relevant social forces" (Somers 1992: 604–605, cited in Katznelson 1997: 96). Configurational macroanalysis situates institutions as "middle-level mediations between large-scale processes and the microdynamics of agency and action" (Katznelson 1997: 84). Configurationalism is very much inspired by "relationalism" in sociology (Emirbayer 1997; Somers 1992, 1998), whose accounts of structure are still more elaborate and flexible and warrant discussion as relationalism makes its way into constructivist IR and in the chapters included in this volume by Patrick Jackson and Daniel Nexon.

It seems that the more interpretivist one becomes in epistemology and the more constructivist one becomes in ontology, the more structure—and certainly simple versions of it—disappears. Relationalists find structure to have qualities of both fixity and flux, but understandings of its character and dimensions vary. Structure in the crude sense of stabilized economic or social conditions (as commonly understood in comparativist work before the new institutionalisms) drops almost completely out of relationalist writing (a hugely powerful statement in itself). Relationalist accounts of structure-like qualities so disaggregate them and are so finely drawn that the word loses its meaning. "[S]tructures are empty abstractions apart from the several elements of which they are composed" (Emirbayer 1997: 287–288). Instead, relationalism is replete with contingency, and so relationalists speak of "patternings," "conjunctures," and "settings," all to communicate great fluidity and complexity of connections between networks and loose categories of practices—the political, social, cultural, and economic.

Margaret Somers's work on the appearance of citizenship identity and working class formation in medieval and early modern England (e.g., 1993), for example, has structural elements similar to standard historical institutionalism, yet steps far beyond this. She uses other terms to describe a kind of background context, such as "relational setting"—that is, "a patterned matrix of institutional relationships among cultural, economic, social, and political practices" (1993: 595; also 1992). "[I]nstitutional and relational clusters" are her focus, "in which people, power and organization are positioned and connected" (1993: 595). These interactional networks do not have hard, material structured properties. But institutions are acknowledged and have structural properties. Phenomena such as changes in the law in a public sphere, for example, do perform as if they are structural changes, much as they would in any institutional analysis, though they work themselves out to have varied effects because of flaws, bubbles, and holes in interaction networks.

In sum, constructivist comparativists can tap into at least two accounts of structure, depending on their ontological proclivities: configurational or relational.

"Political Opportunity Structure" in the Social Movements Literature

A different but interesting and transnationalized treatment of structure is found in the new social movement (NSM) literature, one of the most thoroughly developed literatures and analytic approaches of any under consideration here, densely populated by sociologists, but also including political scientists (Krieger 1999; Tarrow 1994, 1996). This literature's treatment of structure as "political opportunity structure" greatly expands upon many understandings of structure. It displays a sensitivity to agent-structure issues, uses structure loosely, as both enabling and constraining, and is pragmatic in that it is replete with examples of the practical use of the agent-structure relation without exploring the depths of the agent-structure debate itself.

Opportunity structures are multifaceted, covering almost any environmental or contextual feature that might shape, enable, or constrain collective action. The dependent variable in these studies is typically the effects upon the appearance and formation of movements, the timing of protest or movement activity, the outcomes of movement activity, and sometimes the form of movements themselves (McAdam 1996). Opportunity structures involve any number of elements. Most broadly, opportunities for collective action vary considerably across history (McAdam 1996). Some constraints/opportunities are based in government institutions and state structure, obvious and parallel to these arguments in political science's institutionalisms.

Also important is the array of other social movements at a given time. Alliances with other movements or with elite figures can affect possibilities for collective action. Many national labor movements were strengthened after the 1890s as women's movements arose and became allies; the civil rights movement in the United States was able to combine energies with the antiwar movement in the 1960s (Markoff 1996). Shifting political alignments can also open and close windows of opportunity, as can breaks in elite cohesion. Some aspects of opportunity structure are policy-specific, referring to policies as opportunities for mobilization. U.S. government sponsorship of Earth Day in 1970 helped form the environmental movement. U.S. foreign policy positions, for example, about American support for freedom and democracy, clearly enabled domestic movements seeking justice and equality in the United States in the 1950s and 1960s (Tarrow 1996). This is very much similar to notions of principled "metaframes," a kind of ideational-cultural structure, which we will examine in more detail below.

Given the NSM's extensive exploration of the possibilities of structure, it should not be surprising that its literature also pays attention to agency, which is neither ignored or undertheorized in this literature. Tarrow (1996) discusses at length how movements make opportunities by, for example, switching tactics periodically, to catch authorities off guard, by planned escalations of activities. Conversely, protest movements can often create opportunities for their opponents to reach new levels of mobilization. There have been competitive ethnic mobilizations in Russia and the former Yugoslavia.

Finally, of course, this notion of opportunity structure can also be applied to international and transnational levels. World War I was an opportunity for labor and women's movements (Markoff 1996). Oberschall (1996) has looked at domestic and international opportunity structures in eastern Europe in 1989, cases in which diffusion of "opposition frames" was key. The "Gorbachev factor" and signals about Soviet nonintervention made a much more favorable environment for opposition movements to form than in the past. Joel Krieger's analysis of the opportunities for egalitarian social movements in Europe today looks at several elements of the international opportunity structure at the more proximate regional layer and in the global one, which enable and constrain their efforts, including the European Union (EU) integration process itself, its more specific effort to achieve the single currency through fiscal standards, and the context of globalization and the pressures for competitiveness (Krieger 1999). These latter studies, incorporating culture, identity, and the transnational, are largely CCP in orientation.

Culture and Its Impacts: New Institutionalisms, Policy as Culture

A second set of literatures central to CCP is the various cultural approaches in the social sciences. Cultural explanations of political outcomes go back to Montesquieu, Max Weber, and before, and have thus been with us for some time. In the recent revival of culturalism, culture returned as a nonrational, nonmaterialist, nonfunctional explanation of outcomes, and it percolated into many literatures, on culturalist approaches to comparative politics, in organization theory in sociology as a policy-as-ritual literature, and several other literatures on meso-level group cultures and national cultures. A key fault line is between those who incorporate cultural elements as "variables" within neopositivism and those who adopt culturalism holistically, viewing the world as "ideas all the way down" in its full implications for ontology and epistemology. The latter embraces constructionism and a social ontology, and makes a considerable leap into constructivism. Unfortunately, culturalists in CP and elsewhere do not always appear certain about where they stand on these issues—another example of the tensions between methodology, ontology, and epistemology.

The new culturalist CP is still underdeveloped and has been found wanting on several counts—for holding undertheorized ontological and epistemological positions, for invoking cultural "variables" casually, for providing only very partial understandings of political life, and for a lack of clarity on how the impacts of cultural elements are mediated by interests, institutions, and structure. From some perspectives, and the "messy center" of comparative politics, such charges of ad hocery and undertheorization are not worrisome. On the other hand, if one accepts these critiques yet remains convinced of the validity of culturalism and constructionism in principle, where should comparative politics be going now, to address some of these problems?

The foremost of the pioneering culturalist-constructivist literatures arose among the new institutionalisms in sociology and political science, specifically sociology's so-called new institutionalism (DiMaggio and Powell 1983, 1991; March and Olsen 1984, 1989; Meyer and Rowan 1977). The new sociological institutionalism (SI) offers insights into two areas of relevance to comparativists and CCP in particular: public policy processes and the co-constitution of political actors and structures. Though the major early proponents of interpretivist institutionalism were sociologists, this work can also be read as targeted at the heart of traditional social and political science, even appearing in the *American Political Science Review* in the case of James March and Johan Olsen's 1984 landmark, and is highly significant as a strident source of metatheoretical arguments and guidelines against core suppositions of mainstream, positivist social science. In one sense, the first battle waged by the interpretivist/cultural approach in this literature is to demote economism, utilitarianism, and rationalism from their positions as the assumed starting places of logics of explanation to just another cultural-cognitive frame. The roots of the popularity of constructivism today are here, but the value of SI's ideas to many areas of mainstream political science would not be recognized for years to come (Farrell 1998; Finnemore 1996a).

Policy as Culture: Sociological Institutionalism and Industrial
Political Economy

Since the 1970s, sociological institutionalism has been an innovative leader in understanding actors, institutions, and the implications of structures. "Institution" for SI means most fundamentally institutionalized, accepted ways of doing things, sometimes equated to "norms," though SI's use of that term differs from elsewhere. It is argued that rather than careful calculations of choice, most behavior is rule-governed and routinized, and features *post hoc* rationalizations based on shared understandings of appropriateness. Beginning from within organization theory and organizational psychology and then spreading to many policy areas, SI's earliest work is on bureaucratization and rationalization in organization. Though its roots lie deeper,[15] the modern founding statement of this work is Meyer and Rowan's "Institutionalized Organization: Formal Structure as Myth and Ceremony" (1977). Their interest is in "formal structure" of organizations and the reasons why it tends to be similar across many organizations. They find that formal organizations often scarcely follow their supposedly set procedures, purportedly adopted because they were efficient and functional, and that norms of rationality should not be assumed to be present in bureaucratic organizations.

As compared with the early structuralism and institutionalisms in political science, SI is structure (formal and informal institutions) plus culture and interpretivist elements. One of its central arguments is that the "norm of rationality" or rational-bureaucratization is typically a norm in organizations not because it is functional, but because it becomes the accepted and legitimate form—it has ceremonial legitimacy. They thus challenge Max Weber's argument that bureaucratic rationalization is an iron cage spreading inexorably with modernity and industrialization, because it is the most efficient form.

Two other concepts, "organizational field" and "isomorphism," flesh out the perspective, and enhance SI as a theory of much of social life (DiMaggio and Powell 1983). The notion of an organizational field refers to a specific sector in which accepted forms and practices appear and operate. These may be categorized by sector of an economy or by profession, for example. SI scholars highlight the tremendous homogeneity within organizational fields, but also ask what explains homogeneity. SI posits that the typical "structuration" of a field, as they use Gidden's term, procedes as follows. At the beginning in a new industry, policy area, or profession, there is considerable uncertainty, competition, and innovation, and norms and standard practices are emergent. However, as the sector settles down, accepted ways of doing things are established, professionalization occurs, and these become institutionalized. At this point, unless a field remains subject to intense competition, these rules, norms, and practices will be adopted automatically by new entrants to the field, not because they are functional, but because they are the accepted "culture" of the field; considerable homogeneity of form and action, or isomorphism, is produced.

Though beginning as observations on bureaucratic procedures in organizational theory, these insights were clearly applicable to most public policy areas. The process of isomorphism in a given field has been researched in several: in national welfare systems, hospital development, public education policy, the radio broadcast industry, and so forth. The perspective presents a tremendous challenge to other ways of thinking about policy making—based on the strength of interests and contestation, for example. In addition, two other lines of investigation of the Stanford School appeared in this early phase: How and with what effects does isomorphism work on a global scale, across national boundaries? What are the basic meta-principles underlying the Western rational-bureaucratic culture that has spread so well around the world? These issues have received further attention recently (Boli and Thomas 1997, 1999; Meyer et al. 1997), and are discussed in a later section.

The insights and concepts of SI are clearly applicable elsewhere. One subject related to the culture of an organizational field is the notion of "policy paradigms" in specific areas; that is, national policy paradigms that persist long after background conditions have changed. One early breakthrough in treatments of policy paradigms as learned cultures was Charles Sabel's 1982 book *Work and Politics*, a landmark in interpretivist comparative political economy, in industrial policy and the sociology of capitalism that is heavily cited by followers (e.g., Dobbin 1993, 1994; Berk 1990).[16] Its subject is theories of worker behavior and workers, jobs, and class politics in industrial countries after WWII, during boom and bust. As its opening puzzle, Sabel finds that several theories had passed in vogue by the time he was writing—notions of the embourgeoisement of workers and the waning of revolution, strident consumerism as class motivator, theories of cycles of protest and quiescence. But all suffered from the same metatheoretical problems, which Sabel in turn had to address, specifically central elements of modern social science analytic method: technological determinism, reductionism, and essentialism. Technological determinist arguments hold that a society that wishes to industrialize must adopt specific organizational structures, forms of political rule, and ways of doing business; the reductionist account of ideology was that it goes away with modernization, when in fact it persists and mutates. What Sabel is left with to help him explain labor politics is the notion of a "world view," acquired by individuals through socialization processes which construct social facts and common sense that in turn can explain away social facts like "class injustice," at certain times in certain places. Sabel found that workers' world views shaped their perceptions of what was worth fighting for, in part because they included constructed expectations of just behavior and fair treatment (1982: 14).

Finally, this early interpretivist work makes a strong debut in political science thanks to two other important pioneers from organizational sociology, James March and Johan Olsen, and their oft-cited 1984 article on "The New Institutionalism," which appeared in the *American Political Science Review*. Their stated focus is an argument for the autonomy of political institutions, but their most powerful observations are about mainstream political science of the time and what interpretivist institutionalism in particular implies for it. They lay out many interpretivist and social constructivist critiques of "theories of politics since about 1950," the latter having, they argue, forgotten the wisdom of the "old" institutionalism and turned far too much to a choice perspective on political life. Forgotten are "the ways in which political life is organized around the development of meaning through symbols, rituals, and ceremonies" (735). This leads them to an extended attack on mainstream political science explanation that pulls together the insights of SI and organizationalists at the time. They attack common simplifying assumptions of analysis that mask the ritual character of daily life, including: (1) *reductionism*—the tendency to see political phenomena as "the aggregate consequences of individual behavior" rather than as mediated by organizational structures and rules of appropriate behavior; (2) *utilitarianism*—the choice metaphor; a vision of human life as characterized by deliberate decision making and calculations of self-interest; (3) *functionalism*—the assumption of historical efficiency, that history weeds out maladaptations and permits only efficient, superior social innovations; and (4) *instrumentalism*—the problem of "the primacy of outcomes," or the tendency to view politics as "decision making and the allocation of resources" rather than, as it was more historically, about inculcating identity, belonging, and civic morality. Together, these are the problematic simplifications that characterize much of social science thinking to this day and for which interpretivist new institutionalisms are an important corrective. However, instead of these profound critiques, what many absorbed from this article was the more cautious idea that political institutions had autonomy and their own causal impact.[17]

These early works are quite radical in their implications for positivist-rationalist political science in 1984. At that point, however, the majority of political scientists and comparativists largely ignored these insights, as developments progressed in quantitative and choice theoretic approaches and the expansion of a comparative political economy replete with utilitarianism and instrumentalism (reviewed in Hall 1997). Historical institutionalism at this time was just beginning to disaggregate the monolithic state-as-actor, and Peter Hall's (1986) innovation, for example, was to combine formal institutional structure with ideas.

Work on policy paradigms continues, becoming an accepted alternative to purely interest-based explanation; the latter may describe political contests well, but cannot explain why national policy strategies tend to persist for long periods of time, across coalitional changes and even across regime changes. Kenneth Dyson (1983) discussed the notion of an "industrial culture" as a specific, institutionalized logic of economic organization in a given country. Such a culture constitutes the economic "customs" of a country that structure industries, economies, and industrial policies, often persisting for decades or longer. Peter Hall (1992, 1993) has explored how policy paradigms as communicated cultural bundles dictate questions and answers to policy makers. Frank Dobbin (1993) has written on the social construction of the Great Depression and the proper national policy lessons to be learned from it. As he argues, the depression's shock illustrates the importance of industrial cultural paradigms, because it shook these paradigms so evidently: "in the realm of industrial policy the collapse brought changes because it disproved cultural paradigms of industrial rationality" (1993: 1).

New Social Movements, Culture, and Worldviews: Cognitive Frames

The NSM literature has also taken on interpretivist/culturalist elements, in the work using worldviews and in a related means of characterizing the sets of ideas and assumptions that influence group behavior, a version of Garfinkel's notion of "framing" (Morris and Mueller 1992; McAdam, McCarthy, and Zald 1996). Frames are schemas that interpret and order the world and dictate right and wrong action. Specific frames have been found to mobilize actors, spawn related movements, but also trap movements in particular sets of ideas. Frames are central, and contested, often the subject of disputes within and between movements. These authors also note that certain ideas, like the "freeze" notion in the peace movement of the 1980s, proved much more effective than calls for actual disarmament; the civil rights movement also did very well as long as it focused on equal rights and integration, but when this became "black power," it lost support. And frames include related ideas: Collective action frames, "master frames," help to explain why social movements cluster together in "cycles of protest" (Snow and Benford 1992: 137).

Finally, because it is relatively conscious of these things, the NSM literature is adept at thinking through the theoretical implications of its work, in social theoretic terms. For example, Klandermans (1992) has all the elements of a dynamic, reflexive set of relationships between actors, action, identity, and frames, before it appeared in IR. Frames and opportunity structures balance structure and agency; frames are passive, but people also construct them (Gamson and Meyer 1996).

Culturalism in Historical Institutionalism

> Unlike the postpositivist impulse of postmodernism, historical institution-
> alism has refused to reduce reality to signification; and unlike rational
> choice, it has disallowed the reduction of agency to effectively utilitarian
> individuals *in worlds where both the content and means of rationality vary
> by organizational, cultural, and historical configurations.* (Katznelson 1997:
> 85, emphasis added)

Historical institutionalism began with little or no interest in the cultural-
interpretivist and constructionist insights we have been discussing but, as
the above quote from Ira Katznelson indicates, it has come to be very sensitive to both of them. Some sociologists and political scientists began around
this time to extend their work on the state-as-actor to broader inquiry into
formal institutions and their effects on politics, and a revived political institutionalism and historical institutionalism took off.[18] One of the major contributions here is Theda Skocpol's *Protecting Soldiers and Mothers* (1992),
which is transnational in scope and employs worldviews and identity much
as the social movement literature does. It is in several ways an example of
CCP. Further advances on the ideas set out in Skocpol (1992) are found in
Rueschmeyer and Skocpol (1996) on social knowledge and social policy in
the 1870–1920 period. Katznelson argues that the loose configurative
relationalism that comparative's structuralism has become (a kind of structural constructivism, one might say) can actually save comparative politics'
core from the two evils pointed out in Kohli et al. (1995), microanalytic
choice perspectives and postpositivism.

Use and Problems of Culture in Analysis

The above literatures illustrate the value of cultural elements as variables
and of culturalism as a perspective or paradigm. Yet, several critiques of
cultural explanations are commonly identified. Some have categorical
objections to any kind of cultural "explanation" whatsoever (Lichbach 1997:
257). First, cultural explanations are charged with being highly indeterminate, as there is great difficulty demonstrating the causal impact of culture.
Second, there can be confusion as to culture as a unit of analysis. Which
culture is in question, in a given analysis? Culture is used to denote a spectrum from macroscale civilizational cultures to local cultures in a particular
town or locality. Third, within-culture variation can be substantial. A given
policy process may relate to a variety of contradictory national and organizational cultures, as Kaufman (1998) has argued with relation to U.S. AIDS

policy. Countries do not have monolithic cultures. Farrell (1998) points out an interesting weakness with regard to strategic culture in IR: it is most commonly used to explain puzzles and dysfunctional behavior. Otherwise, in military conflict (high politics with high stakes) one is generally led to employ rationalist models of decision making. Johnston (1999), referring to the strategic culture literature, has warned that we must be sure to allow room for other causal factors beyond cultural norms.

How to deal with these critiques? First, many of them are actually speaking across epistemologies, as neopositivists attack interpretivists who only seek a better understanding of events. Second, within neopositivism we must remind ourselves that cultural explanations in which culture is a variable are always partial; cultures are always multiple and overlapping. They are likely to carry more explanatory power, the more a culture is specified, perhaps at different levels of analysis. At the meso/group layer we have seen some strong and compelling arguments, well supported and well researched. The organizational field cultures of SI are intuitively obvious and powerful and established very well in that literature. We should also allow a role for culture as opportunity structure and enabler (Brysk 1995). Culture writ large, as "national culture," sets loose bounds most of the time, though there are clearly times when culture makes something unthinkable—though in such instances it is probably better to speak more precisely of specific norms and organizational cultures. Kaufman (1998) has a very good point. If we take culture as a socially constructed structure, then of course we should expect to have different cultural codes prevailing simultaneously, especially at high levels of social collectivity like the nation-state, even over specific policy issues. An individual constructivist scholar's epistemological proclivities will make some of the above critiques more biting than others.

Identities

Research and writing on questions of "identity" is another pioneering area of interpretivist scholarship very relevant to CCP. This work concerns the gamut of actors and entities to which identities can attach: individuals and several kinds of group-collective identities: community, ethnicity, social class, social movement, nation, locality, region, and others. Identity politics and research have taken off in a particularly marked way in response to changes in the world's politics, in the rise of new social movements, new nationalisms, ethnic identities, and ethnic self-determination since the 1970s.[19] In most of these literatures a main reason for bringing identity in is the classic interpretivist insight—the need to explain the appearance and actions of groups when interests are no longer assumed as given and material. As we've seen, one of the first things rejected by interpretivist social science is rational actor notions and material interest-based explanation. In fact, a fundamental point is that "rationality" is actually a learned behavioral code (characteristic of modernity itself), and therefore so is interest-based action. This problematizes our understandings of action, since the simplifying assumptions of interests and rationality must be replaced by more individualized, particularistic cognitive frames. Individual and collective identity are brought to bear to provide the "reference by which costs and benefits are defined" and the framework within which preferences are constructed (Eisenstadt and Giesen 1995: 73).

Identity literatures have found that identity, at any level of collectivity, shapes preferences about most everything, certainly shapes the probability and character of many varieties of conflict, and stimulates group rights claims and assertions of self-determination. The process of the construction and reconstruction of identities in and of itself has also become a subject of investigation, for example, of national identity after colonial independence, of subnational and ethnic identity with democratization, of new group identities in post-industrial society, or as subject to globalization or economic crisis. Identity is especially important when it changes, spawning new societal cleavages, interests and actions that can reshape history: changes in religious identity with the Reformation, the appearance of nationalism in Europe.

Collective Identity as State or Nation

National identity in comparative politics most often refers to "nationalism" and a kind of exclusivist phenomenon, based on ascriptive characteristics (race, ethnicity, language). Structural theories of nationalism were the most common prevailing explanations for the appearance of nations and nationalism in the industrial West, positing nations as the result of industrialization and modernization and the breakdown of parochial connections, leading to a larger national consciousness that would fade with deeper modernization and global integration. In a counter to these, perhaps *the* pioneering effort in publicizing the notion of social constructionism and in stimulating new work on national identity is Benedict Anderson's *Imagined Comunities* (1991) and the broader study of nationalism, ethnicity, and ethnic conflict. As strong national feeling persisted and even grew throughout late modernity, scholars began to abandon notions of this identity as primordial and shift to national identity as an enduring social construction. A portion of the literature on nationalism and ethno-national identity takes national identity as its dependent variable, and is simply about the construction process itself, either in the abstract or in specific cases—evidence of excitement and controversy about the identification of this new social process.

Within and accompanying Anderson's broad notion of "imagining" communities, a debate has sprung up in comparative politics and sociology regarding the sources of ethnic/national identity and the "primordial" versus "instrumental" nature of national identity. The primordial perspective places emphasis on the more natural, material elements of identity, such as place, food, language, kinship, or race, while an instrumental position accepts a loose constructionist interpretation but specifically emphasizes elite manipulation of identity codes for political and economic gain. Very few still hold a wholly primordial view of ethnic identities as purely natural in origin. Eisenstadt and Giesen (1995), using a self-described macro constructivist framework, examine in multistep detail how national identity is constructed. They combine perspectives, noting for example, that instrumental reasons (competition for resources) may be a factor promoting an identity project. They argue that primoridality itself is largely a social construction, rooted in natural features perhaps, but maintained by rites and rituals and other group actions (p. 78). Virginia Tilley (1997) has also weighed in on this debate, arguing that the beauty of constructivism as an analytic method is that it allows one to see how much ethnic identity is primordial and how much it is instrumental. Some features of identity are definitely less constructed vis-a-vis an "other," for example.

State/National Identity in Comparative Politics

Like all identities, state identity has presocial, intrinsic, domestic elements. But it is also very much relational, derived from social interaction between states in a global society of states that has its own structure of norms, roles, and institutions. Both comparative politics and international relations deal with state identity in both ways, though CIR explores state social identity more fully. Beyond the extensive literature on nationalism as an identity in comparative politics, there is also a literature on national identity as adhering to a given country, building upon a much earlier "national character" perspective.[20] This second comparativist state identity literature has recently revived somewhat, is provocative and useful for CCP, and features the two strands mentioned above—of identity from within and without—but is also about more proximate national political traditions, ideological movements, and an interesting theme of "isms" and their effect in constituting national characters. I examine these two strands separately for convenience—all identities are constructs of both, always—with an eye toward understanding some of the constitutive elements and processes invoked in discussions of each and some observations on what identity in these literatures explains.

From within, national identity is a composite of many elements. There is a rough consensus that internal national identities are built from basic, primordial, and constructed elements such as (though not limited to) a traditional territory or homeland, common myths and historical memories, a common public culture, a common set of rights and duties for members, and a common economy. The constituent elements of national *political* identity over time might include powerful political ideologies and the individual imprints of major political figures, national heroes, and their myths. Some view national constitutions as a sort of national narrative (Berezin 1997). Anderson highlighted other aspects, with a focus on national language and construction of discursive communities in his accounts of the importance of the establishment of national languages and the expansion of printing and reading in early modern Europe. He and others have found that national identity construction is, for example, something elites typically play a heavy role in: political leaders, intellectuals, and cultural figures. There is, at the extreme, an "official nationalism" devised by governments from the top down in cases such Czarist Russia (Anderson 1991), involving the establishment of official languages and national public education with identity content, official ideologies, creation of an expanded public sector, establishment of broad military conscription, and so forth. Many countries have founding fathers or key figures that play an important role in fashioning and representing national identity. However, defining and redefining national identity is also often subject to struggles between different groups in a given society (Prizel 1998; Radcliffe and Westwood 1996).

A few examples illustrate these points about the internal sources of national identity. In an analysis of the early establishment of U.S. national identity after the revolutionary war, Tarver elaborates on many of the above construction processes and elements. During the revolutionary war, Americans were very worried about breaking their ties to England, for economic reasons in particular, but were forced to build nationalism later, as the war raised hatreds so much (Tarver 1992), through speeches, writings, poems, songs, and cartoons. Then after the war, the "Federalist elite" played a crucial role in bringing a more centralizing constitution to form the new country from fractious states (76–84), in a phase of conscious construction by elites (92). Radcliffe and Westwood (1996) have explored how national identity articulates with race, geography, gender, and sexuality in contemporary Ecuador, and the role of literature and media in representing "the nation" there. Primarily elites and the military have taken on the role of nation-building, and use it to their advantage.

Another theme of this literature is the special ideologies or "isms" that typically help to constitute national political identity, as national identity is also used to mean, in effect, a national *political culture* with an identity component. In Turkey, Kemal Attaturk and Kemalism date from early in the twentieth century but are still very much a force today, as a kind of urge to force modernization (Yörük 1997). Similarly, in his discussion of the role of national identity construction in political development and democracy, Spektorowski has written of Argentina's mobilizatory political tradition, as contrasted with Ururguay's more liberal party democracy (Spektorowski 1998). Both were very much influenced at their inception by key political figures: "Yrigoyenism" in Argentina and "Battlism" in Uruguay. These, at formative periods, rewrite national stories, establish new formal institutions, perhaps new constitutions, which hardwire informal norms and practices into national culture and identity as well.

National identity from without, state "social" identity, also appears in the non-IR literature. Most every identity is formed from basic models and also in contrast to an "other," which most studies of national identity make reference to. An interesting exemplar is Carlos Waisman's recent discussion of national identity and "others" in Argentina (1998). Waisman uses the notion of National Identity Frames, borrowed from the NSM literature, and composed of three parts: a sense of the "other," a sense of the self, and the actions implied by the frame. Waisman tracks three National Identity Frames in Argentina in recent times, including that of "emerging market." Waisman is clear about the impacts of these frames on policy, including some interesting effects on Argentinian foreign policy, pushing the country to promote integration schemes regionally and embrace the international political economy; a specific set of disparate policies may in part be driven by a specific identity goal.

As Virginia Tilley (chapter 5 of this volume) recounts, sometimes national identities are based on codings and representations borrowed from without. Definitions of the nation exclude some groups and de-define them, keeping them out of politics as a group. Bruce Magnusson (chapter 6 of this volume) notes that Beninois identity is in part simply "not Nigerian."

What does state/national identity "explain" to comparativists? Many of these studies are more configurative than explanation-oriented, filling in "how-possible" questions. National identity sets limits of possibilities, and its imprint can be seen on major political processes, the course of democratizations, for example.

State/National Identity in Constructivist IR

Much constructivist IR (CIR) pursues state identity in a very different way from comparative politics. While the substantive *topics* of CIR in this area may be of less interest to comparativists, the greater attention to the details of construction and the dissection of elements and processes demonstrates that CIR is arguably better in its method. CIR's standards of evidence and explanation also tend to be more specified.

The term "constructivism" was introduced into IR by Nicholas Onuf (1989) and first popularized by Onuf and Alexander Wendt (1987), and now a host of other followers. CIR is an analytic approach to, rather than a substantive theory of, international relations (Onuf 1998: 58). It is a set of ontological innovations in particular, with which constructivist theories of war, cooperation, and community among states might be built. The basic positions of CIR mirror those we've seen in other literatures. The structure of the global system is a social structure. Structures and agents—states primarily (for some constructivists), but also many other kinds of social actors—are co-generative: Actors shape and are shaped by each other and their environments. Actors' interests and preferences (important to a field concerned with national interest and foreign policy), are therefore not considered fixed or exogeneous to explanation, but rather originate and alter during the process of social interaction; structure and interaction thus not only constrain behavior, but go beyond that to *constitute* interests. More profoundly, state identity, though also shaped by "domestic" factors, is constituted by social interaction.

There are several different understandings of identity in CIR, though most agree that identities are multiple and relational and most use identity to refer to *state* identity. Identity is important for CIR because, as we have seen with other literatures, it is a way of endogenizing actor interests in analysis, instead of assuming them as neorealist IR does—attention to identity is one of the distinctive innovations of CIR then. Alexander Wendt draws heavily from social psychology and symbolic interactionism and defines identities as "relatively stable, role-specific understandings and expectations about self" (1992: 397). As Wendt describes it, actors "acquire" identities from collective meanings and institutions generated through social interaction. What is especially important for IR scholars is that identities are also "the basis of interests" (398), and in his well-known article on anarchy in the international system Wendt discusses how the *constructed* (not natural) institution of self-help in anarchy shapes state identity and interests.

In many treatments of state identity in CIR a basic and important distinction is made between generic identities—that is, a generic classification of state or kingdom or empire—and more specific identities such as "liberal power," "leader of the free world," or "satellite power" (Ruggie 1998: 14), though the generic-specific categories are not well elaborated in the CIR literature. The notion of generic identity is important to IR in describing and understanding system transformations, as in the historical advent of states and the periods before (medieval) and perhaps after states. Some generic forms are prescribed by international norms and practices—the territorial state in the past (Hall 1999), the nation-state in more modern times and today. Other generic identities may become effectively proscribed over time, such as colonies, or city-states.[21] Wendt (1994) also suggests other dichotomies relevant to identity: (1) *corporate* state identity/interests (presocial, inherent to states) versus *social* state identity/interests (formed in interaction with other states and systemic intersubjective meaning structures); and, (2) *domestic* elements of state identity (stemming from relations with society—"liberal," "democratic") versus elements stemming from a state's relations in *international* society ("hegemon" and "balancer" are his examples).

In some senses these shed further light on the state identity concept, but also provide additional parameters that muddy things. For example, before turning to identity in explanation of action, we should ask what can be said of the specific varieties of identities, such as the liberal, democratic, hegemon, and balancer labels Wendt mentions? Other labels appear elsewhere—colonial power, "civilized" nation—but rarely are the implications of any of these worked out. Granted that identities are always multiple and shifting, naive, practical questions arise, regarding which countries these labels might apply to, the interests that can be attached to these labels, and the policies they suggest. As we will see below, while identity is important, in some analyses it appears as if identity labels are generated and brought forth *deus ex machina*, to provide the crucial missing answer.

On the whole, CIR's forays into identity follow the lines of the two broader subschools within CIR as a whole: a "conventional" or modernist CIR and a more postpositivist, discourse-oriented CIR (Burch, chapter 2 of this volume; Hopf 1998; Katzenstein, Keohane, and Krasner 1999; Wendt 1992: 394). Conventional CIR employs a more positivist, reifying analysis that brackets actors-as-constructions and simplifies, using terms as variables with causal interconnections; this is the more state-centric and norms-oriented constructivism, as epitomized by Wendt and Katzenstein. All relations between these elements are recursive and constitutive, but in a crude sense. Research on identity as an independent variable explores the ways in which it shapes state interests and action. This work in turn follows two subsidiary lines of analysis, one focused primarily on identity's impact on "national interest" in international society, and thus ultimately some aspect of foreign policy behavior (Katzenstein 1996) (probably not of direct interest and relevance to comparativists).[22] The other subtheme concerns how state identity shapes interests and in turn actions that are more related to the domestic and public policy (e.g., Berger 1996; Bukovansky 1997). The latter is very relevant to CCP, as it explores an external-internal link to domestic processes. Work which takes state identity as a dependent variable finds that because state identity is important, we must examine what factors affect it and how. This work in turn has a small but interesting subtheme on state "collective identity" formation, interested in how groups of states form shared bonds and identities, as we would expect to happen in any society (Wendt 1994).

The more neopositivist group in CIR spends considerable time on the construction of identities and the causal and constitutive relationships between identity, interest, and action in useful dissection of processes, identifying new variables and examining the relations between them. How does identity shape interests and action, especially that most relevant to domestic politics? First, state social identities and reputations can be very powerful, making some actions unthinkable, or forcing actions contrary to instrumental interests. Identity also affects "instrumentality"—the way actors connect preferences to policy choices (Kowert and Legro 1996: 464).

The case literature on state identity's influences upon interests and policies illustrates the value and problems of identity analysis. Thomas Berger (1996), for example, examines the effects of the new identity enforced upon Japan and Germany after World War II by the conquering Allies. Berger finds compelling evidence that identities change and pull interests and policies along with them. Both countries have become antimilitaristic to the core, such that this quality is now integral to their sense of self, and is also in turn embodied in domestic norms and institutions. Similarly, Herman (1996) examines how Soviet reformers sought to reconstruct national identity in the 1980s; the changes under Gorbachev are effectively an identity shift, which brings radical recalibration of interests. And Price and Tannenwald (1996) have argued that commitment to being a "civilized" nation *reinforces* acceptance of international norms defining chemical and nuclear weapons as illegitimate. Persistent identities (specific national cultures, in a sense), can also lock in interests and policy courses that become difficult to deviate from.

Secondly, identity is of interest as a dependent variable, in discussions of identity construction through various processes and of state/national identity as a subject of political contestation. Berger (1996) discusses how politics in Germany and Japan consciously became about identity after World War II, and in both states global models of legitimate state and national identities shaped a deliberate identity reconstruction process. In the early United States, political leaders used role and identity conceptions drawn from extant ideas, international and domestic law, and philosophy, to construct a "principled identity" that marked America as distinct from the rest of the world (Bukovansky 1997).

Conversely, a more linguistic and poststructuralist approach to identity is taken by the postmodern constructivists, relying much more on discourse analysis and the symbolic representation of actors in discourses. For David Campbell (1993), it is foreign policy that reproduces state boundaries and identity. Identities are performances, ongoing productions of discursive practices. This second literature is also much more sure that identities are multiple and in constant flux, and criticizes Wendt, for example, for reifying states and speaking of interests as knowable (Weldes 1997). Instead interests are constructed from representational vocabularies available inside and outside domestic society (Jackson, chapter 8 of this volume).

Group Collective Identity

Moving beyond the state level, the new identity politics of group identities is all about a rearticulation of politics away from the old divisions of class and toward the new divisions of ethnicity, gender, sexual preference, environmentalism, and so forth. In the North this has in part been the result of the "postmaterialist" politics of affluence and postindustrial society. In Latin America, it has meant a shift away from the old "national-popular" project of the popular sectors, workers and campesinos, and leftist intellectuals (Hale 1997). The appearance of NSMs and of new nationalisms were both unanticipated, even not supposed to happen—they seemed driven by sentiments that would be done away with by modernization and industrialization and the "cultural" victories of the latter over premodern and unanticipated postmodern notions. The rise of the new identity politics also proved confusing for the political Left, as class identities and relationships to capital have retreated in salience (Cohen 1985). In both these literatures it was not that material, rational, instrumental factors were not present, but that they were clearly not the whole story, or even a substantial part of it.

The study of social movements was taken over by the "resource mobilization" perspective in the early 1970s, but this school was rationalist, and it focused largely on the collective action problem of social movements and free riders. However, by the late 1970s, research on new social movements brought many interpretivist and constructionist insights to bear. What initially confused analysts was that the NSMs of the 1970s were not class- or worker-based; they were based around feminists, ecologists, peace activists, and youth. These were also typically careful, good citizens within a "civil society" that sought not to seize the state, but to pluralize public space and relations within the state (Cohen 1985). Second-wave NSM analysts would not take grievances, goals, or preference structures as given (Mueller 1992), nor conflicts as "natural."

Identity was interesting as a reason for collective action, brought in be-cause rational, interest-based approaches were found partially or largely in-adequate in many circumstances and many of the NSMs were and are more manifestly driven by identity concerns. Individuals and NSMs are motivated by the desire for recognition of difference, with symbolic and cultural stakes, rather than material ones, often paramount. As Mueller (1992: 5) has ob-served, "the new actor is conceptualized as socially embedded with loyal-ties, obligations, and identities that reframe issues of potential support for collective action." Cohen (1985) asserts that the NSMs can only be under-stood through interpretive analysis of movement identity, specifically of movement "self-understandings."

A recent direction for identity in the NSM literature, one that is empiri-cally persuasive if complicating, is the notion of "modular politics" (Krieger 1999; Tarrow 1994), which finds that identities in today's movements are multiple and deployed strategically. Movement members and leaders pull together different identities at will, as part of strategy, to aid in struggles for specific goals, such as wage increases or new rights claims; one finds "Swed-ish wage-earner feminism" in a world of identity politics where "identities are hybrid, fluid, and context dependent; they are also strategic" (Krieger 1999: 78).

Summary: The Utility of Identity

What compelling reasons do these literatures give us to pay attention to iden-tity? Many perspectives reject rationalist/instrumentalist assumptions of in-terests, but what do we gain in problematizing interests with identity? It is clear that identity and worldviews add an important dimension to any at-tempt to explain and understand actions or processes, a crucial dimension that can no longer be left out. And from the characterizations of national identities we can also see clearly the importance of differences in identity from country to country: Each is unique and significant in its own way.

Critiques correlate with epistemological positions. A common critique of culture-identity explanations is that they are tautological, and this is prob-lematic for those firmly rooted in positivist, modern social science. Can identity arguments be disproved? If one is a postpositivist, a charge of tau-tology bounces off, but for the modernist branch of CIR, for example, the problem would be more severe. Terminology and conceptual clarity is also vital. It may be that generic state/country identity is useful, for example, but could be expressed in another way (e.g., as Wendt's unit-type), while very specific identity labels are on thinner ground. Kowert (1998) points out that identity and theories of political identity must be important and needed, since there is so much competition to define identity domestically and internationally. Chapters in this volume by Tilley, Goff, and Magnusson are testimony to this. Marc Ross concludes that in any rivalry between culturalist and interest-based or institutional explanations, what is best is to undertake a "multi-method search for convergence," rather than abandon culture-identity altogether (1997: 61).

How can we summarize and come to some conclusions about the role of identity vis-à-vis interests and action? We cannot take actions to simply reflect interests, and thus ignore identity, as so many have in the past. It is clear that there is an identity dimension to any issue, but we have more to learn about identity's proper place. How should we best understand when identity changes and how that will affect interests and action? Can its effects be expressed differently? Skeptics will ask if identity is so privileged in interpretivist ontologies that we feel we have to find a role for it. On the other hand, what other explanations for interests are there? Does all policy/action affect identity? Is there an identity core that precludes some extreme actions? How much latitude does identity allow for action? At the group and state levels, what is the conceptual relationship between identity and culture? There are still many questions.

Governance in a Global Social System

An important shortcoming of many of the institutionalist and culturalist literatures just discussed, and symptomatic of most comparativists as well, is their relative lack of attention to a global social system beyond the state. Certainly almost no comparativist work is based in a developed systemic perspective with a sophisticated account of the global system, its evolution over time, and causal and constitutive relationships between the system, its agentic and structural elements, and state/"domestic" actors in it. What is the systemic order in which "polities" exist, and indeed which constitutes polities? Comparativists need better answers to these questions if they are going to conduct analyses in a new global society. Two notable efforts to think about actors and the global system and provide a theory of the whole are sociological institutionalism's "world polity" school and CIR.[23] Though dating from the 1980s, as they have developed intensively in the late 1990s, they increasingly converge in their fundamental assumptions, use of specific concepts, processes, and language. My treatment of each will only brush the surface of the burgeoning complexity developing in the CIR literature, for example. I focus especially on what both can offer comparativists and CCP. Broadly speaking, CIR offers an approach that is increasingly sophisticated in method and metatheoretical debates, while substantive case research lags behind. The world polity approach is simpler and more structuralist, holist, and tends to be overdetermined in its account of the power of a specific global culture.

Sociological Institutionalism's "World Polity" School

As we have seen, SI early on emphasized the importance of the cognitive dimension in organizations: particular organizational forms and practices are adopted not necessarily because they are functional, but because they fit existing standards and practices and the expectations of the bureaucrats and professionals that design and staff them. But what is the character and origin of the cognitive menu from which bureaucratic actors draw their ideas and by which they judge their creations? Here, some sociological institutionalists have focused upon the level of the "world society" or "world polity," which provides the crucial social and cultural context for processes and outcomes at the state level.[24] From early works in the 1980s, this perspective was amazingly constructivist (citing Berger and Luckman and Goffman), concerned at that time to challenge the economistic accounts of the world system perspective which viewed the world in terms of economic exchange, with the political and cultural as superstructure. The puzzle of interest was the "striking isomorphism" of the world's states, public services, economic sectors, and more.

What the world polity school came up with was a structuralist-culturalist explanation of the similarities in form of economic, political, and social organization across the globe. In brief, the world polity school views the modern world as a social system:

> For a century or more, the world has constituted a singular polity . . . a unitary social system, increasingly integrated by networks of exchange, competition and cooperation. . . . Like all polities, the world polity is constituted by a distinct culture—a set of fundamental principles and models . . . defining the nature and purposes of social actors and action. (Boli and Thomas 1997: 172)

This single-world culture has a specific character underlain by a handful of basic principles: universalism, individualism, rationalization, notions of progress, notions of world citizenship (Boli and Thomas 1997). This culture is "Western-originated" but not dominated by Western nations or elites exclusively (Boli and Thomas 1997). Rather, it is "embedded" in organizations, and especially international nongovernmental organizations (INGOs), which are venues for interests from throughout the world and which fairly frequently promote insurgent interests.

These world cultural principles in turn produce and reproduce the common phenomena we see around us: rational-bureaucratization, technical progress, states, markets, and capitalism. The taken-for-granted aspirations of modern life are omnipresent also: desire for efficiency, fairness, development as accumulation of wealth and goods. Fundamentally, the world polity explanation operates by revealing and "denaturalizing" common sense about the social world, states, the public sector, economic life, and so forth, much as do Foucauldian critiques of the state (Mitchell 1991) and, with a narrower agenda, CIR (Hopf 1998: 182). Thus, universalism and rationalism permeate actors' thoughts and logics at an elemental level, making them receptive to the next improvement in a given issue area. International Organizations (IOs), and INGOs in particular, serve to communicate the legitimate, appropriate forms and new standard models of policy and organizational structure to individuals around the world. Like Arturo Escobar's critique of the profound reframing of categories, discourse, and cognitive frames when the development "machine" comes to a postcolonial country (1995), the Western-rational logic is powerful and accepted with little reflection. In a sense, the systemic environment's cultural content is independent of the actors within it, and it is powerful enough to have constitutive powers, to create specific legitimate categories of actors, like nation-states.

The world polity school has focused on isomorphic patterns across polities, in several policy areas: K-12 education, rational bureaucracies throughout the state, which expand in similar ways when new tasks are invented (or suggested from outside), standing militaries with similar organizational structures, and weapons arrays. Criticisms of the world polity school include that it is far too structurally-determinist, missing agency, and that it is better able to explain organization form and functioning than origins and transformation. We will return to these in a moment.

Constructivist IR—The Global System and Construction
of Identity and Interests

CIR is a less deterministic and more dynamic perspective than the world polity school and has in recent times been probably the most vibrant area of constructivist-oriented work. It is increasingly adept at dealing with identity and interests in explaining action, and through its burgeoning interest in norms, policy propagation in the global system as well. Most importantly, as CIR fans out to a variety of topics, the potential for synergies and cross-fertilizations with comparativists increases dramatically. By comparison with work in comparative politics, international relations scholars are far out in front in exploring the theoretical underpinnings and implications of constructivist ideas.

The CIR literature has come out of nowhere to become *the* challenger to the hallowed and maligned realism/neorealism in the field. And it already contains competing subperspectives as well, which will probably reproduce themselves in CCP. Most identify two or three broad camps: conventional, critical, and postmodern (Hopf 1998; Jepperson, Wendt, and Katzenstein 1996; Katzenstein, Keohane, and Krasner 1999). Kurt Burch (chapter 2 of this volume) has developed a schema to categorize the constructivist IR literature along different lines, identifying "NOC, SOC, and ROC"—that is, norm-oriented constructivism (NOC), structure-oriented constructivism (SOC), and rule-oriented constructivism (ROC). The conventional versus critical constructivist distinction is an important one. Conventional CIR basically comprises Burch's norms-oriented and structure-oriented constructivisms. The chief proponent of SOC is Alexander Wendt, and it focuses much more on hard structures and is most positivist. Postmodern or radical constructivism in IR is the label reserved for textualists such as David Campbell, conforming most closely to Burch's ROC, which is devoted to rules and conceptual histories, and leans the most towards the interpretive and poststructural.

The claim to distinctiveness for ROC is that it has theorized the way in which action produces structure: Through the invocation, following, or flouting of social rules, actions reinforce or challenge and replace the rules that are social structure. NOC, in a sense, starts with norms and tracks their effects, and therefore might be considered to have less sensitivity to agency. ROC might actually be more distinguishable by its penchant for conceptual histories, of sovereignty or property rights for example, and the way that these key concepts constitute structural features.

The Utility of Global Social-Structural Approaches to Comparative Politics

How are these useful to comparativist work? There are some basic ways in which SI and CIR compare and contrast. One basic difference between constructivist IR and the world polity school is that SI is much more structuralist than CIR. Some conventional constructivists label themselves as structuralists, because of their interest in the influence of structural features such as norms on action, but they do not go as far as the holist-structuralist world polity perspective. Second, they differ markedly in their specification of the content of world social structure. As Martha Finnemore (1996a, 1996b), someone who tries to bridge CIR and SI, has pointed out, CIR, while it adopts structurationism and a social-structural view of the global system, fails to make "any particular claims about the content" of that social milieu.

This is a crucial issue for comparativists, who are interested in explaining substantive state-level political processes in history, such as democratization, the development of civil society, and major policy change.

Culture and Principles, Not Norms

CIR is much more fixed on the term and concept of "norm" as a useful device which links individual action to a social context. The world polity perspective, on the other hand, employs terms such as culture, principle, and institution predominantly (the latter for them is roughly equivalent to "norm"). The difference is significant, more than semantic, representing two very different ways of looking at the global social system. The fixation with principles and particularly a few "metaprinciples" allows for considerable simplification of processes and for state-level change to be read off of systemic principles. This difference of approach is in no small part due to the fact that the world polity school comes out of a world culture perspective (Finnemore 1996a), from the macrolevel down, whereas CIR comes out of a regime and liberal institutionalist frame, in which the focus is on very specific issue areas. What can and should comparativists draw from these different positions? It seems sensible to argue for attention to both. The isomorphism hypothesis is an important one, one that should be in the back of comparativists' heads all the time, especially if their work immerses them in the details of a country case. (Finnemore is very correct to admonish other perspectives for not rising to these questions more regularly and pointedly [1996a, 1996b].) Conversely, analysis of norms and norm propagation is progressing quickly, along neopositivist scientific lines (Cortell and Davis 2000). This kind of work will undoubtedly appeal to many comparativists, and is something in which comparativist area and country expertise is much needed.

Agent Versus Structure in Explanation

One troubling issue in the world polity school is the overdetermined nature of world culture—it is relatively monolithic and, for most states and situations, simply received from above. If agency is ignored, agents can be simply reduced to structure in explanation, leaving out the obvious possibilities for interplay between the two. This is not a problem the school is oblivious to, especially in more recent accounts of the school's perspective as it grows sensitive to the issue. Agency is not completely missing from the equation, but it is neglected and undertheorized, defiantly so. As we have seen, national-level outcomes are strongly determined by systemic cultural codes, and SI's focus is on the systemic level, where it emphasizes a kind of inexorable convergence in socio-political and bureaucratic forms—their "isomorphism hypothesis." A defense of SI's position might counter that these conclusions are justified based on the empirical evidence. The initial puzzle is, why is there so much isomorphism across polities at different levels of development, with different histories and cultures? This, as they argue, is surely a sign of a powerful common influence running over national particularities. How else is isomorphism reproduced? What would a more agency-oriented SI look like? Agency for SI is relatively passive, but comes from many sources. It is provided above all by INGOs, but also by IOs. They point out that INGOs do most of the initiating of action then taken up by states and domestic groups.

To the extent that IR scholars view the state as a black box, the externalist determinism of the world polity school may be less troublesome, but for comparativists the obvious question is, what happened to process and policy contestation? And domestic interests? And national institutional structures? One suspects that SI would counter on several grounds: these things are more important in some countries than in others; the details of policy differences are less important than the broader models and their amazing ubiquity. On the other hand, the world polity school does definitely serve to bridge over some of traditional comparativism's search for difference. People share ideas and mindsets across polities, and SI shows us how this shared culture shapes outcomes. It is quite useful as a corrective and reminder for this reason, the antidote to the comparative institutionalist's obsession with difference and variation.

CIR's Relevance to Comparative Politics

CIR is clearly about international relations and the debates and subjects which concern IR scholars. Large portions of it have tended to be state-centric and to focus on explications of IR topics: the supposed anarchy of the international system (Wendt 1992), foreign and national security policy (Bukovansky 1997; Katzenstein 1996), cooperation among democracies (Risse-Kappen 1995). But many topics in CIR also have something to offer comparativists, and a structural change in the subfield itself portends for more, in the sense that one of the wonderful innovations of CIR is that the structure of the international system is no longer viewed simply as the distribution of material power capabilities—we now have a *social* structure of multiple ordering principles, norms, and accepted practices. With this innovation, we get two important developments: discussion of the "constitution" of international society (Onuf 1994) and of a governing structure over international society, an "international state" (Wendt 1994: 392–393), as particles of international government accumulate. This may be the most exciting area of work for constructivist comparativists (see Bukovansky 1999; Burch 1998; Hall 1999 and chapter 4 of this volume; Reus-Smit 1997), an area in which comparativist scholars own efforts have been disparate and isolated, only rarely making use, for example, of any notion of systemic scripts from which state actors draw cues for action.

As IR moves to conceive the international system as a social system, it is also much more able to share insights with CP, and join with it; before this break out of realism, there was little room for connection between the two. (The earliest of this was the extensive CIR literature in the 1990s on the principle of sovereignty.) Some of this synergy can be seen in issues of identity and interest. As we have seen, for CIR most discussions of identity refer to the identities of states or national identity, though this is not always and increasingly not at all the case, as CIR makes a conscious effort to embrace other actors besides states—an opening for comparativist work. In addition, the notion of state identity is perhaps at least along one dimension about political regime type, but moving into typologizing along these lines will probably not prove useful. Overall, comparativists have a much more sophisticated understanding of domestic political processes. Comparing and combining CIR and CCP, we should have a much better sense of both internal and external sources of identity.

Finally, comparativists have much to learn about what might be termed "transsocietal political orders" and the "international state." Constructivists have been compared unfavorably to sociological institutionalists for investigating disparate pieces of social structure with little attention to "the possibility of overarching social structures or of a single coherent structure that coordinates international interaction" (Finnemore 1996b: 16). Though once true, this problem has been addressed of late, with some very innovative work on the constitution of systemic political orders over time, systemic orders which in turn shape the characteristic, identities, and actions of actors in those systems—an area which holds great potential for comparativists to benefit from in the growing CIR literature. This also includes analyses of the way in which political institutions come in and out of history, and the ways in which some periods promote a particular set of modal and preferred political forms: kingship, the state, the nation-based state, etc.

Constructivist Comparative Politics

The purpose of this lengthy literature review has been to discuss what comparativists are already doing that is oriented to a constructivist approach, hopefully also showing a steady progression of developments that make a move to CCP the logical next step. Finally, it says a little bit about how a key feature of CCP, integration of the national and the international, can learn from two important perspectives on political life in a global social system.

CCP makes the most basic of ontological claims required of a constructivist perspective, that the world is socially constructed, that actors create the world by creating shared intersubjective meanings (culture, norms, common understandings) through interaction in a community, but also in turn derive their very identities and roles from these constructions. There is a real world out there, but it is not entirely determined by the physical and material; rather, it is socially constructed by shared meanings and understandings, and assumptions about the world that vary across human collectivities. This in turn involves attention to agent-structure relations, their co-constitution and structurationism.

Further, CCP can be distinguished from much of comparativist work by its differing methodological and analytic positions, about the relevant elements to be incorporated into analysis and the relations between them, along culturalist and transnational themes. CCP is convinced of the value of intersubjectivisms for understanding actors and action and fully incorporates interpretivist elements such as identity, culture, worldviews and cognitive frames, norms, principles, ideas, and new understandings of causal relationships in the world. In addition, CCP drops the "internal/external" barrier between state and international system that is often assumed in comparative analysis, transnationalizing all comparativist inquiry. Given constructivism's emphasis on the social, it seems advisable to adopt a view of the world of countries as a global social system, of overlapping webs of social interaction and politics. The world polity school and CIR offer excellent ideas on where this reconceptualization can lead and how to accomplish the integration of comparative politics and IR. On a different note, CCP also employs the agent-structure relation as a guide to better theory and a means of integrating comparativists to core debates in the social sciences.

Finally, in light of the new metatheoretical sophistication throughout the social sciences, comparativists must become more reflexive about their positions on epistemological and ontological questions. CCP as described here does not impose any orthodoxies, though some positions are more logical than others. I have suggested that the goal of investigation is causal *and* constitutive explanation *and* understanding, through thick description and analytic dissection of processes, and that CCP should be sensitive to the possibility of more generalizable conclusions, beyond the specificities of case studies. Also, true to its comparativist heritage, CCP should seek to produce compelling concepts that can be carefully applied to illuminate phenomena across cases. These constitute minimum first steps, ones that all the essays in this book take. The path beyond them is open and a rich agenda of issues and possibilities awaits.

The Chapters That Follow

This book is divided into two sections, one devoted to broader theoretical issues and the other to more case-oriented investigations. Each of the four theoretical chapters is especially devoted to communicating the possibilities of constructivism, particularly from constructivist international relations but also from sociology, to comparativists who may be unfamiliar with the approach. Kurt Burch's chapter provides a much more expanded discussion of CIR than my own, focusing especially on ROC, with an example of the "conceptual history" of property rights and their constitutive effects on early modern European politics and society. He lists several elements of CIR that are directly valuable to comparative politics. Patrick Jackson and Daniel Nexon highlight the impact of globalization on social science work, and suggest that for comparativists this is profound—the very units we traditionally compare are challenged and a shift in approach and methods is needed. The answer is a processual-relational one, their discussion of which provides an excellent explication of key issues in identity, ontology and epistemology. On the issue of the global-historical context of politics inside polities, Rod Hall discusses the development of collective identities, their social orders, and their institutional forms across five hundred years of European and world history. These describe the "templates" or modal forms that have guided actors in their sense of the legitimate and proper forms of politics in this period, to the "national-sovereign order" currently under challenge.

The "case-study" chapters touch on themes central to CCP, including identity, culture, and polities in a global-systemic context. Virginia Tilley's chapter concerns the effect on national politics of systemic norms and understandings about proper state form. Her focus is indigenous peoples and the ethnic coding of the supposedly neutral modern state. Bruce Magnusson's chapter on Benin is also emblematic of CCP, looking at how democratization in Africa has been a transnational process in which systemic influences are reconfigured by national-cultural lenses. Patricia Goff looks at identity as well, though in this case how identity is constructed, literally, in national cultural policies in the United States, the European Union, and Canada. Goff also shows how identity, interests, and rational calculi are not mutually exclusive, but interact. Finally, Patrick Jackson's chapter on the reconstruction of Germany after World War II reviews the ontological, epistemological, and methodological breaks with mainstream IR and comparative approaches needed to understand the role of "occidentalism" in Germany in this period. Jackson in some ways operationalizes the relational approach to constructivist comparative politics in his analysis, also employing an important set of research tools, in discursive analysis and actors use of "symbolic technologies," to understand his case.

Together, our chapters seek to illuminate key issues in comparative politics in the new millennium, and propose a constructivist approach as the best suited to these challenges. We hope also to accelerate the dialogue between comparative politics and international relations and cause comparativists to focus anew, with new analytic lenses and metatheoretical tools, on their changing discipline.

Notes

1. From the introduction to Lichbach and Zuckerman (1997: ix), which strikes a general tone of disappointment and crisis. Their comparisons of comparativists with American and IR scholars are particularly telling: "Unlike students of American politics, comparativists do not draw on methodological advances to power their scholarship. Unlike students of international politics, comparativists do not debate grand questions of theory. A field established by the founders of social thought and reinvented by some of the most important political scientists of the postwar era needs to be discovered yet again."
2. For one effort to understand patterns of simultaneous political change, see Green (1999, 2000).
3. A useful metaphor for this new world is "neo-medievalism," which achieved considerable currency in international relations theory a few years ago (Ruggie 1986, 1993). Before the consolidation of the centralized sovereign state, there was a "nonexclusive form of territoriality" in medieval Europe, with multiple, overlapping, competing, and incomplete layers of power: the Roman Catholic Church and Holy Roman Empire and its chain of ecclesiastical powers, kings of weak, nascent nationstates, and of course the multitude of local lords and potentates yet to be absorbed or subjugated by central states.
4. Useful treatments of the influences of the interpretivist and cognitive revolutions include Gibbons (1987), Giddens and Turner (1987), DiMaggio and Powell (1991: 11–27), Rosenau (1992, chapter 1), and John Hall (1993). Perhaps the most influential development for the consuming academic public came out of phenomenology and the oft-cited landmark of *The Social Construction of Reality* by Peter Berger and Thomas Luckmann (1966). Phenomenology holds that reality is only "appearance and experience" (Waters 1994: 31), such that what is interesting is how people take sense data and allocate it to categories of phenomena—a bicycle, a divorce, social injustice. Particularly appealing to later proponents of interpretivist institutionalisms is Berger and Luckmann's extensive discussion of how human activity and their meanings are habitualized, shared, and institutionalized by human collectivities, to become effectively real "objective facticities" (1966: 18, 47–92).
5. Interpretivism's move has also been described as a revolt against the sin of

"foundationalist decontextualization"—that is, the assumption that the drives of actors are fixed and can be assumed regardless of context (Steinmetz 1999: 20–21).

6. Interpretivism has in recent years won considerable ground against contending perspectives, forcing small paradigmatic shifts in rationalists and structuralists, for example (Adams 1999; Katznelson 1997; Levi 1997).

7. My distinction between constructionism and constructivism does not hold for other disciplines. For other accounts, see Crotty (1998: 57–58) and Hacking (1999: 40–49).

8. Perhaps a moment of opportunity, also, to unite comparativists with Americanists, international relations scholars, and others (Katznelson 1997: 81–83).

9. The plea to transnationalize comparative politics has been made time and again (Gourevitch 1978; Kahler 1984; Caporaso 1997; Janos 1997), but it remains to be acted upon by most comparativists. This book suggests that in part the problem may have been pseudomethodological, awaiting a constructivist solution. CCP offers a means of integrating comparative with international relations (in particular via CCP's natural companion, constructivist international relations), and therefore, should facilitate the task.

10. Katznelson (1997: 86) reminds us that a lack of metatheoretical sophistication has handicapped structuralism, making it vulnerable to charges of functionalism and teleology.

11. Lichbach (1997: 245) describes ontology as "certain presuppositions about the way the world is constructed . . . about the nature of existence: the entities and their properties that populate our lives." For Kubálková, Onuf, and Kowert, "[o]ntology deals with essence and appearance, the nature of things and how they are related, and how this affects the way that things appear to us" (1998: 14). Comparativists are beginning to use such terms more readily, though quantitative/qualitative debates have always had ontological and epistemological implications. For some of these comparativist discussions, see Laitin (1995), Lichbach (1997), Hall (2001), Hall and Taylor (1998), Hay and Wincott (1998).

12. Thus, to the argument that interpretivists are only interested in "understanding" and not explanation (Lichbach 1997; Price 1994; also Hollis and Smith 1990), I argue here for doing both. This is sympathetic to Wendt (1998, 1999), who argues that the distinction between the two is not a clear one and that any political scientist is really interested in doing both. Similarly, Walter Carlsnaes (1992) claims to have united explanation and understanding by resolving the agent-structure problem with bracketing of agent and structure and a temporal sequencing of interactions between the two. See also Price and Reus-Smit (1998).

13. Indeed, Alexander Wendt's recent book (1999) is a monument to this realization, as he spends a full two hundred pages explicating his ontology and epistemology.

14. By this logic, deploying evidence to make claims of accuracy means that one has become a positivist, perhaps an unfair cognitive leap. By this criterion most are guilty. But this is also a very thin definition of the core of positivism.

15. Antecedents include Simon (1945) and Selznick (1957).

16. In part because his work was pioneering, Sabel's inspirations and supporting citations are few: Max Weber, Clifford Geertz (The Interpretation of Culture, 1973), and Pierre Bourdieu (Outline of a Theory of Practice, 1977), plus E.P. Thompson's landmark study of working class culture in England (1963), but not much more. By comparison, constructivist international relations certainly did not suffer from this trouble, even at the outset, being packed with metatheory and philosophy of science (Wendt 1987; Dessler 1989; Onuf 1989).

17. March and Olsen, in their 1989 book *Rediscovering Institutions*, elaborate upon their rejoinder to rational choice by suggesting alternative mechanisms for explaining actions, such as "logics of appropriateness" and "logics of consequentiality."

18. Useful surveys of this institutionalist literature include Hall (1997), Koelble (1995), and Pontusson (1995).

19. See Hollinger (1997), on the origins of identity studies in the United States in the 1970s. Hale (1997) is a very good introduction to identity politics as well.

20. For example, on the American national character literature, see the citations in Tarver (1992).

21. While the boundaries between and varieties within the generic and social identity categories are relatively unexplored, there may be a useful connection between generic identity and the world polity school, though SI's descriptions of the modern modal state form are highly detailed. In CIR, the expectations for modal state type vary, but mainly get more narrowly defined, approaching the detail of SI (Ruggie 1998). These two literatures overlap and exchange ideas on this point (see Eyre and Suchman 1996; Jepperson, Wendt, and Katzenstein 1996: 35–36).

22. Problematization of state interests is exciting for IR theorists because domestic policy processes are commonly assumed away, except in foreign policy studies, where the policy process is central. But for comparativists, if interested, national interests in international relations would obviously be the subject of a policy process, interest group contestation, institutional structures, etc; neither exogenous nor a puzzle.

23. Martha Finnemore (1996b: 14–28) also provides an extremely useful comparison of these two perspectives, plus a third global social-structural perspective, the "English School" of international relations and the work of Hedley Bull, Martin Wight, and others. For reasons of space and because developments in the other two have been extensive and promising of late, I leave the English School out here.

24. Just as with political science's institutionalists, many sociological institutionalists do not pay attention to or incorporate the global social system in their explanations. Those sociological institutionalists that have definitively turned to world culture explanations are a smaller subset: John Meyer, John Boli, George Thomas, Francisco Ramirez, and others. On other sociological institutionalist work, see DiMaggio and Powell (1991).

Bibliography

Adams, Julia. 1999. "Culture in Rational-Choice Theories of State Formation." In *State/Culture: State-Formation after the Cultural Turn*, ed. George Steinmetz, 98–122. Ithaca: Cornell University Press.

Adler, Emanuel. 1997. "Seizing the Middle Ground: Constructivism in World Politics." *European Journal of International Relations* 3: 319–363.

Almond, Gabriel, and Stephen Genco. 1977. "Clouds, Clocks, and the Study of Politics." *World Politics* 29: 489–522.

Anderson, Benedict. 1991. *Imagined Communities*. 2^d ed. London: Verso.

Armstrong, David. 1998. "Globalization and the Social State." *Review of International Studies* 24: 461–478.

Axford, Barrie. 1995. *The Global System: Economics, Politics and Culture*. New York: St. Martin's.

Bates, Robert H. 1997. "Area Studies and the Discipline: A Useful Controversy?" *PS* 29: 166–169.

Berezin, Mabel. 1997. "Politics and Culture: A Less Fissured Terrain. In *Annual Review of Sociology* 23: 367–383. Palo Alto, CA: Annual Reviews.

Berger, Peter, and Thomas Luckmann. 1966. *The Social Construction of Reality*. New York: Anchor Books.

Berger, Thomas U. 1996. "Norms, Identity and National Security in Germany and Japan." In *The Culture of National Security*, ed. Peter Katzenstein, 317–356. New York: Columbia University Press.

Berk, Gerald. 1990. "Constituting Corporations and Markets: Railroads in Gilded Age Politics." *Studies in American Political Development* 4: 130–168.

Boli, John, and George M. Thomas. 1997. "World Culture in the World Polity: A Century of International Non-Governmental Organization." *American Sociological Review* 62: 172–190.

———, eds. 1999. *Constructing World Culture: International Non-Governmental Organizations since 1875*. Stanford: Stanford University Press.

Bukovansky, Mlada. 1997. "American Identity and Neutral Rights from Independence to the War of 1812." *International Organization* 51: 209–243.

———. 1999. "The Altered State and the State of Nature–the French Revolution and International Politics." *Review of International Studies* 25: 197–215.

Brysk, Alison. 1995. "'Hearts and Minds': Bringing Symbolic Politics Back In." *Polity* 27: 559–606.

Burch, Kurt. 1998. *"Property" and the Making of the International System*. Boulder: Lynne Rienner.

Cable, Vincent. 1995. "The Diminished Nation-State: A Study in the Loss of Economic Power." *Daedalus* 124: 23–53.

Campbell, David. 1993. *Politics Without Principle: Sovereignty, Ethics, and the Narratives of the Gulf War*. Boulder: Lynne Rienner.

Caporaso, James A. 1997. "Across the Great Divide: Integrating Comparative and International Politics." *International Studies Quarterly* 41: 563–591.

Carlsnaes, Walter. 1992. "The Agency-Structure Problem in Foreign Policy Analysis." *International Studies Quarterly* 36: 245–270.

Cerny, Philip G. 1990. *The Changing Architecture of Politics: Structure, Agency, and the Future of the State*. London: Sage.

———. 1995. "Globalization and the Changing Logic of Collective Action." *International Organization* 49: 595–625.

Cohen, Jean. 1985. "Strategy or Identity: New Theoretical Paradigms and Contemporary Social Movements." *Social Research* 52: 633–716.

Cortell, Andrew P., and James W. Davis, Jr. 2000. "Understanding the Domestic Impact of International Norms: A Research Agenda." *International Studies Review* 2: 65–87.

Crotty, Michael. 1998. *The Foundations of Social Research: Meaning and Perspective in the Research Process*. London: Sage.

Dessler, David. 1989. "What's at Stake in the Agent-Structure Debate?" *International Organization* 43: 441–473.

———. 1999. "Constructivism within a Positivist Social Science." *Review of International Studies* 25: 123–137.

DiMaggio, Paul J., and Walter W. Powell. 1983. "The Iron Cage Revisited: Institutional Isomorphism and Collective Rationality in Organizational Fields." *American Sociological Review* 48: 147–160.

———. 1991. "Introduction." In *The New Institutionalism in Organizational Analysis*, ed. Walter Powell and Paul DiMaggio, 1–38. Chicago: University of Chicago Press.

Dobbin, Frank. 1993. "The Social Construction of the Great Depression: Industrial Policy during the 1930s in the United States, Britain, and France." *Theory and Society* 22: 1–56.

———. 1994. *Forging Industrial Policy: The United States, Britain, and France in the Railway Age*. Cambridge, UK: Cambridge University Press.

Dyson, Kenneth. 1983. "The Cultural, Ideological and Structural Context." In *Industrial Crisis: A Comparative Study of the State and Industry*, ed. Kenneth Dyson and Stephen Wilks, 26–66. Oxford: Martin Robinson.

Eisenstadt, Shmuel N., and Bernhard Giesen. 1995. "The Construction of Collective Identity." *Archives Européenes de Sociologie* 36: 72–102.

Emirbayer, Mustafa. 1997. "Manifesto for a Relationalist Sociology." *American Journal of Sociology* 103: 281–317.

Escobar, Arturo. 1995. *Encountering Underdevelopment: The Making and Unmaking of the Third World*. Princeton: Princeton University Press.

Eyre, Dana P., and Mark C. Suchman. 1996. "Status, Norms, and the Proliferation of Conventional Weapons: An Institutional Theory Approach." In *The Culture of National Security*, ed. Peter Katzenstein, 79–113. New York: Columbia University Press.

Farrell, Theo. 1998. "Culture and Military Power." *Review of International Studies* 24: 407–416.

Finnemore, Martha. 1996a. "Norms, Culture and World Politics: Insights from Sociology's Institutionalism," *International Organization*, 50: 325–347.

———. 1996b. *National Interests in International Society*. Ithaca: Cornell University Press.

Gamson, William A., and David S. Meyer. 1996. "Framing Political Opportunity." In *Comparative Perspectives on Social Movements*, ed. Doug McAdam, John McCarthy, and Mayer Zald, 275–290. Cambridge, UK: Cambridge University Press.

Gibbons, Michael T., ed. 1987. *Interpreting Politics*. New York: NYU Press.

Giddens, Anthony, and Jonathan Turner, eds. 1987. *Social Theory Today*. Stanford: Stanford University Press.

Gourevitch, Peter. 1978. "The Second Image Reversed: The International Sources of Domestic Politics." *World Politics* 32: 881–912.

Green, Daniel M. 1999. "The Lingering Liberal Moment: An Historical Perspective on the Global Durability of Democracy after 1989." *Democratization* 6: 1–41.

———. 2000. "Liberal Moments and Democracy's Durability: Comparing Global Outbreaks of Democracy—1918, 1945, 1989." *Studies in Comparative International Development* 34: 83–120.

Grendstad, Gunnar, and Per Selle. 1995. "Cultural Theory and the New Institutionalism." *Journal of Theoretical Politics* 7: 5–27.

Hacking, Ian. 1999. *The Social Construction of What?* Cambridge, MA: Harvard University Press.

Haggard, Stephan. 1988. "The Institutional Foundations of Hegemony: Explaining the Reciprocal Trade Agreements Act of 1934." In *The State and American Foreign Economic Policy*, ed. John Ikenberry, David Lake, and Michael Mastanduno, 91–119. Ithaca: Cornell University Press.

Hale, Charles. R. 1997. "Cultural Politics of Identity in Latin America." *Annual Review of Anthropology* 26: 567–590. Palo Alto, CA: Annual Reviews.

Hall, John A. 1993. "Ideas and the Social Sciences." In *Ideas and Foreign Policy: Beliefs, Institutions and Political Change*, ed. Judith Goldstein and Robert Keohane, 31–54. Ithaca: Cornell University Press.

Hall, Peter A. 1986. *Governing the Economy: The Politics of State Intervention in Britain and France*. New York: Oxford University Press.

————. 1992. "The Movement from Keynesianism to Monetarism: Institutional Analysis and British Economic Policy in the 1970s." In *Structuring Politics: Historical Institutionalism in Comparative Analysis*, ed. Sven Steinmo, Kathleen Thelen and Frank Longstreth, 90–113. Cambridge, UK: Cambridge University Press.

————. 1993. "Policy Paradigms, Social Learning, and the State." *Comparative Politics* 23: 275–296.

————. 1997. "The Role of Interests, Institutions, and Ideas in the Comparative Political Economy of the Industrialized Nations." In *Comparative Politics: Rationality, Culture, and Structure*, ed. Mark Irving Lichbach and Alan S. Zuckerman, 174–207. Cambridge: Cambridge University Press.

————. 2001. "Aligning Ontology and Methodology in Comparative Research." Forthcoming in *Comparative Historical Research*, ed. James Mahoney and Dietrich Rueschemeyer.

Hall, Peter A., and Rosemary C.R. Taylor. 1996. "Political Science and the Three New Institutionalisms." *Political Studies* 44: 936–957.

————. 1998. "The Potential of Historical Institutionalism: A Response to Hay and Wincott." *Political Studies* 46: 958–962.

Hall, Rodney Bruce. 1999. *National Collective Identity: Social Constructs and International Systems*. New York: Columbia University Press.

Hay, Colin, and Daniel Wincott. 1998. "Structure, Agency and Historical Institutionalism." *Political Studies* 46: 951–957.

Herman, Robert G. 1996. "Identity, Norms, and National Security: The Soviet Foreign Policy Revolution and the End of the Cold War." In *The Culture of National Security*, ed. Peter Katzenstein, 271–316. New York: Columbia University Press.

Hollinger, David A. 1997. "The Disciplines and the Identity Debates, 1970–95." *Daedalus* 126: 333–351.

Hollis, Martin, and Steve Smith. 1990. *Explaining and Understanding International Relations*. Oxford: Clarendon Press.

————. 1994. "Two Stories about Structure and Agency." *Review of International Studies* 20: 241–251.

Hopf, Ted. 1998. "The Promise of Constructivism in International Relations Theory," *International Security* 23: 171–200.

Janos, Andrew. 1997. "Paradigms Revisited: Productionism, Globality and Postmodernity in Comparative Politics." *World Politics* 50: 118–149.

Jarvis, Anthony P., and Albert J. Paolini. 1995. "Locating the State." In *The State in Transition: Reimagining Political State*, ed. Joseph Camilleri, Anthony Jarvis and Albert Paolini, 3–19. Boulder: Lynne Rienner.

Jepperson, Ronald, Alexander Wendt, and Peter Katzenstein. 1996. "Norms, Identity, and the Culture of National Security." In *The Culture of National Security*, ed. Peter Katzenstein, 33–78. New York: Columbia University Press.

Johnson, Chalmers. 1997. "Preconception vs. Observation, or the Contributions of Rational Choice Theory and Area Studies to Contemporary Political Science," *PS* 29: 170–174.

Johnston, Alastair Iain. 1999. "Strategic Cultures Revisited: Reply to Colin Gray." *Review of International Studies* 25: 519–523.

Kahler, Miles. 1984. *Decolonization in Britain and France: The Domestic Consequences of International Relations.* Princeton: Princeton University Press.

Katzenstein, Peter, ed. 1996. *The Culture of National Security.* New York: Columbia University Press.

Katzenstein, Peter, Robert O. Keohane, and Stephen D. Krasner, eds. 1999. *Exploration and Contestation in the Study of World Politics.* Cambridge, MA: MIT Press.

Katznelson, Ira. 1997. "Structure and Configuration in Comparative Politics." In *Comparative Politics: Rationality, Culture, and Structure,* ed. Mark Irving Lichbach and Alan Zuckerman, 81–112. Cambridge, UK: Cambridge University Press.

Kaufman, Jason Andrew. 1998. "Competing Conceptions of Individualism in Contemporary American AIDS Policy: A Re-Examination of Neo-Institutionalist Analysis." *Theory and Society* 27: 635–669.

King, Gary, Robert Keohane, and Sidney Verba. 1994. *Designing Social Inquiry: Scientific Inference in Qualitative Research.* Princeton: Princeton University Press.

Klandermans, Bert. 1992. "The Social Construction of Protest and Multiorganizational Fields." In *Frontiers in Social Movement Theory,* ed. Aldon D. Morris and Carol McClurg Mueller, 77–103. New Haven: Yale University Press.

Koelble, Thomas A. 1995. "The New Institutionalism in Political Science and Sociology." *Comparative Politics* 27: 231–243.

Kohli, Atul, Peter Evans, Peter J. Katzenstein, Adam Przeworski, Suzanne Hoeber Rudolph, James C. Scott, and Theda Skocpol. 1995. "The Role of Theory in Comparative Politics: A Symposium." *World Politics* 48: 1–49.

Kowert, Paul. 1998. "Agent versus Structure in the Construction of National Identity." In *International Relations in a Constructed World,* ed. Vendulka Kubálková, Nicholas Onuf, and Paul Kowert, 101–122. Armonk, NY: M.E. Sharpe.

Kowert, Paul, and Jeffrey Legro. 1996. "Norms, Identity, and Their Limits: A Theoretical Reprise." In *The Culture of National Security,* ed. Peter Katzenstein, 451–497. New York: Columbia University Press.

Krieger, Joel. 1999. "Egalitarian Social Movements in Western Europe: Can They Survive Globalization and the EMU?" *International Studies Review* 3: 69–84.

Kubálková, Vendulka, Nicholas Onuf, and Paul Kowert. 1998. "Constructing Constructivism." In *International Relations in a Constructed World,* ed. Vendulka Kubálková, Nicholas Onuf, and Paul Kowert, 3–21. Armonk, NY: M.E. Sharpe.

Laitin, David. 1995. "Disciplining Political Science."*American Political Science Review* 89: 454–457.

Levi, Margaret. 1997. "A Model, a Method, and a Map: Rational Choice in Comparative and Historical Analysis." In *Comparative Politics: Rationality, Culture, and Structure,* ed. Mark Irving Lichbach and Alan S. Zuckerman, 19–41. Cambridge: Cambridge University Press.

Lichbach, Mark I. 1997. "Social Theory and Comparative Politics." In *Comparative Politics: Rationality, Culture, and Structure,* ed. Mark Irving Lichbach and Alan S. Zuckerman, 239–276. Cambridge, UK: Cambridge University Press.

———. 1998. "Contending Theories of Contentious Politics and the Structure-Action Problem of Social Order." In *Annual Review of Political Science* 1: 401–424. Palo Alto, CA: Annual Reviews.

Lichbach, Mark Irving, and Alan Zuckerman, eds. 1997. *Comparative Politics: Rationality, Culture, and Structure.* Cambridge: Cambridge University Press.

Lyons, Gene M., and Michael Mastanduno, eds. 1995. *Beyond Westphalia? State Sovereignty and International Intervention*. Baltimore: Johns Hopkins University Press.

Mahoney, James, and Richard Snyder. 1999. "Rethinking Agency and Structure in the Study of Regime Change." *Studies in Comparative International Development* 34: 3–32.

Mamdani, Mahmood. 1996. *Citizen and Subject: Contemporary Africa and the Legacy of Late Colonialism*. Princeton: Princeton University Press.

March, James G., and Johan Olsen. 1984. "The New Institutionalism: Organizational Factors in Political Life." *American Political Science Review* 78: 734–749.

———. 1989. *Rediscovering Institutions: The Organizational Basis of Politics*. New York: Free Press.

Markoff, John. 1996. *Waves of Democracy: Social Movements and Political Change*. Thousand Oaks, CA: Pine Forge.

McAdam, Doug. 1996. "Conceptual Origins, Current Problems, Future Directions." In *Comparative Perspectives on Social Movements*, ed. Doug McAdam, John McCarthy, and Mayer Zald, 23–40. Cambridge, UK: Cambridge University Press.

McAdam, Doug, John D. McCarthy, and Mayer N. Zald, eds. 1996. *Comparative Perspectives on Social Movements*. Cambridge, UK: Cambridge University Press.

McGrew, Anthony G., and Paul G. Lewis et al. 1992. *Global Politics: Globalization and the Nation-State*. Cambridge, UK: Polity.

Meyer, John, and Brian Rowan. 1977. "Institutionalized Organization: Formal Structure as Myth and Ceremony." *American Journal of Sociology* 83: 340–363.

Meyer, John, John Boli, George M. Thomas, and Francisco O. Ramirez. 1997. "World Society and the Nation-State." *American Journal of Sociology* 103: 144–181.

Mitchell, Timothy. 1991. "The Limits of the State: Beyond Statist Approaches and their Critics." *American Political Science Review* 85: 77–96.

Moore, Barrington. 1966. *Social Origins of Dictatorship and Democracy*. Boston: Beacon Press.

Morris, Aldon D, and Carol McClurg Mueller, eds. 1992. *Frontiers in Social Movement Theory*. New Haven: Yale University Press.

Mueller, Carol McClurg. 1992. "Building Social Movement Theory." In *Frontiers in Social Movement Theory*, ed. Aldon D. Morris and Carol McClurg Mueller, 3–25. New Haven: Yale University Press.

Neufeld, Mark. 1995. *The Restructuring of International Relations Theory*. Cambridge UK: Cambridge University Press.

Oberschall, Anthony. 1996. "Opportunities and Framing in the Transition to Democracy: The Case of Russia." In *Comparative Perspectives on Social Movements*, ed. Doug McAdam, John McCarthy, and Mayer Zald, 122–137. Cambridge, UK: Cambridge University Press.

Onuf, Nicholas Greenwood. 1989. *World of Our Making: Rules and Rule in Social Theory and International Relations*. Columbia: University of South Carolina Press.

———. 1994. "The Constitution of International Society." *European Journal of International Law* 5: 1–19.

———. 1998. "Constructivism: A User's Manual." In *International Relations in a Constructed World*, ed. Vendulka Kubálková, Nicholas Onuf, and Paul Kowert, 58–78. Armonk, NY: M.E. Sharpe.

Patomäki, Heikki, and Colin Wight. 2000. "After Postpositivism? The Promises of Critical Realism." *International Studies Quarterly* 44: 213–237.

Pierson, Paul. 1993. "When Effect Becomes Cause: Policy Feedback and Political Change." *World Politics* 45: 595–628.

Pontusson, Jonas. 1995. "From Comparative Public Policy to Political Economy: Putting Political Institutions in Their Place and Taking Interests Seriously." *Comparative Political Studies* 28: 117–147.

Price, Richard. 1994. "Interpretation and Disciplinary Orthodoxy in International Relations," *Review of International Studies* 20: 201–204.

Price, Richard, and Christian Reus-Smit. 1998. "Dangerous Liaisons? Critical International Theory and Constructivism." *European Journal of International Relations* 4: 259–294.

Price, Richard, and Nina Tannenwald. 1996. "Norms and Deterrence: The Nuclear and Chemical Weapons Taboos." In *The Culture of National Security*, ed. Peter Katzenstein, 114–152. New York: Columbia University Press.

Prizel, Ilya. 1998. *National Identity and Foreign Policy: Nationalism and Leadership in Poland, Russia and Ukraine*. Cambridge, UK: Cambridge University Press.

Radcliffe, Sarah, and Sallie Westwood. 1996. *Remaking the Nation: Place, Identity and Politics in Latin America*. London: Routledge.

Reus-Smit, Christian. 1997. "The Constitutional Structure of International Society and the Nature of Fundamental Institutions." *International Organization* 51: 555–589.

Risse-Kappen, Thomas. 1995. "Democratic Peace–Warlike Democracies? A Social Constructivist Interpretation of the Liberal Argument." *European Journal of International Relations* 1: 491–517.

Rosenau, Pauline Marie. 1992. *Post-Modernism and the Social Sciences: Insights, Inroads and Intrusions*. Princeton: Princeton University Press.

Ross, Marc Howard. 1997. "Culture and Identity in Comparative Political Analysis." In *Comparative Politics: Rationality, Culture, and Structure*, ed. Mark Irving Lichbach and Alan S. Zuckerman, 42–80. Cambridge, UK: Cambridge University Press.

Rothstein, Bo. 1992. "Labor-Market Institutions and Worlking-Class Strength." In *Structuring Politics: Historical Institutionalism in Comparative Analysis*, ed. Sven Steinmo, Kathleen Thelen, and Frank Longstreth. Cambridge, UK: Cambridge University Press.

Rueschmeyer, Dietrich, and Theda Skocpol, eds. 1996. *States, Social Knowledge, and the Origins of Modern Social Policies*. Princeton: Princeton University Press.

Ruggie, John Gerard. 1986. "Continuity and Change in the World Polity: Toward a Neorealist Synthesis." In *Neorealism and Its Critics*, ed. Robert Keohane. New York: Columbia University Press.

———. 1993. "Territoriality and Beyond: Problematizing Modernity in International Relations." *International Organization* 47: 139–174.

———. 1998. *Constructing the World Polity*. London: Routledge.

Sabel, Charles F. 1982. *Work and Politics: The Division of Labor in Industry*. Cambridge UK: Cambridge University Press.

Selznick, Philip. 1957. *Leadership in Administration*. Evanston, IL: Row, Peterson.

Simon, Herbert A. 1945. *Administrative Behavior*. New York: Free Press.

Skocpol, Theda. 1979. *States and Social Revolutions*. Cambridge, UK: Cambridge University Press.

———. 1992. *Protecting Soldiers and Mothers: The Political Origins of Social Policy in the United States*. Cambridge MA: Harvard University Press.

Skocpol, Theda, and Kenneth Finegold. 1982. "Economic Intervention and the Early New Deal." *Political Science Quarterly* 97: 255–278.

Smith, Steve. 2000. "Wendt's World." *Review of International Studies* 26: 151–163.

Snow, David A., and Robert D. Benford. 1992. "Master Frames and Cycles of Protest." In *Frontiers in Social Movement Theory*, ed. Aldon D. Morris and Carol McClurg Mueller, 133–155. New Haven: Yale University Press.

Sohrabi, Nader. 1999. "Revolution and State Culture: The Circle of Justice and Constitutionalism in 1906 Iran." In *State/Culture: State-Formation After the Cultural Turn*, ed. George Steinmetz, 253–288. Ithaca: Cornell University Press.

Somers, Margaret. 1992. "Narrativity, Narative Identity, and Social Action: Rethinking English Working Class Formation." *Social Science History* 16: 591–630.

———. 1993. "Citizenship and the Place of the Public Sphere: Law, Community, and Political Culture in the Transition to Democracy." *American Sociological Review* 58: 587–620.

———. 1998. "'We're No Angels': Realism, Rational Choice, and Relationality in Social Science." *American Journal of Sociology* 104: 722–784.

Spektorowski, Alberto. 1998. "Collective Identity and Democratic Construction: The Cases of Argentina and Uruguay." In *Constructing Collective Identities and Shaping Public Spheres in Latin America*, ed. Luis Roniger and Mario Sznajder, 103–122. Brighton, UK: Sussex Academic Press.

Steinmetz, George. 1999. "Introduction: Culture and the State." In *State/Culture: State-Formation after the Cultural Turn*, ed. George Steinmetz, 1–49. Ithaca: Cornell University Press.

Steinmo, Sven, Kathleen Thelen, and Frank Longstreth, ed. 1992. *Structuring Politics: Historical Institutionalism in Comparative Analysis.* Cambridge, UK: Cambridge University Press.

Tarrow, Sidney. 1994. *Power in Movement: Social Movements, Collective Action and Politics.* Cambridge, UK: Cambridge University Press.

———. 1996. "States and Opportunities: The Political Structuring of Social Movements." In *Comparative Perspectives on Social Movements*, ed. Doug McAdam, John McCarthy, and Mayer Zald, 41–61. Cambridge, UK: Cambridge University Press.

Tarver, Heidi. 1992. "The Creation of American National Identity." *Berkeley Journal of Sociology* 37: 55–99.

Taylor, Michael. 1989. "Structure, Culture and Action in the Explanation of Social Change." *Politics and Society* 17: 115–162.

Thelen, Kathleen. 1991. *Union of Parts: Labor Politics in Postwar Germany.* Ithaca: Cornell University Press.

Thelen, Kathleen, and Sven Steinmo. 1992. "Historical Institutionalism in Comparative Politics." In *Structuring Politics: Historical Institutionalism in Comparative Analysis*, ed. Sven Steinmo, Kathleen Thelen, and Frank Longstreth, 1–32. Cambridge, UK: Cambridge University Press.

Tilley, Virginia. 1997. "The Terms of the Debate: Untangling Language about Ethnicity and Ethnic Movements." *Ethnic and Racial Studies* 20: 497–522.

Waisman, Carlos. 1998. "The Dynamics of National Identity Frames: The Case of Argentina in the Twentieth Century." In *Constructing Collective Identities and Shaping Public Spheres*, ed. Luis Roniger and Mario Sznajder, 148–167. Sussex: Sussex Academic Press.

Waters, Malcolm. 1994. *Modern Sociological Theory.* London: Sage.

Weir, Margaret, and Theda Skocpol. 1985. "State Structures and the Possibilities for 'Keynesian' Responses to the Great Depression in Sweden, Britain and the United States." In *Bringing the State Back In*, ed. Peter Evans, Dietrich Rueschemeyer, and Theda Skocpol. Cambridge, UK: Cambridge University Press.

Wendt, Alexander. 1987. "The Agent-Structure Problem in International Relations Theory." *International Organization* 41: 335–370.

———. 1992. "Anarchy Is What States Make of It: The Social Construction of Power Politics." *International Organization* 46: 391–425.

———. 1994. "Collective Identity Formation and the International State." *American Political Science Review* 88: 384–396.

———. 1998. "On Constitution and Causation in International Relations." In *The Eighty Years Crisis: International Relations, 1919–1999*, ed. Tim Dunne, Michael Cox, and Ken Booth, 101–117. Cambridge, UK: Cambridge University Press.

———. 1999. *Social Theory of International Politics*. Cambridge, UK: Cambridge University Press.

Wight, Colin. 1999. "Meta Campbell: The Epistemological Problematics of Perspectivism." *Review of International Studies* 25: 311–316.

Wildavsky, Aaron. 1987. "Choosing Preferences by Constructing Institutions: A Cultural Theory of Preference Formation." *American Political Science Review* 81: 3–21.

———. 1994. "Why Self-Interest Means Less Outside of a Social Context: Cultural Contributions to a Theory of Rational Choice." *Journal of Theoretical Politics* 6: 131–159.

Yörük, Zafer F. 1997. "Turkish Identity from Genesis to the Day of Judgement." In *Politics and the Ends of Identity*, ed. Kathryn Dean, 103–134. Aldershot, UK: Ashgate.

Zuckerman, Alan S. 1997. "Reformulating Explanatory Standards and Advancing Theory in Comparative Politics." In *Comparative Politics: Rationality, Culture, and Structure*, ed. Mark Irving Lichbach and Alan S. Zuckerman, 277–310. Cambridge, UK: Cambridge University Press.

2

Toward a Constructivist
Comparative Politics

Kurt Burch

Introduction

A landmark recent volume on Comparative Politics (CP) declares that the field "has lost its way" and its promise goes unfulfilled (Lichbach and Zuckerman 1997: ix). This dispiriting condition challenges CP in four ways: posing new questions, identifying new research strategies, heightening attentiveness to new theories, and establishing new analytical means. First, new questions eclipse earlier research agendas. Comparativists increasingly explore questions of social *process*, such as the "creation" of identities and of consequent interests and conflicts (e.g., Cash 1996). Other contemporary research explores the "production" of social spaces and places (e.g., "the nation," "the state," cities), boundaries (e.g., national vs. international, public vs. private), and trajectories (e.g., "progress," "modernity"). Such concerns challenge the state-centered intellectual programs of CP's earlier generation of scholars.

Second, comparativists approach questions from three distinct research premises: rationality, culture, and structure. Little communication circulates among the camps. Lichbach and Zuckerman (1997: 13) suggest pursuing "creative confrontations" among these research traditions to stimulate interactions, comparisons, and diffusions of ideas.

Third, critics describe CP scholars as "theoretically challenged" because "self conscious reflection finds almost no home in our field [of CP]. We do not take our theories or our theorists seriously" (Lichbach 1997: 239–241). Nor generally do comparativists explore the affiliated questions of social theory and philosophy of science that underlay their methodological commitments to causal accounts, explanations, and covering laws (Burch, forthcoming). Thus, comparativists attend disproportionately to methods rather than to theory and the standards of explanation (Zuckerman 1997: 281; also

Lichbach 1997: 240). Indeed, some observers quip that comparative politics is a method, not a field. Fourth, given these circumstances, how might CP scholars aptly conduct comparisons (Lichbach 1997: 253–256, 260–267)?

This essay asks how efforts to restructure and reformulate social theory, especially constructivist approaches, may affect CP and the new challenges it confronts. The argument unfolds in four subsequent parts. In the next section, I describe the general themes of a constructivist approach, detail rival versions of constructivism, then outline how constructivism addresses the concerns confronting comparativists. The following section illustrates the contributions of constructivism by exploring a case study of the development of sovereignty and the boundary separating politics from economics in early modern Europe. This case pursues a comparativist injunction to explore the creation of significant social boundaries. The penultimate section details the virtues of constructivism and of conceptual histories for CP. The final section concludes.

Constructivism

A Primer

Constructivism addresses central dilemmas of social theory: how does the interplay of actors and social structures and of material and ideational factors constitute, inform, and explain social life? Drawing from a theoretical ferment apparent in many disciplines over the last several decades, social construction entered International Relations (IR) primarily through the work of Anthony Giddens (1984), Nicholas Onuf (1989), and Alexander Wendt (1992, 1995, 1999) and has now become a scholarly vogue. However, Onuf (1989: 55) describes the phrase "the social construction of reality" as "a cliché, an overworked excuse to say nothing further." To say more requires greater discrimination and precision in one's philosophical, theoretical, and analytical efforts. The "agent-structure problem" addresses one of the facets of social construction that constructivism seeks to address (Wendt 1987; Burch 1999).

In recent years several scholars have sought to outline constructivism's key principles and purposes. The work clarifies details but confuses the broader picture (e.g., Adler 1997; Checkel 1998; Gould 1998; Walt 1998). At root, neither actors nor social structures can be the Archimedean point of social inquiry, since they mutually constitute each other in a *continuous process* of social construction. In that process actors make choices. In contrast, comparativists and IR scholars often privilege either agents or structures rather than the processes of social construction.

Rather than wrestle with the agent-structure dilemma, constructivists seek to transcend it or account for it. Some (e.g., Onuf) attend to the causes and consequences of social action, not to the social actors. Others, described below, take agents and structures (or their "identities" and characteristics) as problematic, so pose questions about their origins. Some seek to explain the constitution of actors' identities and interests as a prelude to understanding their (rational?) choices. Still others seek to account for the constitution of normative structures of meaning—that is, the contexts and understandings that shape identities and behavior. Thus, co-constitution involves three foci: agents, structures, and meanings. These are the foci that Lichbach and Zuckerman identify: rationality (of agents), structure, and culture (as source of meaning). A comprehensive constructivist approach recognizes the co-constitution of conditions (ideas and material conditions), of society (agents and structures), and of subjective meaning among individuals and groups (Onuf 1989: 54–58).

Constructivism shifts attentions away from objects (actors, structures) to processes (constitution, construction, creation, learning), thereby sharing much with new impulses animating CP. Such research highlights three fundamental questions: What is the source of the interests and identities of individual actors? Are prevailing structures material or also social? What are the processes through which agents construct structures and structures constitute agents?

Answers follow from constructivism's three key premises: agents, structures, and social process. *Agents* are least problematic. Traditional scholars hold that agents possess interests, which they rationally pursue given their capabilities. Yet modern society no longer constitutes actors as chivalrous knights, alchemists, samurai, or geishas. Constructivists, however, premise that social structures constitute actors' identities, interests, or capabilities, just as actors' choices constitute patterned social structures.

Structures require more explanation. According to Wendt (1995: 72), "constructivists are structuralists" because the defining structures of world politics are social rather than material. These structures possess two features. First, while structures comprise in part the distribution of material resources and capabilities, such capabilities alone possess no explanatory power unless embedded in a system of meanings and values which define understandings and expectations. "Meaning" is social. Thus, second, the meanings conveyed in socially shared knowledge—whether the comprehensive knowledge conveyed in a culture or the specific knowledge embodied in a rule—structure social relationships. Socially shared knowledge attributes meaning to material conditions and identifies specific social roles and circumstances (Wendt 1999). For example, "[a]mity and enmity are social, not material, relations" (Wendt and Freidheim 1995: 692). Similarly, the material distribution of petroleum reserves did not affect global relations until technological innovations valued oil.

Thus, the meaning of "power" and "interests," for example, or the value of "resources," depends on the structure of shared knowledge. Meanings cause no effects apart from shared valuations. Actors may pursue interests understood as power, but the character of the interests, the basis of the power, and the nature of such understandings derive from actors' shared knowledge and social conditions. However, constructivists do not presume that the character or content of social structures is given. Rather, actors' choices construct social structures.

Both agents and structures exist in and by process. *Process* is the key to constructivist thought; rules are central to the process of social construction (Onuf 1989; Burch 2000). Wendt devotes little attention to the process of social construction, instead inferring it from outcomes (1992, 1995, 1999; Wendt and Friedheim 1995). However, other versions of constructivism attend specifically to processes of social construction by dismantling structures into complexes of rules or norms, which simultaneously organize social relations (via foundational rules or constitutive principles) and guide the conduct of actors (via sanctions or regulations).

As actors make policy choices, they support or erode some norms and rules of the society. Norms and rules convey the shared knowledge of a society, informing members what to do and how to do it: stop for red lights; grant immunity to foreign diplomats; do not shoot down unarmed civilian planes. Actors' choices indicate that norms and rules regulate conduct. Thus, most drivers, diplomats, and pilots operate safely. Actors' specific choices manifest how norms and rules transform or constitute a state of affairs. For example, diplomatic hostages and downed planes may create wholly new situations. Obeyed norms and rules buttress society by reinforcement; ignored or challenged norms and rules reshape society by erosion or demolition; new rules (re)shape society by constitution and construction. Governments condemned Iran's capture of U.S. diplomats; many expressed outrage over the civilian Korean jet downed by the USSR in the early 1980s; and the U.S. government leveled retaliatory sanctions when Cuba shot down a civilian plane in February 1996. Iranian, Soviet, and Cuban violations corroded prevailing norms and rules, but other actors' responses strengthened the violated rule and reinforced social structures. Thus, actors constitute social relations as they make policy choices in terms of existing norms and rules structuring society, yet these precepts simultaneously constitute actors, condition their choices, and shape their roles and interests.

In this light, Onuf (1994: 1) declares that international "society is a thing and a process." Wendt (1992) concludes, "Anarchy is what states make of it." Similarly, the cold war was what the superpowers made of it (Burch 1996). The cold war rivalry was constituted by social structures such as "common knowledge embodied in intersubjective phenomena like institutions and threat systems" (Wendt and Friedheim 1995: 691). Such knowledge and institutions yielded the cold war's well-known rules of the game and a form of indirect global rule marked by a hostile but stable global order. These structures constructed the unique roles of the United States and the USSR, as well as the interests they pursued. In recent years many international relations (IR) and CP scholars, constructivists included, have addressed security concerns in novel ways (e.g., Katzenstein 1996; Adler and Barnett 1998; Hunter 1998; Snyder 1999; and Weldes et al. 1999).

Note the parallel between constructivist premises and CP research agendas. Constructivism connects the three CP research traditions into a holistic approach to social theory. An agent-centered approach analyzes choice making and rationality. Structural approaches declare that institutions and social arrangements cause social effects (e.g., Lichbach 1997: 251–252; Wendt 1999). Attention to process highlights cultural rules and norms, so considers the sociocultural context in which action occurs.

Yet several versions of constructivism currently circulate in Political Science and IR. Each version differently configures the central elements and themes of constructivism. One version explains the mechanisms of social construction by introducing an ontology of rules as the mechanism of social construction. The most distinctive features of constructivism are its ontological premises, which have implications for one's methods, epistemology, and logic of inquiry (Ruggie 1998: 33–34). Different versions of constructivism share important elements: "their underlying philosophical bases and how those relate to the possibility of a social science" (Ruggie 1998: 35). In these terms, Ruggie distinguishes three versions of constructivism (the rows in Table 2.1). I also identify three versions of constructivism, distinguished by their central analytic foci or ontological claim (the columns). Arrayed together, the result is a nine-cell matrix (for alternatives see Onuf 1989: 57; Adler 1997: 331). Each entry (or form of constructivism) lends itself to rule-oriented analysis.

Versions of Constructivism

This section elaborates distinct versions of constructivism. Ruggie (1998: 35–36) distinguishes constructivism in terms of "neoclassical," "postmodern," and "naturalist" forms. *Neoclassical (modern)* versions of constructivism draw from the familiar traditions of Durkheim and Weber, presume a com-

Table 2.1

A Typology of Constructivisms

		ONTOLOGICAL FOCI		
		SOC	NOC	ROC
		State/Structure	Norms	Rules
E P I S T E M O L O G Y	Modern or neoclassical	Adler and Barnett (1998); Katzenstein (1996)	Ruggie (1998); Finnemore (1996); Keck and Sikkink (1998)	Onuf (1989, 1998); Kratochwil (1989)
	Natural	Wendt (1999)	?	?
	Critical or postmodern	Weldes et al. (1999)	Price (1995); Price and Reus-Smit (1998)	Burch (1998, 2000)

mitment to social science, and address intersubjective meanings. Ruggie places most IR and CP constructivists in this camp. *Postmodern (critical)* versions trace a lineage from Nietzsche to Foucault, dismiss the prospects for social science, and focus on the linguistic construction of subjects. Ashley, Campbell, and Walker are prime examples of this approach. The *naturalist* version shares aspects of the other two, but is grounded in the philosophy of scientific realism, hopefully anticipates novel social scientific advances, and addresses "nonobservables" in social life. Wendt and Dessler are the foremost scholars working in this middle ground.

However, one may differently distinguish constructivism's dimensions. I identify three versions distinguished by their ontological foci: structure-oriented, norm-oriented, and rules-oriented constructivism. I label them by the acronyms SOC, NOC, and ROC.

Structure-Oriented Constructivism

According to Wendt (1995: 72), all constructivists are structuralists, and all constructivism is "structural idealism" (1999: 1). Structure-oriented constructivism (SOC) considers how norms construct actors and interests and takes states as central actors. Put crudely, SOC looks at outcomes first (e.g., state-centered interests), then looks at how norms affect them. In Wendt's view, agents rationally employ their material capabilities to pursue interests, yet rationalism explains actors' behaviors only if the social context is fixed.

However, since structures constitute actors' interests and identities, then the context is always fluid, so one must offer alternative explanations. Wendt moves analytically to structures and philosophically to scientific realism. Fundamental, socially significant structures are social rather than material, since material capabilities per se cause nothing and require a social context to be meaningful (Wendt 1995: 73). Thus, structures comprise both material resources and shared knowledge—that is, structures are both material and ideational. We recognize them by their effects.

In CP and IR, SOC addresses specific outcomes (ideational, norm-driven identities and interests) of specific actors (states). This approach enriches the state-centric traditions of neorealism and neoliberalism in CP and IR, although it undermines positivist philosophical foundations. In principle, one could change focus to look at how norms affect structures and, in turn, how structures affect interests and identities of any actors. Thus, one may generalize this approach to "peoples" and other actors (e.g., Tilley 1997). Nonetheless, Wendt's SOC is an idiosyncratic position as gauged by its scientific realist foundations. However, in terms of his attention to the structural properties of norms, Wendt shares ground with a wider circle of constructivist scholars. I call the products of this wider circle norm-oriented constructivism.

Norm-Oriented Constructivism

John Ruggie (1998) and Martha Finnemore (1996) are two notable proponents of norm-oriented constructivism (NOC), also called sociological institutionalism. A landmark volume is Peter Katzenstein's edited collection (1996) titled *The Culture of National Security*. Ruggie, Finnemore, and Katzenstein's collection each offer an "institutionalist" approach that has roots in sociology. For Finnemore (1996: 2, 3) a state's "interests are not just 'out there' waiting to be discovered; they are constructed through social interaction . . . [and] are shaped by internationally shared norms and values that structure and give meaning to international political life." Prominent norms—and changes in those norms—can alter states' interests and behavior, so shift patterns of global relations. Thus, NOC looks at norms first, then at outcomes. Finnemore describes constructivism as a method (3–4) that problematizes actors and interests rather than taking them as given. This method informs causal explanations. In these terms she describes constructivism as a social theory (27). In her view, constructivists attribute causal status to "philosophic principles, identities, norms of behavior, [and] shared terms of discourse" (15). Specifically, she generates structural theory by transforming norms (along with beliefs, discourse, and culture) into social structures (22). She then inexplicably distorts this view by generalizing:

she asserts that constructivism emphasizes "the causal nature of social structures" in general (16). As a result, constructivism is simultaneously method, theory, and metatheory. The latter arises because constructivism raises and answers fundamental "philosophic issues" (5).

Ruggie (1998: 27) agrees. He makes the case bluntly: "Social constructivism in international relations has come into its own during the past decade or so, not only as metatheoretical critique but increasingly in the form of empirical evidence and insights." Ruggie (e.g., 1998: 33) understands constructivism much as Finnemore does. Said simply, constructivists seek to explain the identity and interests of actors by challenging the atomistic, positivist frameworks of traditional analyses. Further, constructivism "attributes to ideational factors, including culture, norms, and ideas, social efficacy over and above any functional utility they may have." In this light, constructivism conceives actors as reflective agents, rather than as programmed rational maximizers, capable of social creation within structured constraints (Ruggie 1998: 4).

In short, NOC declares that "norms count" because they constitute actors' identities and interests, which should be considered endogenous and socially constructed rather than exogenous and given (Ruggie 1998: 16). Said differently, culture and norms are becoming more prominent in the subfields of political science because they have for so long been eclipsed by the ontological polarity of agents (individual, rational actors) and structures (collectivities, having causal, constraining effects) (see Lapid and Kratochwil 1996). Further, drawing on a typology by Goldstein and Keohane (1993: 8–10), Ruggie (1998: 18–22) identifies three types of ideas that are causally significant: worldviews, principled beliefs, and causal beliefs. Also, both Finnemore and Ruggie distinguish types of causation. Finnemore (1996: 29–31) describes "logics of appropriateness" and "logics of consequences"; Ruggie (22) distinguishes "reasons for actions" and "causes of actions."

Ruggie aptly notes that many NOC scholars select a cultural norm, explore the social construction of the norm (that is, how the norm evolved), then see how that norm, once in place, affects social action (e.g., Price 1995; Katzenstein 1996). Yet there is no way to judge or identify prominent norms in advance. Rather, the choice is arbitrary. Thus, no necessary cumulation results, and the social consequences are not clearly comparable, except to catalogue the effects of norms and the results of co-constitution.

What is one to make of Ruggie's claims? His career—combining his scholarship on multilateralism and his practice as a United Nations official— testifies to his long-standing liberal-institutionalist instincts. In what sense is he a constructivist? In what sense has he been a constructivist for decades, as he now claims? He has indeed been interested in the significance and effects of ideas, but is this the hallmark of constructivism? He has also worked closely with Friedrich Kratochwil, but does that work stake out a decidedly constructivist terrain? Is Ruggie leaping atop a bandwagon and claiming the reins by hailing himself an early pioneer of constructivism? Or does he successfully seize, hold, and command a broader "middle ground" (Adler 1997) for social inquiry? Some scholars describe (norm-oriented) constructivism as the new "mainstream" in IR and IPE.

The common, middle ground may be quite broad. For example, given Wendt's collaboration with Katzenstein and Jepperson (Jepperson, Wendt, and Katzenstein 1996), it is unclear whether Wendt thinks SOC and NOC represent distinct positions. Similarly, NOC advocates may be structural idealists (SOCs) by default since they take for granted the structural properties of norms as system supports.

An alternative conception of constructivism steps away from causal explanation in two ways: first, by highlighting constitution rather than causality and, second, by describing itself as an analytical framework rather than a theory.

Rule-Oriented Constructivism

Nicholas Onuf (1989, 1997, 1998) and Friedrich Kratochwil (1989) are the premier exponents of rule-oriented constructivism (ROC). Social rules play a significant role in select literatures of law, international law, political theory, social theory, domestic politics, and from these, to IR and CP. In IR, attention to social rules developed inextricably from efforts by Kratochwil and Onuf to devise social constructivist theories over the last decade.

For constructivism to tell us anything remarkable about social life, it must identify the mechanisms of co-constitution that entwine agents with structures and enmesh material with ideational factors. Onuf offers unique answers because he offers a novel ontology that identifies social rules as the medium of social construction and social rule as the outcome. Also, Onuf links rules to the discursive practices of actors, since all social activity passes through the concepts and syntax of language (also Kratochwil 2001: 1, 16). In this regard, ROC is an analytical framework attentive to language, concepts, and discourse, but it is not a specific theory.

From linguistic premises concerning speech acts (e.g., Searle 1969), Onuf deduces three types of rules. Actors always make their choices about how to act in the context of social rules, whether formal laws or informal norms. Indeed, social structures are intricate complexes of rules, norms, and principles. In turn, the rulelike character of social relations always entails forms of social rule, also of three types corresponding to the typology of rules.

Thus, actors confront what appears to them to be a relatively fixed set of social relations embodying a mix of rules and consequent rule. As actors make decisions, they choose, in effect, to abide, evade, or assault specific rules. The result either strengthens or erodes specific rules, thereby shifting the shape and character of society and altering ultimately the dominant form of rule. To explain any specific instance of co-constitution and change requires a specific theory directed at the contingent issues. For example, to explain change in the Westphalian state system, Ruggie invokes theories of multilateralism; Susan Strange (1996), of technological change; Hendrik Spruyt (1994), of unit-change (see Burch 2000: 192–196).

Rules are significant because they link the material and ideational aspects of social structures. Property rights are particularly noteworthy since rules deploy resources. Similarly, other prominent concepts (such as authority, sovereignty, citizenship, etc.) may be subject to social rules and/or consequent rule. In this sense, ROC promotes a conceptual analysis of prominent organizing principles of social structures. Though NOC and SOC, in principle, conduct similar analyses of organizing principles, ROC focuses such inquiry since it further locates the prominent concepts within social rules. Those analysts who conduct conceptual histories recognize how valuably the approach complements ROC (e.g., Burch 1998).

What Can Constructivism Contribute in Particular to CP?

Constructivism offers four contributions to CP (see Table 2.2). First, new questions in CP increasingly address the "social production" of conditions (Table 2, column 1). Attention to social construction offers immediate analytical leverage and assists the latent critical impulse in much comparative work to challenge "givens." In column 1, I draw examples from my own work (e.g., Burch 1998) and my interest in the boundaries that mark the modern global political economy. In particular, I explore the conceptual split between politics and economics and the conceptual development of sovereignty, which demarcates domestic from international (or, in Walker's [1993] terms, demarcates inside from outside). Together, these conceptual boundaries constitute what I call conceptual "crosshairs" marking modernity and the state.

Many of the most exciting and most compelling controversies involve the construction of conceptual boundaries. Others include the construction of "nations" and "ethnicities" or the distinctions between "public" and "private" or between "quackery," "common sense," and "science."

Second, constructivism speaks simultaneously to matters of rationality, culture (ideational context), and social structures. Attention to actors raises

Table 2.2

Examples of Contributions of Constructivism to Comparative Politics

(1) Posing new questions:	(2)	(3)	(4a)	(4b)	(4c)	(4d)
the social construction of space and boundaries	Linking three traditions: rationality, culture, and structure	Attending to (meta) theory and explanation	Comparing processes of social construction	Comparing conditions of rules and rule	Comparing changes in rules and rule	Comparing conceptual histories
Crosshairs	*Agents act* (rationally) but not in narrowly utilitarian terms	Science is multitiered, including foundations, theory, and empirical findings	Social construction is a function of:	Social construction informs the exercise of rule, so the exercise (or reconstitution) of authority:	Feudalism: overlapping heteronomy and abridged hierarchy	Property informs:
Production of sovereignty			—agents' choices			—personal character
Production of politics/economics split	*Acting is structurally* constrained and *structurally* empowering; identities and interests are *structurally* influenced (e.g., the state, state-building)	Constructivism offers a set of novel ontologies, theoretical applications, and unique findings	—rationality and unintended consequences	—extends heteronomy	Modernity: domestic hierarchy, international heteronomy, global cultural hegemony	—personal possessions
Production of the state			—structures	—advocates liberal hegemony		—relationship to possessing and possessions
			—ideas and norms			—mobile and immobile possessions

71

Culture shapes decision-making calculations, structural forms, and dominant norms; i.e., culture affects rationality, structure, norms, and rules

Constructivism braids diverse explanations and causes: rationality, culture, structure; positivism, interpretation, scientific realism, rule-orientation

—rules

—reinforces hierarchy

—informs sovereignty and public life

Postmodernity: reconfiguration of international heteronomy and global cultural hegemony

—tangible and intangible possessions

—intellectual property

questions about rationality. Constructivism offers opportunities to conceive rationality in terms less beholden to narrowly utilitarian principles. Similarly, constructivists conceive structures in analytically insightful ways, though the character of structures may vary according to the analyst: sets of norms, institutions, complexes of rules. Also, constructivists consider culture in terms of the relative dominance or centrality of particular ideas, norms, or rules and in terms of the structuring effects of cultural values and worldviews. In any case, culture introduces "ideas," whether incorporated into actors' worldviews or into the character of social structures. Table 2.2, column 2, identifies how agents (rationality), structures, and culture may be individual or joint foci.

Third, constructivism fosters more self-conscious, explicit attention to matters of theory and explanation. Witness the frequent complaints that constructivists are too theoretical and/or metatheoretical. Witness also the exhaustive attention to matters of (meta)theory in the work of Wendt and Onuf.

Fourth, constructivism also offers a specific subject of comparison and a means of comparing. NOC draws attention to socially prominent norms. SOC does much the same. ROC focuses on rules, sets of rules, consequent social rule, and the conceptual subjects of those rules. More specifically, a ROC comparativist can seek to compare the set of rules and consequent rule that prevail in a particular social setting, across settings, or across time. In this sense constructivism helps comparativists explore social change. For example, one may conduct comparisons by looking at shifts in prevailing rules (Burch 2000) or by tracing conceptual histories (Burch 1994, 1998).

The following case study of the social construction of sovereignty, the state, and the boundary between politics and economics illustrates these contributions. The case explores the social production of the boundaries separating "politics" from "economics" and demarcating "national" space from "international." We recognize the latter boundary as sovereignty.

Attention to the social construction of boundaries contributes to CP by addressing topics frequently obscured by CP scholars. Traditionally, CP addresses only territorial boundaries as markers of conceptual space. For example, "cultures" were often thought to be located within state boundaries, as in studies of "political culture." Also, area studies were often premised on the view that one could identify different regions in terms of distinctive cultures. Studies of "structures" were often conducted in similar ways. Examples include studies of Latin American authoritarianism, European fascism and corporatism, and the ever-popular comparisons of democratic practices in the United States, the United Kingdom, and the European continent. However, such studies miss a good deal that is of interest to CP scholars. For example, how do ethnicities get demarcated and (self-) identified? What distinguishes "politics" from "law" or "ethics"? Is a postmodern or post-Enlightenment world in the offing? Many scholars declare that globalization blurs, breaks, and reconfigures boundaries, but how and to what effect? CP opens itself to a broader range of concerns by engaging the many compelling questions associated with the marking and shaping of conceptual space and its boundaries.

The following section addresses such questions.

Property, Sovereignty, and the Split Between Politics and Economics

This section recounts a conceptual history of "property" and "property rights" to explore the social construction of prominent social boundaries in northwestern Europe in the seventeenth century. Conceptual histories chronicle and evaluate changing meanings of concepts over time and circumstance. Prominent examples include a landmark survey of conceptual change by Ball et al. (1989), Hart's (1961) study of law, Macpherson's (1962) exploration of possessive individualism, Pocock's (1975) and Onuf's studies of republicanism (1998b), Lincoln's (1994) treatment of authority, Dryzek's (1996) study of democracy, and Pipes's (1999) investigation of property and freedom.

I argue that sixteenth- and seventeenth-century actors in what is now England, France, and the Netherlands did not conceive distinct political and economic realms because there existed no conceptual apparatus for discriminating property rights to landed, tangible properties from mobile, intangible ones (Burch 1994, 1998). Once the prevailing conception of property rights bifurcated into distinctly landed and mobile forms in the late 1600s, the split established the conceptual foundations for tangible, geographically centered politics (estates, the state, landed rights) and intangible, noncentered economics (markets, capitalist exchange, rights to mobile property). These early modern actors operated in a social system of conceptual and practical unity, which entailed social understandings and behaviors that maintained this unified worldview until material and conceptual changes altered the framework of understandings. In deed and in concept, their social system was constructed (constituted) as a unity.

Property and Sovereignty

Property rights were a means for recrafting authority and institutionalizing sovereignty in western Europe in the seventeenth century. This section draws on and elaborates earlier work by Burch (1994, 1997, 1998).

Revolution and regicide shattered the era. The significant crises of the

early half of the century generated a widespread need to reconstruct authority. In England political authority collapsed after the beheading of King
Charles in 1649. To reconstitute authority was to pose questions about the
principles by which society constituted political personality. On what basis
can one claim or recognize authority? On what basis should individuals obey?
What property rights (civil liberties) would citizens possess?

Property and property rights provided answers via their specific vocabulary and substantive focus (Tuck 1979). The solution was to concentrate
political authority, yet to justify sovereign *political* authority in terms of relatively exclusive *property* rights was to bring into public debate imperial notions of authority versus liberalized notions of exclusive rights. As a result,
political bargains led to the social construction of two forms of sovereignty
and two forms of property. A monarch exercises *royal sovereignty* over a
state and subjects; an individual exercises limited *personal sovereignty* over
herself and her possessions. A monarch exercises sovereignty on condition
the ruler respects individuals' private, personal property and personal liberty. *Real property* set the foundation for the claims by states' rulers to be
territorial rights-bearers—that is, landholding sovereigns. Emerging notions
of *mobile property* underscored merchants' claims to be rights-bearers, too—
that is, citizens possessing personal sovereignty, liberty, and exchangeable
goods. In the process, a stable, unitary conception of property metamorphosed
into the multiple and overlapping property rights that currently construct
social life.

Why would subjects and rulers engage in such a bargain? Amid the tumult of the times, citizens craved social order and effective authority. Simultaneously, early modern rulers lacked substantial physical resources and
personal influence. Royal resources rarely sufficed to satisfy public functions, so severely limited royal authority (de Jouvenal 1957: 178–180; Wilson 1977: 131–132; see also Howat 1974 and Kenyon 1978). Rulers went
hat in hand to parliaments and to individual citizens. Those asked negotiated
for favorable conditions or enhanced rights. "[B]efore the days of parliament there was no real sovereignty at all: sovereignty was only achieved by
the energy of the crown in parliament" (quoted by de Jouvenal 1957: 177).
Sovereigns were many, but sovereignty was rare. Sovereignty as we currently understand it was being socially constructed.

In political and rhetorical terms, the decisive move allied bourgeois elements with those advocating strengthened centralized authority. The bourgeoisie, freer of feudal bonds and increasingly able to participate in the
commercial revolution, now sought to protect its property and rights by but-
tressing public authority as a weapon against lingering feudal relations (de
Jouvenal 1957: 181).

Actors struck bargains. Rulers granted property rights to prominent bourgeois citizens and restless merchants to forge an institutional alliance to bring finances to royal coffers. Individuals transferred resources to the monarchy in exchange for rights. Through grants, rulers dispensed commercially advantageous property rights in politically beneficial ways (Burch 1994). Such exchanges transformed the monarchy into the crown state. "Sovereignty became a distinct institution when the claim to supreme authority was coupled with a specific *rule of allocation* for exercising this authority" (Kratochwil 1995: 25; italics added). Absolute or unqualified sovereign authority never existed because sovereignty was always conditioned in two ways: by the royal need for resources and by the royal commitment to respect citizen's property rights. Thus, political "sovereignty" represents *claims* of rights, specifically the right to rule and rights of authority.

As a property right, "sovereignty" is the highest, most complete right of ownership. To call such property rights "absolute sovereignty" in the seventeenth century connoted not absolute power or authority, but absolute (pure, uncontested) *claims to property*. Further, a socially advantageous fiction arose from citizens' guarded recognition of supreme authority on the basis of enhanced property rights for themselves and "absolutely sovereign" monarchical claims to property. Since monarchs possessed the strong titles (property rights), then their claims to authority seemed most likely to succeed, so most likely to reconstitute authority, reconstruct society, and protect blossoming liberal relations. Bourgeois citizens exacted an exchange. "Unless men inherited or acquired property, it was hard to see how they acquired an obligation to obey the laws of society. . . . [F]reedom must have a material base: that a man must own himself if he were not to be owned by another" (Pocock 1977: 27).

Such claims to sovereign political authority, sufficiently grounded in legal property rights claims, satisfied many domestic groups' craving to create a stable, workable, tolerable social order. Since alternative claims to authority were too contentious or too slight, only hierarchical arrangements could reframe society. Hierarchical authority drew from well-established idioms and had roots in existing social rules, especially property rights. Further, the hierarchical form would be nominally but never practically absolute. Thus, actors constructed hierarchical arrangements of absolute sovereignty in the seventeenth century in an effort to reconstitute political authority.

In the cumulative, conflicting efforts to reconstruct political authority by myriad actors, the state emerges as an agent of order and reason. In seventeenth-century terms: "What God is to Nature, the King is to the State" (Toulmin 1990: 127). Only in the context of the state does sovereignty become a constitutive principle of modern civic life. At the dawn of the seventeenth century, a prominent French jurist declared in thoroughly modern terms that "sovereignty is entirely inseparable from the state. . . . Sovereignty is the summit of authority, by means of which the state is created and maintained" (quoted in de Jouvenal 1957: 180). To this degree, states and sovereignty are distinctively and solely modern (Onuf 1991: 426). In the transition to modernity wrought by profound material and conceptual change, actors construct mobile property, states, sovereignty, "possessive individualism" (Macpherson 1962), reconstitutued authority (Pocock 1975), and liberalism. Knowledgeable, diverse, conflicting actors constituted these elements through practices derived from bifurcating property rights into real (tangible) and mobile (intangible) forms. In short, "properties are the foundation of constitutions" and constituting (quoted in Macpherson 1962: 139).

In the social tumult of the seventeenth century, Hobbes' citizens fear not the Leviathan, but the social chaos unleashed by ruthlessly self-centered, morally unrestrained, politically unchecked individuals. Political necessity demanded the centralized, reconstructed authority of the *sovereign state*, which required the expansion and protection of *personal sovereignty* and *individual liberty*. Simultaneously and inextricably, establishing and defending personal liberty required a powerful authority. Thus, "sovereign authorities" guarantee general and specific (property) rights in return for support, deference, and contributions to the coffers. Thus, both sovereign authority and individual liberty are reciprocally and suspiciously truncated. As such, "the rights of the ruler, no less than those of the community, succumbed to the doctrine of the sovereignty of the state itself" (Hinsley 1986: 126; also de Jouvenal 1957: 198). The modern era and worldview arrive because sovereignty in itself constitutes the state and state system.

This view of property rights and social relations suggests that the origins of the modern state is based not upon sovereignty (Ruggie 1983; Kratochwil 1995), but upon specific property rights, of which sovereignty comprises a distinct set. Sovereign property rights simultaneously yield states and the state system as a matter of definition and social practice (Kratochwil 1995: 25). The conditions and social practice of sovereignty construct and rule modernity. Simultaneously, the conditions and social practice of sovereignty demarcate national realms of sovereign authority. Yet this is only part of the story, since the political system of authority separated from a system of exchange (of rights). Again, property rights help us see the split.

Property and the Split Between Politics and Economics

In Western Europe prior to 1600 there was no clear distinction between the state system and capitalism, between polity and economy. By approximately

1700, however, commercial expansion, transferable entitlements, and the diversity of social practices created distinctly real and mobile forms of property, hence novel applications of property rights (Pocock 1957; Burch 1994). During the 1600s, states, a state system, and capitalist social relations developed.

Attempts to define, control, and constitute property rights animated these changes. Monarchs extended property rights to reinforce royal rule and domination. Also, burgeoning states required resources effectively attained by fostering mobile property and capitalist exchange. Beneficiaries profited from the social stability and effective rule.

The bifurcation in property rights established the conceptual division between the state system (real, tangible property) and the capitalist system (mobile, intangible property). Upon this conceptual foundation, and with the development and recognition in practice of mobile property, capitalism becomes a system of fluid exchange (Pocock 1985: 69). Thus, the institution of property rights contributes to the constitution and unity of capitalism and the interstate system (Chase-Dunn 1981; Burch 1994). Differences between real and mobile property contribute to the differences between capitalism and states. Crucial to this development is the interplay of ideas and practice.

As a matter of ideas, seventeenth century disputes over property were inextricable from contemporaneous disputes over rights generally, sparked by the growth of market society and profound transformations in law, morality, authority, commerce, philosophy, and worldviews. England was the crucible (Tuck 1979; Shapiro 1987).

Property was a wedge that split the spheres of society and a tie that bound them. New conceptions of property rights transformed the "political" world and laid the foundation for an "economic" realm that burst forth from household or manorial production to become society's prime mover. Market society vanquished the classical view of participatory politics and replaced it with alienated politics. Actors no longer understood politics as the relations among (equal) individuals in a civic community. Instead, politics entailed hierarchical relations. By analogy, authorities are to subjects as owners are to property possessions.

As a matter of practice, mobile property rights helped sovereign authorities marshal resources. Systemic competition and domestic pressure spurred bureaucratic development in both England and France. By exercising sovereign property rights, rulers directed the competitive state toward acquisitive, defensive, and aggressive ends. Since resources were scarce, the state fostered institutions that could effectively acquire money and materiel. Again, the practice and ideas involved property.

The crown extended property rights—as grants, monopolies, charters, use rights, exemptions, and many other benefits—to induce companies to bear investment risk, to pursue foreign policy interests, and to meet national needs. In exchange for property rights the Crown attained goals, promoted social order, and received necessary resources, goods, services, and specie. Monarchs specifically solicited, promoted, and often created companies to redress the problem of chronic national insolvency in the period 1500–1800. The chronic poverty of national treasuries also encouraged state leaders to encourage but co-opt successful companies (Wilson 1977: 131–132). Joint stock companies date to as early as 1450, become prominent by the 1550s, and become prime movers by roughly the 1650s. Merchants understood the risky circumstances, so profited by, for example, extending high-interest loans to the Crown. By the last half of the seventeenth century the English *state* comprised an institutional-legal order inextricably wed to joint stock companies receiving monopoly concessions.

The development of entwined institutional networks comprising central banks, joint stock companies, and legal infrastructures in England, France, and the Netherlands occurred at similar times and under similar circumstances during the seventeenth century. Whether told as stories of state-building, interstate rivalry, capitalist expansion, or colonization, seventeenth-century citizens understood these experiences and conducted related practices in terms of property rights. Indeed, the uncertain seventeenth-century distinction between statecraft and economic activity illustrates the degree to which the separation of politics from economics comprises an ideological premise that coalesced in the following century. After 1700 the development of liberal thought and modern practices further encouraged the view of these as distinct realms.

From this view, seventeenth-century actors constructed—through the discourse and rules of property—the seeming separation of economics from politics. They also constructed their separate characteristics. One distinguishes them by the character of the property rights appropriate to each. The emergence of distinctive economic rights heralds the arrival of the modern era and liberal market society.

Benefits to Comparative Politics

The Virtues of Constructivism

The rule-oriented, conceptually historicist constructivist approach used in the case study makes problematic a prevailing ideological and conceptual framework, offers critique, integrates approaches, and collects empirical data. Such an investigation also maintains scientific integrity by providing comprehensive explanations in terms of select fundamental principles subject to public scrutiny (Fay 1987: 26; Tooze and Murphy 1996: 696). Thus, the constructivist *approach* is at once scientific, critical, interpretive, and empirical. These are characteristics of "restructured social theory" (Burch, forthcoming 2002). Constructivism is an analytic framework, not a theory. ROC is a refinement. Theories of property and property rights convey the explanations. The method involves conducting conceptual histories. The question asked reveals a critical stance. Asking actors' contingent understandings implies attention to interpretation.

Second, this account of property, sovereignty, and conceptual split between politics and economics addresses issues currently relevant to comparativists. The conceptual history of property explains the social construction of a pair of significant social boundaries, links the pair, and situates them within the social construction of "the state" and early modern "nationalism."

Third, the conceptual history addresses understandings of "rationality," but does not presume that such rationality is universal or utilitarian. Rather, it locates rationality within a specific historical and conceptual context, informs that context via conceptual histories, and specifies "rational" choice making in terms of decisions to abide (or not) with prevailing rules. Indeed, all social action involves actors making rule-constrained choices. Thus, rationality is contingent upon cultural context. Constructivism understands culture in terms of prevailing rules and norms that constitute a state of affairs and a worldview. The conceptual history of property and the attention to rules inform an underlying early-modern worldview.

Fourth, theories erected atop constructivist foundations are generally more attentive to the ideological foundations and theoretical frameworks that inform social explanations. This again refers to the characteristics of restructured social theory. In particular, ROC is attentive to the inextricable, complementary relations between the ideological and analytical tiers of social inquiry.

Fifth, ROC is amenable to comparative inquiry. ROC directs comparativists to sets of rules and consequent rule. One may compare the rules or rule across time and/or place. Similarly, tracing conceptual histories is also potentially comparative since one could compare conceptual meaning and significance in different times, places, or cultures. Thus, the case study emphasizes the virtue of conducting conceptual histories as a comparative technique.

The Virtues of Conceptual Histories

Comparative methods engage theoretical controversies. For example, Skocpol (1984) argues that the comparative method can approximate the rigor of "scientific" inquiry. However, Wallerstein (e.g., 1974) and Tilly (1984) suggest "interpretive" comparisons that illuminate significant connections among phenomena. They also encourage approaches that challenge prevailing categories. How then to proceed? Do we simply reprise the debate over "explaining" versus "understanding" (e.g., Hollis and Smith 1991)? How can we compare phenomena through space and time when space and time are variable, when analytical units and categories are drawn from them? How can we compare changes *of* time and space (McMichael 1990)?

Wallerstein argues a spatial concern in holding that world-systems are the proper units of analysis and comparison. Tilly argues that the processes of the state system and global capitalism are the proper comparative units. Both suggest "encompassing comparisons" (Tilly 1984), which locate focal, usually large-scale, phenomena within social structures that transcend specific cultures, societies, or states. Alternatively, "incorporated comparisons" construct social wholes from historical phenomena. "[T]he whole emerges via comparative analysis of 'parts' as moments in a self-forming whole" (McMichael 1990: 386). Said differently, McMichael inductively constructs a whole from parts, while Wallerstein and Tilly deduce parts from wholes.

The distinction is significant, but shares a scientific outlook on theory and comparison. Wallerstein, Tilly, and McMichael all view social wholes and parts through a microscope of sorts, from outside or above the phenomena of interest. This objective distance provides analytic advantages. The greater the distance, the broader the perspective. Indeed, to apprehend large scale changes or to conduct macro comparisons demands considerable distance, thereby blurring discrete details but bringing into relief dominant structures and shaping forces.

An alternative is to embed oneself in the flux, to interpret rather than explain, to stand within (e.g., Pettman 1996, 1997). In balancing objective distance with subjective meanings, we complement our scientific explanations of causality with understandings (*verstehen*) of the reasons motivating social action. Such understandings involve social interpretation. Astride explanations, interpretive accounts introduce alternative comparisons and a novel view of social change. In seeking to explain particular phenomena, theorists compare circumstances by applying a set of criteria (or a model of relationships) to different eras, areas, or cultures. Rather than constructing the model out-of-context, then applying it, one might also construct it in-context. In constructing the conceptual histories of "property" and "property rights," I attempt to (re)build the conceptual framework of the relevant era. I seek to interpret conceptual meanings and consequent behaviors within the confines of the subjects' worldview. I seek to understand their behavior and their motivating choices. I do not peer through a microscope so much as I join a milieu.

To appreciate their worldview, I enter their world through their language. I explore what they thought and the conceptual materiel through which they could think it and constitute it. Thus, I investigate how their ways of thinking influenced their behaviors. Others call this "folklore" or *l'histoire des mentalities*. Scholars call it "historical sociology" (Abrams 1981) or simply "history in the ethnographic grain" (Darnton 1984). Such work:

> begins from the premise that individual expression takes place within a general idiom, that we learn to classify sensations and make sense of things by thinking within a framework provided by our culture. It therefore should be possible for the historian [and other social scientists] to discover the social dimension of thought and to tease meaning from documents by relating them to the surrounding world of significance, passing from text to context and back again until he has cleared a way through a foreign mental world. . . . So historians should be able to see how cultures shape ways of thinking, even for the greatest thinkers. (Darnton 1984: 6)

Such work perhaps sounds like conceptual anthropology and ethnography. Max Weber called it the study of "world-images" (Callinicos 1999: 164). Clifford Geertz (1973) calls it "the interpretation of cultures." Jurgen Habermas (1987: 132) calls it the study of "ideologies." The concepts and ideas that inform these images, cultures, and ideologies establish ways of life and outlooks on the world that construct meanings, constitute identities, and shape social practices. Such ideas—ideological premises—are templates that shape sociocultural arrangements and provide the authoritative categories and concepts by which individuals and groups understand the world and by which science and politics become meaningful (Geertz 1973: 218). Shared ideological premises constitute a "broader matrix of social practices that gives meaning to the way that people understand themselves and their behavior. . . . [They] generate categories of meaning by which reality can be understood [conceived] and explained" (George 1994: 29–30).

In the study of ideas and concepts, I am strongly wedded to the implications of the "linguistic turn" in philosophy. I take seriously the claim that the "limits of one's language mark the limits of one's world" (Ball et al. 1989: 2) and that "behavior has no meaning at all outside of discourse" (Doty 1996: 25). To understand social life, I attend to the concepts and conceptual frameworks that comprise worldviews. Three elements are key: conceptual histories, constitutive principles (key concepts), and social construction. My method underscores a substantive orientation: social construction and the linguistic constitution of social life (see Burch 1998: 10–15).

I explore the concepts "property" and "property rights" because they occupy a central place in conceptions of "politics" and "economics." Moreover, actors' understandings of "property" and property rights will affect, and perhaps constitute, their worldview and behaviors. By this conceptual history I explore the emergence of the state (system) and capitalism in seventeenth-century England. I use the concepts to reconstruct a seventeenth-century understanding of the emerging modern world, the relationships of politics/states to economics/capitalism in constituting the system, and the consequent behaviors which (re)produced it. Thus, we see the emergence of the modern world through the eyes and concepts of contemporaries, rather than as we conceive it several hundred years later. Seventeenth-century evidence (both original and secondary) shows that global capitalism and the state system comprise a single coherent social reality—the modern world— rather than two distinct realms.

The possibilities for comparison proliferate since one can conduct all standard comparisons, but also one may compare subjects' (self-)understandings to the theorists' (weakly determinist) explanations. The larger the social structures and forces, the less likely that theorists will regard individuals as *analytically* significant. Addressed interpretively, though, theorists can compare eras and areas, as well as actors' conceptions of their time and place. The shift is valuable because how might one otherwise explain the existence or reproduction of social structures? Social structures arise from patterned human behaviors and the frameworks of meaning which motivate consistent behavior. Thus we encounter rules, conventions, traditions, customs, rituals, bromides, and maxims. We encounter the material of cultural history ranging from folklore to high culture. Of course the social world comprises much more than the limited understandings of individuals or cultures. And of course we cannot hope to understand the world solely by attention to their worldviews and judgments. But just as clearly we can neither know nor construct the social world solely from structures, dynamics, trends, rates, levels, and quanta. So we compare and contrast.

If our theoretical explanation compares favorably with our conceptual understandings, we feel corroborated. With an interpretive approach we discover that the worldviews of seventeenth-century European actors conceived no discrete social realms of politics and economics. A conceptual history of property and property rights demonstrates that the seventeenth-century worldview saw a "unified" systemic reality that splintered into discrete fragments only by 1700. However, if differences emerge between our explanations and interpretations, then we focus our attentions. Some important difference looms. For this we turn to history to apprehend the changes. I suggest we turn to conceptual histories.

Conceptual histories yield unique historically and contextually contingent understandings. Such histories encourage us not to take for granted the meanings of concepts or interpretations of circumstances. *Conceptual* histories allow us to reconstruct frameworks of meaning and understanding. Conceptual *histories* afford us the opportunity to compare understandings and map changes in them. Changing meanings reciprocally cause and manifest changes in material conditions and key relationships. The grander the material or structural changes, the more likely they should appear as alterations in the conceptual apparatus of the era. Behaviors change only as our understandings change.

By conducting conceptual histories, we tap into conceptions of change, rather than into the outcomes. Momentous changes will leave their mark on the material landscape and upon prevailing worldviews. In both cases, behaviors will change. In seeking to explain the causes of social change, we can peer into the worldviews by which actors frame their choices and make judgments. In seeking to understand social change, we can experience it indirectly through actors' changing conceptions of their world. As we compare eras and systems, we can do so from the inside out as easily as from the outside in. With conceptual histories, we track and generate social change. We thereby expand our comparative options as we enhance our current theoretical models.

Conclusion

This essay asks how efforts to restructure social theory, especially constructivist efforts, may affect CP and the challenges it confronts. The essay answers that constructivism addresses several of the most prominent challenges facing CP scholars. The essay begins with a constructivist primer that distinguishes several versions of constructivism. The essay briefly describes structure-oriented, norm-oriented, and rule-oriented constructivisms (SOC, NOC, and ROC).

Constructivism makes four specific contributions to CP. First, constructivism provides analytical leverage upon "new questions" in CP (see Table 2.2). Such questions include the creation or social production of identities, spaces, places, and physical and conceptual boundaries. Second, constructivism connects the three seemingly distinct traditions of CP analyses (rationality, culture, and structure) into a coherent process of social construction. These connections and relationships encourage scholarly interactions, comparisons, and confrontations. Third, in response to the claim that CP scholars are "theoretically challenged" (Lichbach 1997: 239–241), constructivism (re)introduces self-conscious attention to matters of theory and explanation. Fourth, constructivist premises and analyses suggest specific subjects to compare and novel means of comparison. To illustrate these points, the essay offers a case study of the development of sovereignty and the boundary separating politics from economics. The case study draws from a conceptual history of "property" and "property rights."

The essay ends with an inventory of constructivism's virtues for CP and of several virtues of conceptual histories as a form of comparative analysis.

Bibliography

Abrams, Philip. 1981. *Historical Sociology*. Ithaca: Cornell University Press.

Adler, Emanuel. 1997. "Seizing the Middle Ground: Constructivism and World Politics." *European Journal of International Relations* 3(3): 319–363.

Adler, E., and M. Barnett, eds. 1998. *Security Communities*. New York: Cambridge University Press.

Ball, Terence, et al., eds. 1989. *Political Innovation and Conceptual Change*. New York: Cambridge University Press.

Burch, Kurt. 1994. The 'Properties' of the State System and Global Capitalism." In *The Global Economy as Political Space*, ed. S. Rosow, N. Inayatullah, and M. Rupert, 37–59. Boulder: Lynne Rienner.

———. 1996. "Illustrating Constructivism: George Kennan and the Social Construction of the Cold War." *Swords and Ploughshares* 6(1): 3–22.

———. 1997. "Constituting International Political Economy and Modernity." In *Constituting International Political Economy*, ed. K. Burch and R. Denemark. 21–40 (vol. 10 of the *International Political Economy Yearbook* series). Boulder: Lynne Rienner.

———. 1998. *"Property" and the Making of the International System*. Boulder: Lynne Rienner.

———. 1999. "Agent-Structure Issues." In *Encyclopedia of International Political Economy*, ed. R.J. Barry Jones. London: Routledge.

———. 2000. "Changing the Rules: Reconceiving Change in the Westphalian System." *International Studies Review* 2(2): 181–210.

———. Forthcoming. "The Promise and Practice of Restructuring Social Theory." In *Odysseys: Adventures Across the Borders of International Political Economy*, ed. M. Tetreault. New York: Routledge.

Callinicos, Alex. 1999. *Social Theory: A Historical Introduction*. New York: New York University Press.

Cash, John Daniel. 1996. *Identity, Ideology, and Conflict: The Structuration of Politics in Northern Ireland*. New York: Cambridge University Press.

Chase-Dunn, Christopher. 1981. "Interstate System and Capitalist World-Economy: One Logic or Two?" *International Studies Quarterly* 25(1): 19–42.

Checkel, Jeffrey T. 1998. "The Constructivist Turn in International Relations Theory." *World Politics* 50: 324–348.

Darnton, Robert. 1984. *The Great Cat Massacre and Other Episodes in French Cultural History*. New York: Basic Books.

de Jouvenal, Bertrand. 1957. *Sovereignty: An Inquiry into the Political Good*. J.F. Huntington, trans. Chicago: University of Chicago Press.

Doty, Roxanne. 1996. *Imperial Encounters: The Politics of Representation in North-South Relations*. Minneapolis: University of Minnesota Press.

Dryzek, John S. 1996. *Democracy in Capitalist Times*. New York: Oxford University Press.

Fay, Brian. 1987. *Critical Social Science*. Ithaca: Cornell University Press.

Finnemore, Martha. 1996. *National Interests in International Society*. Ithaca: Cornell University Press.

Geertz, Clifford. 1973. *The Interpretation of Cultures*. New York: Basic Books.

George, Jim. 1994. *Discourses on Global Politics*. Boulder: Lynne Rienner.

Giddens, Anthony. 1984. *The Constitution of Society*. Berkeley: University of California Press.

Goldstein, Judith, and Robert Keohane, eds. 1993. *Ideas and Foreign Policy*. Ithaca: Cornell University Press.

Gould, Harry. 1998. "What *Is* at Stake in the Agent-Structure Debate?" In *International Relations in a Constructed World*, ed. V. Kubalkova, N. Onuf, and P. Kowert, 79–98. Armonk, NY: M.E. Sharpe.

Habermas, Jurgen. 1987. *The Philosophical Discourses of Modernity: 12 Lectures*. F. Lawrence, trans. Cambridge, MA: MIT Press.

Hart, H.L.A. 1961. *Concept of Law*. New York: Clarendon Press.

Hinsley, F.H. 1986. *Sovereignty*. 2nd ed. New York: Cambridge University Press.

Hollis, Martin, and Steve Smith. 1991. *Explaining and Understanding International Relations*. New York: Clarendon Press.

Howat, G.M.D. 1974. *Stuart and Cromwellian Foreign Policy*. New York: St. Martin's.

Hunter, Allen, ed. 1998. *Rethinking the Cold War*. Philadelphia: Temple University Press.

Jepperson, Ronald L., Alexander Wendt, and Peter J. Katzenstein. 1996. "Norms, Identity, and Culture in National Security." In *The Culture of National Security*, ed. P.J. Katzenstein, 33–75. New York: Columbia University Press.

Katzenstein, Peter J., ed. 1996. *The Culture of National Security: Norms and Identity in World Politics*. New York: Columbia University Press.

Keck, Margaret, and Kathryn Sikkink. 1998. *Activists Beyond Borders: Advocacy Networks in International Politics*. Ithaca: Cornell University Press.

Kenyon, J.P. 1978. *Stuart England*. New York: Penguin Books.

Kratochwil, Friedrich. 1989. *Rules, Norms, and Decisions*. New York: Cambridge University Press.

———. 1995. "Sovereignty as *Dominium*: Is There a Right of Humanitarian Intervention?" In *Beyond Westphalia?: State Sovereignty and International Intervention*, ed. G.M. Lyons and M. Mastanduno, 21–42. Baltimore: Johns Hopkins University Press.

———. 2001. "Sovereignty, Property, and Propriety: The Generative Grammar of Modernity." Paper delivered at conference on "History, Systemic Transformation, and International Relations Theory," Gregynog, Wales, April.

Lapid, Yosef, and Friedrich Kratochwil, eds. 1996. *The Return of Culture and Identity in IR Theory*. Boulder: Lynne Rienner.

Lichbach, Mark. 1997. "Social Theory and Comparative Politics." In *Comparative Politics: Rationality, Culture, and Structure*, ed. M. Lichbach and A. Zuckerman, 239–276. New York: Cambridge University Press.

Lichbach, Mark, and Alan Zuckerman, eds. 1997. *Comparative Politics: Rationality, Culture, and Structure*. New York: Cambridge University Press.

Lincoln, Bruce. 1994. *Authority: Construction and Corrosion*. Chicago: University of Chicago Press.

Macpherson, C.B. 1962. *The Political Theory of Possessive Individualism*. New York: Oxford University Press.

McMichael, Philip. 1990. "Incorporating Comparison within a World-Historical Perspective: An Alternative Comparative Method." *American Sociological Review* 55: 385–397.

Onuf, Nicholas. 1989. *World of Our Making: Rules and Rule in Social Theory and International Relations*. Columbia: University of South Carolina Press.

———. 1991. "Sovereignty: Outline of a Conceptual History." *Alternatives* 16: 425–446.

———. 1994. "The Constitution of International Society." *European Journal of International Law* 5(1): 1–19.

———. 1997. "A Constructivist Manifesto." In *Constituting International Political Economy*, ed. K. Burch and R. Denemark, 7–17. Boulder: Lynne Rienner.

———. 1998a. "Constructivism: A User's Manual." In *International Relations in a Constructed World*, ed. V. Kubalkova, N. Onuf, and P. Kowert, 58–78. Armonk, NY: M.E. Sharpe.

———. 1998b. *The Republican Legacy in International Thought*. New York: Cambridge University Press.

Pettman, Ralph. 1996. *Understanding International Political Economy with Readings for the Fatigued*. Boulder: Lynne Rienner.

———. 1997. "The Limits to a Rationalist Understanding of IPE." In *Constituting International Political Economy*, ed. K. Burch and R. Denemark, 155–168. Boulder: Lynne Rienner.

Pipes, Richard. 1999. *Property and Freedom*. London: Harvill Press.

Pocock, J.G.A. 1957. *The Ancient Constitution and the Feudal Law: A Study of English Historical Thought in the Seventeenth Century*. New York: Cambridge University Press.

———. 1975. *The Machiavellian Moment: Florentine Political Thought and the Atlantic Republican Tradition*. Princeton: Princeton University Press.

———. 1977. "Historical Introduction." In *The Political Works of James Harrington*, ed. J.G.A. Pocock, 1–152. New York: Cambridge University Press.

———. 1985. *Virtue, Commerce, and History*. New York: Cambridge University Press.

Price, Richard. 1995. "A Genealogy of the Chemical Weapons Taboo." *International Organization* 49(1): 73–103.

Price, Richard, and Christian Reus-Smit. 1998. "Dangerous Liaisons?: Critical International Theory and Constructivism." *European Journal of International Relations* 4(3): 259–294.

Ruggie, John. 1983. "Continuity and Transformation in the World Polity: Toward a Neorealist Synthesis." *World Politics* 35(2): 261–285.

———. 1998. *Constructing the World Polity: Essays on International Institutionalization*. New York: Routledge.

Searle, John. 1969. *Speech Acts*. New York: Cambridge University Press.

Shapiro, Ian. 1987. *The Evolution of Rights in Liberal Theory*. New York: Cambridge University Press.

Skocpol, Theda, ed. 1984. *Vision and Method in Historical Sociology*. New York: Cambridge University Press.

Snyder, Craig A., ed. 1999. *Contemporary Security and Strategy*. New York: Routledge.

Spruyt, Hendrik. 1994. *The Sovereign State and Its Competitors: An Analysis of Systems Change*. Princeton: Princeton University Press.

Strange, Susan. 1996. *The Retreat of the State: The Diffusion of Power in the World Economy*. New York: Cambridge University Press.

Tilley, Virginia. 1997. "The Terms of the Debate: Untangling Language about Ethnicity and Ethnic Movements." *Ethnic and Racial Studies* 20(3): 497–522.

Tilly, Charles. 1984. *Big Structures, Large Processes, Huge Comparisons*. New York: Russell Sage Foundation.

―――, ed. 1975. *The Formation of National States in Western Europe*. Princeton: Princeton University Press.

Tooze, Roger, and Craig Murphy. 1996. "The Epistemology of Poverty and the Poverty of Epistemology in IPE: Mystery, Blindness, and Invisibility." *Millennium* 25(3): 681–707.

Toulmin, Stephen. 1990. *Cosmopolis: The Hidden Agenda of Modernity*. New York: Free Press.

Tuck, Richard. 1979. *Natural Rights Theories: Their Origin and Development*. New York: Cambridge University Press.

Walker, R.B.J. 1993. *Inside/Outside: International Relations as Political Theory*. New York: Cambridge University Press.

Wallerstein, Immanuel. 1974. *The Modern World-System I: Capitalist Agriculture and the Origins of the European World-Economy in the Sixteenth Century*. New York: Academic Press.

Walt, Stephen. 1998. "International Relations: One World, Many Theories." *Foreign Policy* 110: 29–46.

Weldes, Jutta et al., eds. 1999. *Cultures of Insecurity: States, Communities, and the Production of Danger*. Minneapolis: University of Minnesota Press.

Wendt, Alexander. 1987. "The Agent-Structure Problem in International Relations Theory." *International Organization* 41(3): 435–470.

―――. 1992. "Anarchy Is What States Make of It." *International Organization* 46(2): 391–425.

―――. 1995. "Constructing International Politics." *International Security* 20: 71–81.

―――. 1999. *Social Theory of International Politics*. New York: Cambridge University Press.

Wendt, Alexander, and Daniel Friedheim. 1995. "Hierarchy Under Anarchy: Informal Empire and the East German State." *International Organization* 49(4): 689–721.

Wilson, Charles. 1977. "The British Isles." In *An Introduction to the Sources of European Economic History, 1500–1800*, ed. C. Wilson and G. Parker, 115–154. Ithaca: Cornell University Press.

Zuckerman, Alan. 1997. "Reformulating Explanatory Standards and Advancing Theory in Comparative Politics." In *Comparative Politics: Rationality, Culture, and Structure*, ed. M. Lichbach and A. Zuckerman, 277–310. New York: Cambridge University Press.

3

Globalization, the Comparative Method, and Comparing Constructions

Patrick Thaddeus Jackson and Daniel Nexon

It has become a piece of American folklore that while ideals of women's weight change, standards of hip-to-waist ratios remain constant. Sociobiologists and evolutionary psychologists advance a number of explanations for this preference, including its impact on hormone production and male perceptions of female fertility. Others have suggested that these ratios have nothing to do with biology, and everything to do with culture. They claim that exposure to Western media produces perceptions of beauty and socializes men and women to see such ratios as ideal. In 1998, the *Economist* reported on a study designed to evaluate these two claims. Dr. Douglas Yu conducted research on an isolated tribe in Peru—the Matsigenka—with no access to outside cultural influences. Yu found that the Matsigenka "preferred women with wider waists than the 'Western' norm." In fact, among indigenous groups in Peru, "as contact increased, men's preferences shifted rapidly to coincide with those of men in the United States." The author of the article concluded that "the argument is far from over. But as Dr. Yu points out in his article, it may not go on much longer. As globalisation works its magic, isolated groups such as the Matsigenka are becoming harder to find. The great hourglass debate is, sadly, running out of time" (*Economist* 1998: 86–87).

Yu's study intersects three critical themes in this volume and our chapter: social constructionism, the comparative method, and globalization. To argue that a phenomenon is socially constructed is to hold that "X need not have existed, or need not be at all as it is. X, or X as it is at present, is not determined by the nature of things; it is not inevitable" (Hacking 1999: 6). The debate over standards of beauty in women's hip-to-waist ratios centers around whether these ratios are given by the nature of human beings, or are the relatively changeable product of cultural processes. Yu attempted to test this proposition through comparative logic: by isolating groups through which culture could be controlled as an independent variable. In this regard, his study provides good evidence that standards of beauty with regard to women's hip-to-waist ratios are indeed socially constructed rather than a function of human nature.

However, Yu's study also demonstrates quite nicely how globalization *challenges* the comparative method. A growing number of scholars recognize that globalization calls into question the traditional distinction between comparative politics (CP) and international relations (IR)—a distinction premised upon the assumption that state boundaries create a clear difference between domestic and international political processes. Globalization involves a shift in the balance of power between economic and political forces in the world in ways that undermine the power of locally bounded entities such as the sovereign territorial state: the internationalization of production, the rise of transnational forces, and the erosion of local and state power. Processes of globalization simultaneously internationalize important aspects of domestic politics and domesticate international politics, making it difficult to clearly differentiate between the subject areas of comparative politics and international relations.

Fewer scholars recognize that these shifts present a more profound challenge to ordinary comparative political inquiry. This challenge is nicely summarized by Charles Tilly (1997: 50), who argues that the comparative method is "ontologically inadequate" in the context of globalization. The comparative method presumes distinct and symmetrical objects of comparison, such as cultures, civilizations, states, regions, ethnic groups, or social movements. In order to compare phenomena, they must be "autonomous and coherent" with respect to one another, so that we can treat them as distinct cases. They must also be "symmetrical" in the sense that they have essential characteristics which justify their comparison as two examples of similar phenomena. As Yu points out, processes of globalization erode our ability to consider groups like the Matsigenka as both distinct from and symmetrical with other cultural communities—and, thus, our ability to treat such groups as cases for use in a comparative study.

In this respect, dynamics associated with globalization are not particularly unique. As Kurt Burch and Rodney Hall make clear in their contributions to this volume, processes of social construction have long configured and reconfigured the social relations that comprise units of comparison. The production and diffusion of nationalism, liberal property rights, religious affiliations, social class, and other networks that tie actors together into categories create topographies of similarity and difference. They inform our commonsense assumptions about whether two clusters of actors are both distinct and symmetrical, and thus give rise to both the political reality of comparison and our methodological presupposition that such actors *can* be compared. This is the common link between the concrete processes by which Italian nationalists in the nineteenth century mobilized on the grounds that they (unlike the French or the British) lacked a unified state, and our social-scientific assumption that contemporary Italy and France constitute cases that can be compared with reference to such features as their gross domestic product (GDP), population, or divorce rate.

This class of dynamics, of which those associated with globalization constitute a subset, may be termed processes of *mapping* and *remapping*, in that they cordon off subsets of social relations and bundle them together to produce relatively coherent units. These processes can produce new maps of political life, or they can work to reproduce existing maps. Normal comparative political inquiry takes our contemporary maps of political life for granted, and engages in comparison based upon those preexisting maps. By contrast, in our view the task of a constructivist comparative politics (CCP) is to analyze, understand, and elucidate the causal and constitutive effects of mapping and remapping. This requires not the comparison of the variable attributes of stable entities, but the comparative analysis of processes.

This chapter is divided into four sections. In the first we examine the basic assumptions at work in standard versions of the comparative method. We argue that the comparative method, as routinely practiced in CP and IR, carries with it a metageography tied to specific presumptions about the contours of political life. In the second, we assess the limitations of the comparative method for constructivism, focusing on three tensions generated through its marriage to constructivist inquiry. In the third section, we argue for a modified comparative method centered around the comparison of processes and political relations. We illustrate comparative process analysis through a short account of Polish national mobilization in the nineteenth century. In the fourth section, we return directly to the issue of globalization and argue for the importance of process analysis in understanding and evaluating key issues at stake in contemporary political change.

The Metageography of the Comparative Method

According to Martin Lewis and Kären Wigen (1997: ix), "every global consideration of human affairs deploys a metageography, whether acknowledged or not." The notion of "metageography" refers to "the set of spatial structures through which people order their knowledge of the world: the often unconscious frameworks that organize studies of history, sociology, anthropology, economics, political science, or even natural history." Every map has a metageography, and the maps presupposed in comparative politics and the comparative method are no different.

The maps presupposed by the comparative method derive their plausibility either directly or indirectly from the metageography of the sovereign territorial states system (Tilly 1997: 50). According to Reinhard Bendix (1978: 267–268), the idea of a "Spanish" society and an "English" society as aggregate, comparable units emerged in tandem with the formation of early modern states. The defining feature of this system is the compartmentalization of politics, society, and culture into discrete territorial borders. Since we generally presume that each sovereign territorial state is equivalent with respect to a set of essential characteristics, the sovereign territorial state system creates an immediately plausible case for the symmetry of political communities. This logic enables us to easily conceive of contained communities subject to differentiable norms, rules, and structures (Mann 1986: 1–3, Tilly 1984). Even though linguistic, national, ethnic, and religious affiliations seldom conform to the boundaries of nation-states, "most of our encyclopedias, textbooks, atlases, and almanacs portray states as holistic entities, unified and distinct" (Lewis and Wigen 1997: 8).

Despite the current interdependency of sovereign territoriality and the metageography of the comparative method, the former is not necessary for the latter. In classical Greece, where processes of political and social life were oriented toward relatively bounded city-states, philosophers such as Aristotle and Plato engaged in comparative political inquiry very similar to that of contemporary scholars. Aristotle both compared city-states with reference to their constitutional principles (the "natural" forms of monarchy, aristocracy, and polity and the "perverted" forms of tyranny, oligarchy, and democracy) and compared Greeks to barbarians. The comparison of civilization to barbarism has also been a ubiquitous feature of empires from Rome to Ming China (Gong 1984).

Nevertheless, what this contrast tells us is that *historical forms of comparison* have varied greatly in terms of the objects of comparison and the distinctions drawn between those objects. In other words, we are dealing with different (but genealogically interrelated) metageographies. These are not *simply* questions of rhetorical representation, but of concrete social and political practices that map the world into sovereign territorial states, ethnic groups, and other discrete, symmetrical, and coherent objects (White 1992a). In this sense, maps are not just representations of territories, they *are* territories (see Black 1997; Turnbull 1993; Wood 1992).

The Comparative Method

The comparative method is perhaps the most common research methodology in both international relations and comparative politics. A variety of forms of the comparative method exist, but the most popular are drawn from J.S. Mill: the method of difference and the method of agreement.[1] Interestingly, Mill himself cautioned against the appropriateness of using these methods in social-scientific analysis, where linear cause and effect relations either do not exist or are difficult to disentangle. In political and social systems, outcomes rarely reproduce themselves (rendering laboratory conditions impossible), and the existence of multiple pathways of causation forms an insurmountable problem (Mill 1874: 324). Nevertheless, international relations and comparative politics scholars routinely apply Mill's methods to their studies of social phenomena.

As conventionally understood, the comparative method involves the comparison of several *cases* with respect to specified *variables*, which are attributes on which the cases may or may not vary. Recent political science usage has tended to divide these variables into *independent* and *dependent* variables, depending on which variables are being used to explain which others: independent variables explain dependent variables, not vice versa. The distinction between a method of difference (in which cases are sought that are *alike* in all ways except for the independent variable of interest, and the cases are examined to see if the dependent variable is systematically linked to changes in the value of the independent variable of interest) and a method of agreement (in which cases are sought which are *different* in all ways except for the independent variable of interest, and the cases are examined to see if the dependent variable is constant across cases) is often thought to exhaust the possible types of comparison. Most debates about the comparative method in recent years have focused on large-N versus small-N questions (King, Keohane, and Verba 1994), the problems of selecting cases on the dependent variable (Geddes 1990), the uses of counterfactuals as additional cases for analysis (Tetlock and Belkin 1996), and other such technical issues in making the overall analytical scheme work.

One of the most prevalent research strategies in comparative politics is the multicountry study. Several states are collected into a set, data is collected on each state (type of regime, for example, or GDP, or extent of internal fragmentation), and the states are compared with one another. Some examples in comparative politics include Peter Hall's (1986) study of economic policy making, Theda Skocpol's (1979) studies of revolutions, and countless other works. Examples of this type of study appear in international relations as well, particularly in the emerging literature on "two-level games" (Evans, Jacobson, and Putnam 1993), the domestic sources of foreign policy (Snyder 1991; Milner 1988), the "second image reversed" (Gourevitch 1986), and studies of regime type and war, such as those found in the debate over the "democratic peace" (see Brown et al. 1996).

States are directly mobilized as cases in these studies; in particular, they are used as *containers* in which various values of variables may be found. For example, Peter Hall's (1986) book *Governing the Economy* is subtitled "The Politics of State Intervention *in* Britain and France" [emphasis added]; Britain and France are locations in which Hall's key independent variable of "institutional factors" can play themselves out and take on different values. The causal logic of Hall's argument, like that of most other comparative analyses of states, is not that the *case itself* was different, but that *particular attributes of the case* varied, and that this variance accounts for the preferred dependent variable: it matters not at all to Hall's account that Britain and France *are* "Britain" and "France," but only that they share similarities on many of the relevant variables, and differ in the matter of domestic institutional configuration. If another state (say, Germany or China or India) were found to display the same pattern of variables (similarity on most, difference in domestic institutional configuration), it could be compared to Britain or France just as meaningfully. Peter Gourevitch's (1986: 67) book *Politics in Hard Times* displays this same logic with a twist: one of the common features displayed by all of the states he analyzes is that they all face a common external phenomenon: an economic crisis of worldwide proportions. In addition, Gourevitch is careful to include among his cases only those states which "had economic actors with rough similarities of placement in the world economy," making his study a good example of the method of difference mode of comparison.

There is an interesting circularity to the logic of case selection in such studies. On the one hand, cases are chosen because of their variance on several variables that the analyst believes to be important. A comparison of France and Germany, for example, might look productive because of the similarity of France and Germany on many matters, combined with their variance on other matters of interest. On the other hand, cases appear in these studies to be nothing other than *collections of variables*, locations in which these variables can take on different values. France and Germany are therefore collections of variable attributes that happen to occur in the same territorial container; in particular, they are collections of the particular variables deemed important by the analyst. Cases are *constructed* by the decision of the analyst with respect to which possible attributes to concentrate on; these cases are then *compared* with one another in order to see if some of the chosen variables have a significant effect on the chosen dependent variable. Hence the circularity: *cases that are to be compared on various variables are first constructed out of those variables*, ignoring others that might have an impact on the dependent variable. (Incidentally, this was Mill's original critique of applying comparative methods to the study of social phenomena: one never knows in advance what is going to be important, and one cannot control precisely as in the experimental sciences.)

The circularity of case selection is answered in various ways by practitioners in international relations and comparative politics. A popular response is the 'neopositivist' approach, explicitly articulated by Gary King and his coauthors in their methodological manual *Designing Social Inquiry*: move away from "cases" to "observations," which are "measures of one or more variables on exactly one unit." "Observations" are the fundamental element of research, they argue, and approvingly quote Harry Eckstein's argument that an analyst should not focus on "concrete entities but at the measures made of them" (King, Keohane, and Verba 1994: 52–53). Hence any determination of what constitutes a case is a *pragmatic* judgment about the taking of observations, and depends more on the theory than on the world. Much of their book is concerned with tips and techniques for maximizing the number of observations, even when the number of units or cases is small; the pursuit of a large N (so that statistical techniques can be brought into play) is the overriding thrust of their recommendations. In particular, they urge the use of counterfactual analysis, the search for observable implications of a theory at a lower level of generality (administrative regions rather than state, for instance), and the division of a case by time period (so that "British GDP" becomes "British GDP 1996," "British GDP 1997," "British GDP 1998," and so forth).

However, the neopositivist response is inadequate in one major respect: it provides no guidelines for *which* collections of attributes can be meaningfully compared. Suppose one were interested in the impact of authority structures on the distribution of funds among members of a group, and wished to compare the allowances given by a father to his three children with a redistributionist tax policy pursued by a democratic welfare state; these cases differ on certain variables (particularly structure of authority) and are similar on others (funds are distributed, multiple persons are involved in each group, etc.). Something about this comparison strikes us as absurd, however, and (presumably) no one would ever try to carry out such a comparative study. At the same time, comparing two states or comparing two administrative regions of the same state does not seem as prima facie absurd. The difference between these two kinds of comparisons illustrates the drawbacks of the neopositivist approach to comparison, namely that it ignores something crucial by assuming that the construction of cases is purely pragmatic. There is no way to tell a priori whether two cases are comparable; this is an assumption, albeit a necessary one. As King and his coauthors note, "the notion of unit homogeneity . . . lies at the basis of all scientific [according to their definition] research" (King, Keohane, and Verba 1994: 93). But in practice, this as-

sumption is *not* made in an arbitrary fashion, but according to the lines specified in the underlying metageography held by a researcher.

The Assumption of Unit Stability

We can see the nonarbitrary nature of notions of unit homogeneity more
clearly if we consider the matter of unit *stability*, which is also implicated in
issues of case selection. One of the aims of the comparative method is to
distinguish "systematic" from "random" variation. The kind of causal inference practiced when cases are compared involves looking for *invariant* and
linear causal generalizations: "*x* causes *y*" means that *x* always, or at least
significantly (in a statistical sense), leads to *y*. Although most comparativists
consider their causal claims to be probabilistic rather than truly invariant, the
logic of causal inference follows the same schema. This schema can be com-
plicated by the addition of intervening variables, background variables, interaction effects, and the like. However, the underlying thrust remains the
same. If comparison of some set of cases yields no systematic connection
between the independent and dependent variables, the hypothesis is
disconfirmed and no causal relationship has been established.

In addition to resting on the assumption of discreteness and symmetry,
this approach to explanation assumes that the cases identified are relatively
stable constellations of forces. In other words, it assumes that *variables* (attributes of cases which change) can be easily separated from *systemic conditions* (relatively stable attributes of cases). Thus, the identification of the
"case" itself requires an assumption of stability in terms of some essential,
well-defined, and bounded entity.

The reason for this requirement lies in the distinction between "primary"
and "secondary" attributes, which is required for variable-based comparison
and causal inference. We often forget that variables are technically certain
kinds of properties of an object; they are secondary attributes, properties of
some *thing* that can change without altering the fundamental nature of that
thing. In contrast, primary attributes are the constitutive properties of a thing,
fundamentally linked to that thing's very existence as the kind of thing which
it is. Change a primary attribute, and you are dealing with a different thing
altogether. Take away a bipedal morphology from a human being and replace its hands with paws, and you no longer have a human being. Alter a
human being's hair color from black to yellow, change its age and sex, and
you still have a human being. The former are plausible candidates for primary attributes, the latter for secondary or variable attributes (Rescher 1996).

The elements of cases that enable us to identify them as, for example,
symmetrical and discrete *must be* primary attributes. One state is compa-

rable with another state because it can be thought of as having similar primary attributes, for instance, a government with predominant authority over a given territory. The comparative method then explains differences or similarities between, for instance, trade policy in those two states with reference to variable (secondary) attributes such as the size of the states, their dominant political coalitions, and their respective economic dependency on exports.

It follows that, if we engage in the standard forms of the comparative method, we cannot allow secondary attributes to alter primary ones. If a variable associated with the comparison between two or more cases changes the essential properties of at least one of the cases, then we are no longer dealing with the same class of cases. In such a case, we could no longer assume that the cases were comparable. We would lose our ability to isolate causal variables from systemic conditions, since the changes in question would represent alterations in the very systemic conditions under which we can plausibly claim a linear and invariant causal relation obtains.

How do comparative researchers prevent this from happening in their studies? As we have suggested, the principal technique for distinguishing between primary and secondary characteristics involves accepting the domestic/international divide as relatively fixed, which by implication means accepting the notions that discrete domestic and international systems exist, and that these realms of activity are appropriately characterized as *systems* with relatively stable connections between elements. But this strategy makes sense only in a world that is *in fact* characterized by such a domestic/international divide—a world in which states *are* meaningful discrete units, possessing essential and stable cores that constitute them as such. However, not all periods of history are characterized by such conditions; there was a political world before the state system came into being, and presumably there will be one after that system ends. One simply cannot pick up methods that were fashioned to deal with a particular configuration of social life and apply them willy-nilly, to periods in which those conditions do not obtain (Spruyt 1994: 14). In addition, one cannot use methods that presume stability in the primary attributes of entities in analyzing *whether* alterations in secondary attributes are producing fundamental changes in social and political life, as this possibility is logically ruled out by the presumptions of the method itself. Globalization, whatever else it might be, represents a shift in the processes of mapping that sustain the primary/secondary distinction for sovereign states, calling into question the suitability of case-comparative methods to adequately address such phenomena.

Social Construction and the Comparative Method

In the preceding section, we explored the kinds of maps that underlie standard versions of the comparative method. These maps work to constitute and delimit its research territory. As with all maps, those of the comparative method "are conventional, selective, indexical, embedded in forms of life, dependent on the understanding of a cognitive schema and practical mastery." At heart, "there is something more than something metaphoric about maps and theories; they share a common characteristic which is the very condition for the possibility of knowledge or experience—connectivity" (Turnbull, 1993: 61). In this section, we examine three limitations imposed by the comparative method's map on constructivist research.

Social Construction within the Comparative Method

Constructivists in IR often focus on the causal and constitutive role of norms and identities in international politics (see Adler 1997 and Wendt 1999). Thus, many constructivists assume that if they can demonstrate (a) *that norms and identities explain outcomes in international relations* and (b) that, in turn, *the behavior of actors alters norms and identities*, then we can plausibly conclude that international politics are, in some significant respects, socially constructed (see Katzenstein 1996).

It is not difficult to see how the comparative method can be used to advance such a project. A researcher takes a norm (a social expectation of appropriate behavior in a particular context) or an identity (a definition of who an actor is that carries with it expectations of appropriate behaviors) and treats it as a variable attribute of a case or an actor within a case. Using the comparative method, the researcher then tests to see whether the norm or identity better explains a given outcome than other independent variables.

For example, Thomas Banchoff (1999: 260–261) argues that identity-as-variable explains why Germany, after the collapse of the Soviet Union and German reunification, has neither embraced "a more assertive and independent foreign policy" nor made "an active Ostpolitik a priority over deeper German integration." Although the international environment and structural position of Germany (as a great power) is similar to that of other states that have actively balanced potential competitors, Banchoff (1999: 272–273) argues that German politics constructed a "supranational European identity" that "depicted the FRG . . . as a partner within a developing political union in which norms of cooperation and shared sovereign were paramount." Post-cold war German foreign policy continues to be consistent with that identity. Furthermore, elite discourse surrounding foreign policy decisions regularly *what's inside identity?*

involves narratives associated with a supranational European identity. Thus, Banchoff shows through eliminative inference that some other variables—such as relative material power—fail to account for German behavior, while identity—which remained constant—is a likely candidate for explaining its foreign policy continuity.

Through the comparative method, Banchoff establishes condition (a): identity-as-variable seems like the best explanation for the observed outcome. In fact, his method of doing so should be familiar to practitioners of CP: it is similar to that of the "political culture" framework advanced in comparative politics in the 1960s and 1970s (Steinmetz 1999: 19). But it is also more sophisticated. Banchoff and other constructivists deploy more complex conceptual frameworks, such as a focus on discourse and narrative rather than crude statistical indicators of cultural phenomena. More important, however, is their attempt to demonstrate not simply (a) but also (b)—thereby substituting social constructionism for cultural determinism. How does Banchoff show that the behavior of actors actively constructed norms and identities? Here Banchoff relies on a narrative strategy: he briefly traces the establishment and diffusion of Germany's supranational identity through parliamentary debates.

One common criticism of constructivist work in international relations is that it suffers from omitted variable bias. In other words, it ignores the existence of a number of other potential causes that may not be socially constructed. Another is that "objective" (non-socially constructed) factors actually explain variation in constructivist independent variables. For instance, realists are increasingly likely to argue that military and economic (material) factors themselves account for changes in actors' identities. For example, constructivists frequently argue that the end of the cold war was a result of the dissemination of new ideas among Soviet elites. Realists counter that these new ideas came into being only because those elites recognized that the Soviet Union was in serious military and economic decline (see Brooks and Wohlforth 2000/2001). However, both kinds of criticisms are, as Mill (1874) pointed out, intractable in any application of the comparative method to social and political phenomenon.

The critical link in constructivist arguments is not, as many opponents of constructivism in political science maintain, the correlation between a given norm or identity and an outcome. Rather, the crucial problem for constructivism is to show *both* (a) that social constructions shape international politics and (b) that the conduct of international politics alters or reproduces social constructions.[2] When approached through the comparative method, (a) and (b) involve two distinct objects of inquiry. In the former, identities and norms are independent variables. In the latter, identities and norms are dependent variables.

In response, constructivists in international relations tend to partition their analysis into two different steps. In article-length treatments, this almost always requires them to choose either (a) or (b) and leave the other undertheorized. Many constructivists take Banchoff's route and choose to focus on (a), in part because nonconstructivist explanations in international relations tend to discount the significance of cultural factors in international politics. On the other hand, a growing number of constructivists are turning their attention to (b). For example, Gregory Flynn and Henry Farrel (1999) examine how participants in the CSCE came to an apparent normative consensus on European security concerns. In doing so, they explicitly neglect a thorough assessment of how social constructions shape international political outcomes. In fact, constructivists have begun to construct research agendas surrounding actor socialization and persuasion. Their primary question is under what conditions actors change their minds about norms, values, identities, and appropriate strategies for some particular issue. Some focus on the microprocesses of socialization and persuasion (see Checkel 1997, 1999; Risse 2000). Others examine the structural conditions that make change in collective beliefs more likely (see Legro 2000, 2001).

But the separation between (a) and (b) also carries with it certain costs. Specifically, we wind up with two different theories: one demonstrating and explaining how social constructions shape action, and another demonstrating and explaining how actions transform or maintain social constructions. But are these really two distinct empirical stages? In fact, it seems more plausible that the reasons why social constructions shape action are closely connected to the mechanisms through which they are maintained or transformed. For example, a change in public discourse surrounding national identity may result in the disenfranchisement of a minority group. But the processes—such as debates about national identity—through which minority groups are disenfranchised may themselves be crucial to the transformation of national identity.

In the dynamics of social construction, socially constructed phenomena serve as both independent (causal) and dependent (outcome) variables. A norm is both a cause of behavior and an outcome of that behavior. Thus, it is particularly hard to deal with instances of transformation in socially constructed aspects of politics, because we work ourselves into the muddle of arguing that a determinant cause of behavior in once instance is actually modified by the very behavior it supposedly causes. This is one reason why "norms can be thought of only with great difficulty as 'causing' occurrences" in the manner assumed by the comparative method (Kratochwil and Ruggie 1986: 767; Laffey and Weldes 1997).

In sum, while standard versions of the comparative method are useful for establishing the elements of a social constructionist claim, they are not particularly suited to the development of robust constructivist theories. The heart of constructivist approaches to politics is a double movement: Social action produces and transforms the very conditions that give rise to social action. If we are unable to gain direct leverage over this complex interplay of cause and effect relationships, then constructivist theory remains fundamentally incomplete. In this respect, the methodological requirements of standard comparative political analysis can only take us so far.

The Social Construction of Comparisons

The problems we discussed in the previous section are, in important respects, tied to the assumption of unit stability in the comparative method. Recall that standard, variable-based comparative analysis works through a distinction between primary (invariable) and secondary (variable) attributes. The primary attributes of a set of units (be they individuals, societies, or states) allow us to assume that they are discrete and symmetrical—in short, comparable. The assumption of unit stability also enables us to carve out a set of conditions as systemic and thus ignore them for the purposes of establishing a cause and effect relationship. This is part of the reason why social constructivist analysis *within* the comparative method forces us to treat the effects of a social construction on behavior and the effects of behavior on social constructions as two different objects of inquiry.

However, we can ameliorate this problem without fundamentally challenging the assumption of unit stability by theorizing both the cause and effect properties of social constructions within a particular set of cases. For instance, we could compare the cause and effect relations implicated in the social construction of national identity across multiple social movements or states. Where the assumption of unit stability really gets us into trouble is with respect to what we have called mapping processes: those dynamics that produce and transform the very boundaries that give rise to discrete and symmetrical units.

The most fundamental way in which social construction figures into comparative case analysis is through the establishment of units of comparison. States, societies, nations, tribes, cities, regions, political parties, and social movements are all examples of social constructions in the most banal sense: They cannot exist without being actively produced and reproduced by the social activities of human beings. There is nothing inevitable about them: They disappear, emerge, and reconfigure as a result of social forces that emerge from the contingent decisions made and ideas generated by human beings.

Standard case comparison takes these communities for granted in order to generate discrete and symmetrical units of comparison. Their discreteness and similarity is a social fact resulting from processes of social construction. As long as they are stable, comparing dynamics within them has a certain prima facie credibility. Mapping processes, however, reconfigure social and political boundaries and, in turn, may either change the primary attributes of units or give rise to new units altogether. Globalization, the diffusion of nationalism, and mass immigration are all examples of processes that, at the very least, have the potential to remap social relations and give rise to new units of comparison.

The comparative method can deal with these processes in one of two ways. First, it can compare the effects of mapping processes within extant units. This is a common approach to the study of globalization. For example, scholars explore the impact of some putative aspect of globalization—such as the rise of trade interdependence—upon government policy or interest-group networks. Second, it can compare mapping processes across different kinds of units. For example, a scholar could compare the effects of Germanic immigration into the Roman Empire with Mexican immigration into the United States.

The drawback of the former strategy is that it artificially limits our ability to discern whether mapping processes have altered the nature of units themselves. Because we *begin* our analysis through the assumption of unit stability, we cannot easily inquire into whether those primary attributes which we methodologically held constant have in fact changed. As a result, many of the studies of globalization in this vein wind up concluding that economic interdependence is not seriously eroding sovereign territoriality. But how could they do otherwise, since they analyze the effects of economic interdependence *within territorial boundaries*? Moreover, any finding of remapping always involves stepping outside of the causal relations found through comparative analysis. Since the generation of the causal relationship requires that primary attributes be invariant, they cannot logically be modified by the variable attributes analyzed through the comparative method.

The drawback of the latter strategy is obvious: How can a comparison between the Roman Empire and the contemporary United States plausibly control for the tremendous differences between the times, places, and modes of organization of both units of comparison? From within the standard comparative method, we are likely to either produce a theory so general as to be effectively tautological or fail to find any causal generalization at all (Tilly 1984: 74–86). Comparing the United States and the Roman Empire *as cases* does not seem particularly fruitful, and a constructivist CP must therefore pursue other avenues of inquiry. While the comparative method can draw our attention to mapping processes and their influence upon social relations within relatively stable units, it is far less suited to exploring whether those processes are altering the nature of units themselves.

Contingency and Necessity

The comparative method strives for invariant and linear causal generalizations. For many, this is the goal of political-scientific analysis: to find determinate relations that enable both explanation and prediction. Of course, political scientists who seek lawlike generalizations generally admit that their findings are usually provisional. Since causation, let alone social causation, tends to be complex in nature, it is very difficult to develop truly invariant causal relations. Rarely do outcomes "have a single cause," "causes rarely operate in isolation," and "a specific cause may have opposite effects depending on context" (Ragin 1987: 27, see also Abbott 1988). Nevertheless, the identification of regularities with determinate cause and effect relations is the benchmark for theoretical inquiry in most forms of the comparative method.

The goal of finding invariant causal relationships produces a fundamental tension in constructivist theory. Constructivism is premised upon the significance of contingency in political relations: the belief that any given outcome is not a necessary consequence of the "nature of things" but instead a contingent effect of the interaction between agents and the sociocultural structures generated by their interaction (Shotter 1993). When constructivists seek to develop invariant and quasi-invariant causal laws, they risk undermining the constructivist project.

How can this be the case, when those causal laws frequently involve socialization, persuasion, and the generation of new identities and beliefs? Our argument must seem somewhat strange, considering that most of the generalizations involved in constructivist theory concern the production or impact of social constructions. The difficulty stems from that fact that almost all political science deals with socially constructed phenomena. Even if we hold that politics are primarily shaped by material factors or that human nature is relatively fixed, we still have to admit that the combination of human interactions and historical circumstance makes any particular political event subject to some degree of contingency. From an ontological perspective, political relations are necessarily socially constructed, in that they have no existence outside of social interaction (Dessler 1999: 127). In short, since political scientists do not deal directly with phenomena that have an existence completely external to human social relations—such as gravity, subatomic particles, and the mating habits of finches—there is no grounds for debating whether the objects of analysis are, in some significant respects, social constructions.

In consequence, although Jeffrey Legro (2000, 2001) criticizes process-oriented constructivism for having to rely on contingency to explain variations in collective identity, we believe that constructivists cannot afford to lose sight of the fundamental role contingency plays in their research program. This requires an emphasis on social agency: the contingent ways in which the interaction of human beings shapes political outcomes by producing or transforming the conditions of politics. An emphasis on social agency is not, however, the same as a theory of individual choice. If such a theory is couched in terms of invariant laws of individual behavior, then the theory necessarily contradicts a constructivist interpretation of the phenomenon in question. Such a theory may be correct, but if it is, then we would not do well to argue that the phenomenon in question is best explored through a constructivist lens.

However, there is a specific context in which constructivists should be perfectly comfortable with formulating determinate relations: when social constructions themselves produce regularities in social relations. These "contingent regularities" give rise to apparently robust invariant relations because they involve effective constraints on social agency in particular times and places. In other words, agency itself is socially constructed and thus amenable to constructivist analysis. Rather than challenge constructivist analysis, this class of regularities is frequently the subject of constructivist theory.

Despite these considerations, constructivist research must remain sensitive to the tensions between the formulation of lawlike generalizations in political science and the fundamental importance of contingency in constructivist theory (cf. Dessler 1999: 135–137). There is no clear solution to these tensions, but the epistemological commitments of the comparative method exacerbate them in a way that suggests we need to look for alternatives.

Comparative Process Analysis

The maps at play in the comparative method enable certain kinds of inquiry into the social construction of politics, but, as with all maps, they also bring with them limitations. The comparative method allows us to assess the causal efficacy of socially constructed aspects of political life, such as culture and identity. It does not allow us, however, to fully explore dynamics of social construction. Furthermore, since the maps of comparative political inquiry are themselves the products of processes of social construction, they preclude us from examining some of the most crucial questions raised by the constructivist research agenda. Finally, the emphasis placed in the comparative method on finding linear and invariant causal relations undermines the core emphasis of constructivism upon contingency and complexity.

Under circumstances where these limitations become particularly acute, constructivists should turn toward a form of comparative process analysis derived from sociological relationalism (see Emirbayer 1997; Jackson and Nexon 1999). Many comparative politics textbooks are already turning to processes—such as democratization, state formation, and economic development—as organizational themes. However, comparative process analysis involves a number of key modifications of the standard comparative method.

Processes are the focus of comparison. In standard versions of the comparative method, variable attributes of entities or cases are the focus of comparative analysis. Comparative process analysis seeks to understand how similar processes unfold differently in different contexts. A process is a "coordinated group of changes in the complexion of reality, an organized family of occurrences that are systematically linked to one another either causally or functionally" (Rescher 1996: 38). Processes are simply observable and (usually) regular dynamics. They can operate at any level of analysis, and can involve a great many or a very few occurrences. Political campaigning, for example, is a process in which a candidate engages in certain routine activities designed to win political support for herself or a cause she champions. Socialization is a process whereby individuals internalize expectations of appropriate behavior in some given context, often through or in relation to a particular identity. Warfare is a process in which organized groups mobilize and deploy resources aimed at resolving disputes through violence. Evolution is a process in which various mechanisms—such as natural selection—alter the characteristics of a species and/or lead to the genesis of a new species.

Social ties are created and maintained by processes of transaction. A social tie is a relation between two actors (or "sites"), such as domination, economic exchange, or communication. When taken together, social ties form networks of social transaction—such as hierarchies, organizational networks, scholarly communities, and so on.

Units are particular kinds of configurations of social ties or networks of social relations. While the comparative method treats units as essentially stable entities, comparative process analysis assumes that units, categories, and corporate actors are constituted by dynamic networks of social and political ties. The discreteness and symmetry of units are properties of their underlying network forms. For example, units are discrete when two or more networks are linked by relatively sparse social, political, and/or cultural ties. For instance, when "one site" within each network "has the right to establish cross-boundary relations that bind members of internal ties," then each network constitutes a discrete "organization" (Tilly 1999: 413). Modern states tend to vest their governments (a particular site within the broader country) with the exclusive right to regulate trade, immigration, and so forth, with other states. Cultural communities consist of relatively dense transaction in which common meanings and symbolism circulate, but ties with other communities lack certain critical common meanings and symbolism that serve as a basis for differentiation.

Causal generalization takes place at the level of mechanisms; these mechanisms account for variation in how processes unfold. Instead of attempting to find invariant and linear causal relations between discrete variables, comparative process analysis involves accounting for how common process configure differently in different contexts. An analyst shows "how widely-applicable causes concatenate into substantially different outcomes depending on initial conditions, subsequent sequences, and adjacent processes" (Tilly 1997: 49). This involves a strategy Ira Katznelson (1997: 99) labels an "analytic narrative," in which the very complexity of relationships between elements in a case is filtered through an analytic lens to provide a plausible account of different trajectories in the aggregate process of interest to the researcher (Tilly 1984).

At first glance, identifying a process may appear to be insufficiently rigorous for comparative political analysis. When we identify a process, after all, we are already making judgements about causality. Since the purpose of variable-based comparison is to determine whether there really is a relationship between "occurrences," the standard comparative method may appear to be necessarily prior to process-based analysis. However, there is nothing inherently more suspect about identifying a process than identifying a variable. Common independent variables such as "level of democratization" and "economic growth rates" already involve judgments about the existence of processes. Both variables and processes are simplified, analytical representations of complex dynamics and interaction effects. In this respect, the identification of a process is simply an observation of dynamics we believe to be significant to some set of political relations or outcomes. In fact, to specify an outcome variable—such as ethnic conflict, mass mobilization, or the emergence of democracy—is to presuppose that we can identify a process.

In international relations, there are a variety of different process-oriented approaches. Many of these have dealt with processes of bargaining, persuasion, and socialization. For instance, Jeffrey Checkel (2001) argues that rationalist mechanisms are more likely to account for norm compliance in certain political settings, while socialization and learning are more salient in other institutional contexts. Although Checkel uses the language of variable analysis, his study brings the comparative analysis of processes into focus (see also Risse 2000). The work of many scholars influenced by poststructuralism also highlights the importance of processes in accounting for how social constructions—understood as discursive configurations—both shape and are shaped by the legitimization of interventions (Weber 1995), the deployment of stories about the other (Neumann 1999), and so forth. Discursive configurations create conditions of possibility for political action but only under specific, identifiable circumstances do they overdetermine how social agents act. Similarly, the constructivist approach pioneered by Nicholas Onuf (1998) focuses on the role of rules in maintaining and transforming social relations.[3]

As these examples suggest, processes can be subdivided into constituent process. Similarly, many processes can be aggregated into larger processes. In some cases, macroprocesses such as globalization and the spread of capitalism are perfectly appropriate subjects of analysis. At other times, scholars may wish to focus upon microprocesses of individual bargaining or face-to-face persuasion. How far a scholar aggregates or disaggregates processes is an analytical question related to the nature of her research.

Nevertheless, we favor an approach that, regardless of the level of analysis, searches for mechanisms and processes within patterns of political relations—as opposed to those inside of actors' heads. We believe this represents a sensible division of labor in the social sciences, given that most political scientists lack expertise in cognitive psychology or neurobiology. Furthermore, a focus on patterns of political relations (but not to the total *exclusion* of, for instance, cognitive mechanisms) is well-suited to questions pertaining to the *social construction* of political life (Shotter 1993: 179; Tilly 1999: 410). How do these assumptions play out in practice, and how does the map they generate ameliorate some of the problems posed by the comparative method for constructivist analysis?

The relational analysis of processes allows us to link the issue of how constructions shape political outcomes while, at the same time, such outcomes may transform or reproduce social constructions. Take the following illustration. After the partition of the Polish Commonwealth in the late eighteenth century, many self-identified Poles struggled to mobilize former members of the Commonwealth against their occupiers: Austria, Prussia, and, most frequently, Russia. One of the most pressing problems faced by Polish nationalists was how to mobilize the peasantry. In the Commonwealth, the peasantry enjoyed none of the rights and privileges of citizenship and existed in a state of near slavery. Full citizenship status had been restricted to the nobility. Even the abortive attempt to modernize the Polish constitution in 1791 sought only to "extend gradually the rights and privileges of the gentry to the burghers" (Wandycz 1974: 8).

In the November Insurrection of 1830, which was aimed against Russian control of Polish territory, Polish nationalists made identity claims centered around the restoration of liberty. Initially, the peasantry assumed that the slogan of liberty meant that they would be emancipated from their "compulsory obligations" and prepared to join in the rebellion. The nobility, however, banned spontaneous peasant agitation for fear of social upheaval (Kieniewicz 1969: 83). As the insurrection progressed, and the need for peasant participation grew, the peasantry largely abandoned the national cause. "When called to enroll, the peasants were asking, And what about compulsory labor? Or they might say, The landlords started the fighting: they should fight themselves" (Kieniewicz 1969, 84).

After the failure of the 1830 insurrection, Polish nationalists embraced the so-called romantic notion of national identity. Polish romantic nationalism focused on the multiethnic and multicultural nature of the old Commonwealth. This was a "civic" conception of the nation, aimed at restoring democratic society centered around a romanticized view of the old Commonwealth (Wandycz 1974). This move came, in large part, as a response to the failure of 1830. In a series of upheavals in the 1840s, Polish romantic nationalism failed to resolve the class tensions between the nobility and the peasantry. In Austrian-occupied Poland, the peasantry even turned against their own gentry (Rozdolski 1986). Polish romantic nationalism, when coupled with radical pro-peasant positions, was not incapable of bringing the peasantry to support the nationalists—but such positions usually alienated the landed gentry and caused them to oppose Polish nationalist aspirations (Kieniewicz 1969).

A similar fate befell the January insurrection of 1863 in Russian-occupied Poland. Despite a unified front including the landed gentry, liberals, and radicals, the peasantry split between supporting the rebels, the Russians, and staying out of the conflict (Wandycz 1974: 177–178). What is striking about peasant participation is that it remained motivated by immediate economic and class concerns: in general, the peasantry did not commit to the cause of national self-determination for its own sake (Gemmill 1995).

In fact, "Polish" peasants generally did not consider themselves Poles until a suitably inclusive notion of ethnic identity came to replace a "civic" conception of Polish nationality dependent on the privileges of nobles and the bourgeoisie. This occurred through a series of developments after 1860, involving the spread of literacy, peasant newspapers, and a resulting increase in ethno-linguistic consciousness. In the next few decades moves to suppress Polish culture and the Catholic Church in both Russian and German Poland helped produce a common sense of grievances across class lines. For these reasons, identity claims invoking common language, ethnicity, and religion proved effective at mobilizing the peasantry. But this new identity also had the effect of transforming the aspirations of Polish nationalists and excluding Jews from full membership in the national community (Gemmill 1995; see also Blanke 1981, Kieniewicz 1969, Walicki 1982, and Wandycz 1974).

How would we approach this through comparative process analysis? Many theorists of identity note the importance of "resonance" in the maintenance and transformation of identities. An identity claim resonates when it activates preexisting understandings of social obligation, justice, and grievances. Of course, these understandings are themselves shaped by already existing frameworks of identity. Resonance has the potential to both transform and reproduce existing identity frameworks—when a sufficiently novel identity claim resonates, it transforms identity. In this respect, resonance is a dialectical process: When an identity claim resonates, it both fits with past experiences and identities and reconfigures them to create new expectations and identities.

In this brief sketch of Polish nationalism, resonance operates as an important process that captures both the causal role of a social construction (Polish national identity) in explaining outcomes and the impact of those outcomes on that social construction. The failure of successive claims about Polish national identity to reconfigure social ties and, hence, to overcome the tremendous network-gaps between the gentry and the peasantry doomed Polish uprisings against Russia, Prussia (later Germany), and Austria. Each failure caused committed nationalists to draw upon discursive resources in order to reconceptualize what it meant to be a Pole. While each new conceptualization of Polish nationalism was a contingent combination of discursive resources, these resources were shaped by the constraints imposed by past nationalist failures. After the 1861 uprising, the suppression of Polish culture and religion in Russia and Germany created common grievances that new identity claims could exploit.

In addition, bans on overt Polish political activity led to programs such as "Organic Work" which stressed the modernization of Poland—in large part through the education of the peasantry (Kieniewicz 1969). The Organic Work program (both a contingent and constrained development) involved both literacy education and the production of newspapers to serve the needs of the peasantry. These newspapers, in fact, created a network of social ties of the type that Benedict Anderson (1991) calls an "imagined community" (Gemmill 1995). Ethno-linguistic conceptions of national identity both emerged out of these changes and piggybacked on them. The notion that being a Pole consisted of a common religion, ties to Polish soil, and language activated and deepened common identity ties across class networks and produced the understanding of what it is to be a Pole that we now take for granted.

Obviously, both our account and processes of resonance are insufficient to explain the full contours of Polish national mobilization and resistance—for that we would need an understanding of other relevant processes centered around bargaining, communication, and so on. However, the difficulty with even a detailed empirical account of processes of resonance and identity is that it is almost impossible to tell, in a predictive and *a priori* sense, whether the particular content of a given claim about identity will, in fact, resonate. As a result, resonance is both a critical process of identity transformation *and* one that generally must be determined *a posteriori*.[4]

It would be problematic, for example, to take each kind of national identity claim and treat it as an independent variable. Removing each claim from the historical context that generated it would do violence to the historical processes that shaped both the kinds of identity claims put forth by Polish nationalists and accounted for how they resonated with different groups. The alternative kind of causal relationship found through comparative analysis—that an identity is more likely to take hold if it resonates—is at best unhelpful and, at worst, tautological. If the civic conception of Polish nationality had triumphed, we would be arguing instead that *it* resonated.

This is the difficulty with process analysis, but it is also its virtue. Rather than test resonance or other processes, we take them as consistent dynamics with respect to the phenomenon we wish to explain. We then show, as in the case above, how the context in which these processes operated altered or reinforced existing social relations, and how those social relations shaped the unfolding of the processes themselves. Generalization operates at the intersection of the networks generated by social ties, the dynamics they generate, and how they interact with the processes identified for study by the researcher.

Comparative process analysis provides one way of mediating between the social-scientific goal of causal generalization and the constructivist emphasis on contingency. In the Polish nationalism illustration, we emphasized the contingent role of social agency in combining different discursive resources. While historical events and developments shaped the available options for Polish nationalist claims and strategies of mobilization, processes of nationalist mobilization varied given somewhat contingent and historically generated social relations.

Causal generalization at the level of mechanisms and processes is, of course, a more humble approach than that sought through the specification of invariant laws. It shares parallels both with rational choice theory and with the poststructuralist emphasis upon conditions of possibility. Rational choice theory, for example, generalizes at the level of choice mechanisms but is agnostic about specific outcomes. Although its emphasis on stability (equilibrium outcomes) and its fixed assumptions about human decision-making processes means that rational choice approaches are of limited utility when studying the social construction of politics, it supplies one plausible mechanism at work in specific configurational contexts.

Relational forms of process analysis hold that significant regularities arise from similarities in social relations. Generalizations can be drawn from analogies in societal forms, but these generalizations operate at the level of dynamics associated with those forms. As Georg Simmel (1971: 26) observes, "Superiority, subordination, competition, division of labor, formation of parties, representation, inner solidarity coupled with exclusiveness toward the outside, and innumerable similar features are found in the state as well as in a religious community, in a band of conspirators as well as an economic association, in an art school as in a family." The association of regular dynamics with social forms/network configurations should not be surprising: each persists as a result of more-or-less routine processes of transaction. Nevertheless, in any concrete historical context, social forms are frequently (1) embedded in different networks and (2) sustained by different meanings and material flows (Tilly 1999: 411).

Thus, relational analytic narratives focus our attention on particular dispositional properties—mechanisms—generated by social relations and how they interact with processes of interest in comparative politics and international relations. Social agency sustains and activates these dynamics, provides one of the sources of indeterminacy that defies their reduction to invariant laws, and, in consequence, can transform social relations themselves. As we discussed above, the scope of social agency is both constrained and produced by the location actors hold in political networks. For instance, to be a leader in a social movement is to occupy a particular location in a network. In some respects, leaders have greater social agency than their followers, but, in other respects, they may face greater restrictions upon their ability to influence outcomes. These are, of course, questions that must be resolved through empirical analysis.

Constructivists tend to be particularly interested in the symbolic and cultural aspects of social relations, such as rules, norms, identities, stories, and so forth. These patterns may carry with them their own dynamics and logics, but we are not convinced that it makes sense to separate them from the material dimensions of social interaction. At the very least, analysts should be prepared to evaluate the causal ramifications of overlap and disconnect between material flows and the cultural significance attached to them. It is, after all, the disjunctures and incompleteness in social relations that make possible historical change (White 1992b).

Comparative process analysis allows a methodologically consistent approach to mapping and remapping. Recall that mapping processes are social dynamics that maintain or transform basic categories of comparison. In this sense, mapping processes play what constructivists refer to as a constitutive role in political life: They define basic categories, social roles, and ways of knowing, and generally contour the parameters and nature of actors and agency.

The disaggregation of units into networks of political transaction is critical to the study of mapping processes. If we consider political institutions and categories to be relative stabilities in patterns of interaction, then it is possible to theorize alterations in the boundaries between them while taking them seriously as social facts. Institutions, categories, and other units of political life can be extremely durable, highly routinized, and supported by a multiplex of overlapping social relations that reinforce boundaries (see, e.g., Tilly 1998b). But, at heart, they must be maintained by concrete social, political, and economic interactions, and thus even the most stable unit is built on dynamic processes that work to maintain its stability. Through an understanding of what dynamics maintain the stability of the boundaries between discrete actors and institutions, we can conceptualize how and what kinds of processes are likely to reinforce or disrupt their stability.

For instance, Andrew Abbott (1996: 861–862) argues that, "in formal topology, boundaries and entities are more or less logically equivalent. Either one could be primal." Therefor, one need not begin with completed entities, but with "the more general notion of 'difference of character' or 'sites of difference.'" These sites of difference are the raw material out of which potential boundary lines can be drawn. Sites of difference, he argues, are "things that emerge from local cultural negotiations. That is, local interaction gradually tosses up stable properties defining two 'sides.'" In this respect, extant units always provide potential alternative locations for boundary drawing. From a social perspective, "the work of creating an entity must also be seen as the work of rationalizing these various connections so that the resulting entity has the ability to endure, as a persistent thing, in the various ecologies in which it is located" (Abbott 1996: 870–872).

In the Polish nationalism example, resonance can also be treated as a mapping process, in that identity claims seek to reorder or reinforce social relations between actors. Depending on which social ties were reinforced or transformed through the resonance of specific identity claims, the map of the (imagined) Polish community shifted or remained stable. Treating resonance as an *analytically independent* process playing out across different network configurations allows us to theorize what kinds of interactions produce new political maps.

While some mapping processes are generated by social relations within units of comparison, mapping processes cannot be said to operate simply within those units because they either maintain or transform the boundary

conditions of political life. Some mapping processes, however, clearly operate both through and across putatively discrete units. The dynamics associated with globalization may constitute such a set of mapping processes.

Globalization as Process

Claims about globalization center around at least two distinct but interrelated questions. First, is globalization altering the nature of international and
domestic political interactions? Second, is globalization eroding the centrality of the sovereign territorial state in favor of new corporate actors such as
international organizations, multinational corporations, transnational movements, and world-cities? Both these questions bear fundamentally on comparative politics. If the nature of international political interactions are
changing, then new forces are at work in domestic political dynamics. Similarly, if sovereign territoriality is eroding as an organizing principle of the
international system, then the disciplinary boundaries between CP and IR
are increasingly anachronistic to the study of politics. Moreover, new units
of comparison will replace the traditional focus of comparative politics on
intrastate politics.

Consider the claims about globalization made by contemporary scholars.
There are at least three categories of such claims. The first is the contention
that processes of globalization—from rising economic interdependence to
changes in international norms and collective identification—are displacing
the centrality of the sovereign territorial state and undermining the explanatory power of anarchy as an organizing principle of international relations
(Milner 1993; Goldstein et al. 2000; Wendt 1994). National, ethnic, and religious conflicts that might once have been seen as primarily domestic affairs
increasingly have international dimensions as a result of terrorism, migration, and the speed of global telecommunications. Environmental problems
with potentially destabilizing implications fail to respect state boundaries.
At the extreme, some suggest that the state "is in decline. . . . Many existing
states are either combining together into larger communities or falling apart."
Even where stable states persist, "already many of their functions are being
taken over by a variety of organizations which . . . are not states" (Van Creveld
1999: vii). Thus, the basic argument is that globalization means the irrelevance of the individual state because of increasing "internationalization"
(Milner and Keohane 1996). Internationalization is simply an increase in the
interdependence of state economies, which can take place without ever calling the existence of state boundaries into question; increases in capital mobility and cross-cultural interchanges are the hallmarks of such a change.

A second group of claims involves the notion that globalization has to do

with fundamental alterations in the connections between the individual, the
state, and society, as a result of which the post-1945 synthesis of political,
economic, and cultural authority behind the banner of the sovereign nation-
state (Giddens 1987: 289–291) may be coming apart. In this respect, increases in capital mobility may have far greater effects than a reduction in
the (always circumscribed, even in the best of circumstances) ability of state
governments to control "their" domestic economies. Instead, the lateral movements of capital across state borders deprive the sovereign territorial state of
the rationale which once guided its actions: the protection of regimes of social citizenship from external threats (Bamyeh 2000: 77–79). In a fundamental way, the core of the state as an actor is altered, and its boundaries
cease to be "boundaries" in any meaningful sense.

A third set of claims is characteristic of those social theorists who have
begun to speak of the contemporary period as a period of late modernity,
hypermodernity, or reflexive modernity. Briefly, this means that the traditional social formations of industrialism are breaking down and being replaced; it is "a *radicalization* of modernity, which breaks up the premises
and contours of industrial society and opens paths to another modernity"
(Beck, Giddens, and Lash 1994: 3). For some, the most powerful evidence
of this is an acceleration of everyday life, especially as witnessed in the
global media; for others, it is the replacement of tradition by "invented tradition" and marketing of nostalgia (Harvey 1989); for still others, the key lies
in the "compression" of space and time by new technologies (Giddens 1984).
Robertson (1992: 100) has argued that what we are witnessing in the contemporary world is nothing less than an increasing consciousness of the world
as a single place, and that this breaks down into two simultaneously occurring processes: "*the universalization of particularism and the particulariza-
tion of universalism.*" At one and the same time, the notion of a universal
(humanity, the globe as a whole) is being incorporated into particular plans
and programs (such as the environmental movement, the feminist movement, etc.), *and* the notion of particular traditions—the notion that everyone
should have unique traditions—has become universally promulgated. These
shifts cannot fail to have profound implications for the maintenance of the
boundaries of legitimate state authority.

In some contexts, particularly in the environmental movement, the globe
has begun to emerge as an *actor* in its own right. Daniel Deudney notes that
the "'whole earth picture,' photographs of the earth from outer space . . . has
emerged as the unofficial icon of the environmental movement." This image
helps such groups to plausibly argue that they are capable of carrying out
action in the name of the entire planet, as opposed to some particular subunit
on its surface (Deudney 1996: 140–141). In other contexts, the globe has

emerged not as an actor, but as a region, a new playing field; this type of characterization is particularly prominent among businesses and those governments that have decided that their proper role is furnishing the conditions under which such globalized businesses can function at maximum efficiency. The very global character of the global region—in that there is something final about the globe, because further expansion is impossible without practical space travel—helps to reinforce the putative inevitability of globalization, and allows political and social actors to plausibly claim that they can do nothing when faced with globalizing tendencies (Hay and Watson 1998).

Against these claims are the arguments of those scholars who see little that is distinctive about globalization. IR "realists" are among the most skeptical of the importance of globalization. They dispute the claim that "the world is increasingly ruled by markets" and that globalization significantly alters the nature of world politics (Waltz 1999: 700). For them, the current international system simply displays characteristics associated with a unipolar distribution of power. Until a state or coalition of states effectively balances against the hegemony of the United States, major international conflict is unlikely. Thus, it is not surprising that nontraditional security threats are at the forefront of international concern, that international organizations and regional integration are relatively robust, and that challengers to the international order rely on terrorism and other strategies that avoid direct military confrontation with the United States. Contemporary developments either bear out core realist assumptions or represent a temporary lull before a return to balance-of-power and realpolitik (see Layne 1993, 1997; Waltz 2000; Wohlforth 1999).

Another set of objections comes from analysts who believe there is nothing particularly new about globalization. They argue that the metageography of the sovereign territorial state system has never been an accurate way of understanding political and social relations in global politics. In fact, the rhetoric of contemporary work on globalization is strikingly reminiscent of writings over a century ago. In 1901, H.G. Wells observed that "the world grows smaller and smaller, the telegraph and telephone go everywhere, wireless telegraphy opens wider and wider possibilities to the imagination." Technology demolishes "obsolescent particularisms" such as national boundaries and will someday lead to the creation of a "world-state at peace with itself." Wells' opinions were not isolated. To take but one example, Marshall McLuhan used the term "global village"—now widely associated with the impact of satellite broadcasting and the internet—to describe the effects of electricity and electronic technologies on social and political culture (Kern 1983: 228–229).

Indeed, the idea of the world as a single place which should not be divided into discrete entities "is at least as old as [Karl] Jaspers's Axial Age . . . in which the major world religions and metaphysical doctrines arose" (Robertson 1992: 113). It is possible to trace the notion of "the globe" back for a number of centuries, perhaps as far back as the classical Greek notion of the "civilization/barbarian" opposition visible in Aristotle and Herodotus, but certainly back to the "standard of civilization" operative in international society from the sixteenth until the early twentieth centuries (Gong 1984). The claim to speak for the world as a whole becomes a standard feature of European great power politics, and the current trend of globalization has roots in European colonialism. It seems difficult to argue that globalization somehow started with the demise of the Bretton Woods system and recent increases in capital mobility. There is a way in which the existence of states as hermetically sealed containers is the *exception* rather than the rule (Giddens 1987). At the very least, what we call globalization may be better thought of as a return to an older constellation of political and economic conditions.

How can we evaluate these claims? Resolving all of these questions will require the use of many methodological techniques, but the comparative analysis of processes provides an important means to do so. The question of whether the nature of domestic and international political interactions are changing is, at heart, a question about processes. We can recast it in the following way: are the *dynamics* of domestic and international politics changing? This question calls attention to processes, rather than to variable attributes of putatively stable units.

In fact, even if some state or group of states succeeded in disciplining capital mobility and clamping down on cross-cultural interchange, this would not imply that globalization was an unimportant phenomenon, or that some kind of natural equilibrium had been restored. From a constructivist perspective, all such moments of relative stability are problems to be explained; this applies to the state system as well as it does to a globalized world. In a way, what is at stake in globalization is what is always at stake in social and political life: the creation and maintenance of actors, boundaries, and patterns of authority. Even if globalization were defeated and the old sovereign territorial map were reinstalled quite authoritatively, this would not mean that analysts should simply go back to operating within the classical comparative method. Globalization, rather, provides us with an opportunity to call the utility of the conventional comparative method into question regardless of the empirical setting.

How the processes discussed in this section concatenate over time will indicate the extent to which globalization is a fundamental change in the configuration of world politics. Although the traditional comparative politics map lends some intuitive plausibility to the conventional comparative method, a process-oriented perspective counsels us to be skeptical of those intuitions. What we need instead is a form of comparison between processes that allows us to note the formal similarities between how boundaries are established and maintained in different empirical settings. Globalization calls attention to the need for such a form of analysis by revealing the contingency of what we had previously taken for granted; this insight should persist *irrespective* of how the current round of state/market struggles plays out. Even if "globalization" turns out to be more hype than substance, the *techniques* which would enable us to determine this would still—ironically—be a better set of conceptual tools to apply, even to situations in which actors *appear* to be quite stable.

Notes

We would like to thank Maia A. Gemmill, Stacie E. Goddard, Daniel Green, Iver Neumann, Herman M. Schwartz, Charles Tilly, and the editors of the series for their numerous helpful suggestions and comments.

1. Mill (1874) also had two *other* methods—the Method of Residues and the Method of Concomitant Variations—but these are not as commonly deployed in CP or IR.

2. For similar criticisms of the disconnect between aspirations and methodologies in constructivist theories, see Jackson and Nexon (2001) and Tilly (1998).

3. As Daniel Green shows in his introduction to this volume, these and other approaches differ greatly in terms of their methodological, epistemological, and ontological commitments. All we wish to highlight here is that process and relational analysis—in many different forms—can help capture the double movement contained in any constructivist claim.

4. In this respect, comparative process analysis falls under the rubric of what David Dessler (1999, 136–137) calls "causal reconstructions." However, we believe it is possible to occupy an intermediate position between covering law generalizations and causal reconstructions.

Bibliography

Abbott, Andrew. 1988. "Transcending General Linear Reality." *Sociological Theory* 6: 169–186.

———. 1996. "Things of Boundaries." *Social Research* 62: 857–881.

Adler, Emmanuel. 1997. "Seizing the Middle Ground: Constructivism in World Politics." *European Journal of International Relations* 3: 319–363.

Anderson, Benedict. 1991. *Imagined Communities: Reflections on the Origin and Spread of Nationalism.* Revised ed. London: Verso.

Bamyeh, Mohammed A. 2000. *The Ends of Globalization.* Minneapolis: University of Minnesota Press.

Banchoff, Thomas. 1999. "German Identity and European Integration." *European Journal of International Relations* 5: 259–290.

Beck, Ulrich, Anthony Giddens, and Scott Lash. 1994. *Reflexive Modernization: Politics, Tradition and Aesthetics in the Modern Social Order.* Cambridge: Polity Press.

Bendix, Reinhard. 1978. *Kings or People*. Berkeley: University of California Press.

Black, Jeremy. 1997. *Maps and History: Constructing Images of the Past*. New Haven: Yale University Press.

Blanke, Richard. 1981. *Prussian Poland in the German Empire*. New York: Columbia University Press.

Brooks, Stephen G., and William C. Wohlforth. 2000/2001. "Power, Globalization, and the End of the Cold War: Reevaluating a Landmark Case for Ideas." *Security Studies* 25: 5–53.

Brown, Michael et al., eds. 1996. *Debating the Democratic Peace*. Cambridge, MA: MIT Press.

Checkel, Jeffrey. 1997. "International Norms and Domestic Politics: Bridging the Rationalist-Constructivist Divide." *European Journal of International Relations* 3: 473–492.

———. 1999. "Norms, Institutions, and National Identity in Contemporary Europe." *International Studies Quarterly* 43: 83–114.

———. 2001. "Why Comply? Social Learning and European Identity Change." *International Organization* 55: 553–538.

Dessler, David. 1999. "Constructivism within a Positivist Social Science." *Review of International Studies* 24: 123–137.

Deudney, Daniel. 1996. "Ground Identity: Nature, Place, and Space in Nationalism." In *The Return of Culture and Identity in IR Theory*, ed. Yosef Lapid and Friedrich Kratochwil, 129–146. Boulder: Lynne Reiner.

Emirbayer, Mustafa. 1997. "Manifesto for a Relational Sociology." *American Journal of Sociology* 103: 281–317.

Evans, Peter, Harold Karan Jacobson, and Robert D. Putnam, eds. 1993. *Double-Edged Diplomacy: International Bargaining and Domestic Politics*. Berkeley: University of California Press.

Flynn, Gregory, and Henry Farrell. 1999. "Piecing Together the Democratic Peace: The CSCE, Norms and the Construction of Security in Post–Cold War Europe." *International Organization* 53: 505–535.

Geddes, Barbara. 1990. "How the Cases You Choose Affect the Answers You Get: Selection Bias in Comparative Politics." *Political Analysis* 2: 131–150.

Gemmill, Maia A. 1995. "The Peasant Question in the National Context: Nation-Building in Nineteenth Century Poland." B.A. thesis, Harvard University.

Giddens, Anthony. 1984. *The Constitution of Society*. Berkeley: University of California Press.

———. 1987. *The Nation-State and Violence*. Berkeley: University of California Press.

Goldstein, Judith, Miles Kahler, Robert O. Keohane, and Anne-Marie Slaughter. 2000. "Introduction: Legalization and World Politics." *International Organization* 54: 385–400.

Gong, Gerritt. 1984. *The Standard of 'Civilization' in International Society*. Oxford: Clarendon Press.

Gourevitch, Peter. 1986. *Politics in Hard Times: Comparative Responses to International Economic Crisis*. Ithaca: Cornell University Press.

Hacking, Ian. 1999. *The Social Construction of What*. Cambridge, MA: Harvard University Press.

Hall, Peter. 1986. *Governing the Economy: The Politics of State Intervention in Britain and France*. New York: Oxford University Press.

Harvey, David. 1989. *The Condition of Postmodernity*. Oxford: Blackwell.

Hay, Colin, and Matthew Watson. 1998. "Rendering the Contingent Necessary: New Labour's Neo-Liberal Conversion and the Discourse of Globalisation." Working paper 8.4, Program for the Study of Germany and Europe, Minda de Gunzburg Canter for European Studies, Harvard University.

Jackson, Patrick Thaddeus, and Daniel H. Nexon. 1999. "Relations Before States: Substance, Process and the Study of World Politics." *European Journal of International Relations* 5: 291–332.

———. 2001. "Whence Causal Mechanisms?" *Dialogue-IO* [online]. Available at <http://mitpress.mit.edu/IO>.

Katzenstein, Peter, ed. 1996. *The Culture of National Security*. New York: Columbia University Press.

Katznelson, Ira. 1997. "Structure and Configuration in Comparative Politics." In *Comparative Politics: Rationality, Culture, and Structure*, ed. Mark Irving Lichbach and Alan S. Zuckerman, 81–112. Cambridge, UK: Cambridge University Press.

Kern, Stephen. 1983. *The Culture of Time and Space: 1880–1918*. Cambridge, MA: Harvard University Press.

Kieniewicz, Stefan. 1969. *The Emancipation of the Polish Peasantry*. Chicago: University of Chicago Press.

King, Gary, Robert O. Keohane, and Sidney Verba. 1994. *Designing Social Inquiry: Scientific Inference in Qualitative Research*. Princeton: Princeton University Press.

Kratochwil, Friedrich, and John Gerard Ruggie. 1986. "International Organization: A State of the Art on an Art of the State." *International Organization* 40: 753–775.

Laffey, Mark and Jutta Weldes (1997) "Beyond Belief: Ideas and Symbolic Technologies in the Study of International Relations." *European Journal of International Relations* 3: 193–237.

Layne, Christopher. 1993. "The Unipolar Illusion: Why New Great Powers Will Arise." *International Security* 17: 5–51.

———. 1997. "From Preponderance to Offshore Balancing: America's Future Grand Strategy." *International Security* 22: 86–124.

Legro, Jeffrey. 2000. "Whence American Internationalism?" *International Organization* 54: 253–289.

———. 2001. "W(h)ither My Argument? A Reply to Jackson and Nexon." *Dialogue-IO* [online]. Available at <<http://mitpress.mit.edu/IO>>.

Lewis, Martin and Kären Wigen. 1997. *The Myth of Continents: A Critique of Metageography*. Berkeley: University of California Press.

Mann, Michael. 1986. *The Sources of Social Power, Volume I*. Cambridge, UK: Cambridge University Press.

Mill, John Stuart. 1874. *A System of Logic*. 8th ed. New York: Harper.

Milner, Helen. 1988. *Resisting Protectionism: Global Industries and the Politics of International Trade*. Princeton: Princeton University Press.

———. 1993. "The Assumption of Anarchy in International Relations Theory: A Critique. In *Neorealism and Neoliberalism*, ed. David Baldwin, 143–169. New York: Columbia University Press.

Milner, Helen, and Robert O. Keohane, eds. 1996. *Internationalization and Domestic Politics*. Cambridge, UK: Cambridge University Press.

Neumann, Iver B. 1999. *The Uses of the Other: "The East" in European Identity Formation*. Minneapolis: University of Minnesota Press.

Onuf, Nicholas. 1998. "Constructivism: A User's Manual." In *International Rela-*

tions in a Constructed World, ed. Vendulka Kubálková, Nicholas Onuf, and Paul Kowert, 58–78. Armonk, NY: M.E. Sharpe.

Ragin, Charles C. 1987. *The Comparative Method: Moving Beyond Qualitative and Quantitative Strategies*. Berkeley: University of California Press.

Rescher, Nicholas. 1996. *Process Metaphysics*. Albany: State University of New York Press.

Risse, Thomas. 2000. "Let's Argue! Communicative Action in World Politics." *International Organization* 54: 1–39.

Robertson, Roland. 1992. *Globalization*. London: Sage.

Rozdolski, Roman. 1986. *Engels and the "Nonhistoric" Peoples: The National Question in the Revolution of 1848*. Critique; 18/19. Glasgow: Critique Books.

Shotter, John. 1993. *Conversational Realities: Constructing Life Through Language*. London: Sage.

Simmel, Georg. 1971. *On Individuality and Social Forms: Selected Writings*. ed. Donald N. Levine. Chicago: University of Chicago Press.

Skocpol, Theda. 1979. *States and Social Revolutions: A Comparative Analysis of France, Russia, and China*. Cambridge, UK: Cambridge University Press.

Snyder, Jack L. 1991. *Myths of Empire: Domestic Politics and International Ambition*. Ithaca: Cornell University Press.

"Sociobiology: A Beauty Contest," 1998. *Economist*. November 18: 86–87.

Spruyt, Hendrik. 1994. *The Sovereign State and its Competitors*. Princeton: Princeton University Press.

Steinmetz, George. 1999. "Introduction: Culture and the State." In *State/Culture: State-Formation After the Cultural Turn*, ed. George Steinmetz, 1–50. Ithaca: Cornell University Press.

Tetlock, Phillip and Aaron Belkin, eds. 1996. *Counterfactual Thought Experiments in World Politics Logical, Methodological, and Psychological Perspectives*. Princeton: Princeton University Press.

Tilly, Charles. 1984. *Big Structures, Large Processes, Huge Comparisons*. New York: Russell Sage Foundation.

———. 1997. "Means and Ends of Comparison in Macrosociology." *Comparative Social Research* 16: 43–53.

———. 1998a. "International Communities, Secure or Otherwise." In *Security Communities*, ed. Emmanuel Adler and Michael Barnett, 397–412. Cambridge, UK: Cambridge University Press.

———. 1998b. *Durable Inequality*. Berkeley: University of California Press.

———. 1999. "Epilogue: Now Where?" In *State/Culture: State-Formation After the Cultural Turn*, ed. George Steinmetz, 407–420. Ithaca: Cornell University Press.

Turnbull, David. 1993. *Maps Are Territories: Science Is an Atlas*. Chicago: University of Chicago Press.

Van Creveld, Martin L. 1999. *The Rise and Decline of the State*. Cambridge, UK: Cambridge University Press.

Walicki, Andrzej. 1982. *Philosophy and Romantic Nationalism: The Case of Poland*. New York: Oxford University Press.

Waltz, Kenneth. 1999. "Globalization and Governance." *PS: Political Science and Politics* 32: 693–700.

———. 2000. "Structural Realism After the Cold War." *Security Studies* 25: 5–41.

Wandycz, Piotr Stefan. 1974. *The Lands of Partitioned Poland, 1795–1918; A History of East Central Europe, v. 7*. Seattle: University of Washington Press.

Weber, Cynthia. 1995. *Simulating Sovereignty*. Cambridge, UK: Cambridge University Press.

Wendt, Alexander. 1994. "Collective Identity Formation and the International State." *American Political Science Review* 88: 384–425.

———. 1999. *Social Theory of International Politics*. Cambridge, UK: Cambridge University Press.

White, Harrison C. 1992a. "Cases Are for Identity, Explanation, or Control." In *What Is a Case?* ed. Charles C. Ragin and Howard S. Becker, 83–104. Cambridge, UK: Cambridge University Press.

———. 1992b. *Identity and Control*. Princeton: Princeton University Press.

Wohlforth, William C. 1999. "The Stability of a Unipolar World." *Security Studies* 24: 5–41.

Wood, Denis. 1992. *The Power of Maps*. New York: Guilford Press.

4

The Socially Constructed Contexts of Comparative Politics*

Rodney Bruce Hall

This chapter will provide a constructivist, "identity-driven" argument about transhistorical change in social orders and social institutions. I have developed this argument elsewhere in an attempt to provide a reconstructive theoretical framework for international relations that seeks to explain historical transformation of the international system (Hall 1999). Integral to the argument are interactions among social forces that operate between societies, as well as within societies. This is a "society-centric" rather than a "state-centric" analysis. This form of analysis transcends the disciplinary boundaries between comparative and international politics. Thus I hope the argument may be of value to scholars interested in constructivist approaches to understanding a range of questions central to the subdiscipline of comparative politics.

What makes an identity-driven argument constructivist? What is critical in constructivist thought is the assertion that the analyst cannot impute a structure of interests and motivations of social actors exogenously. Should the analyst do so, this may say a great deal more about the analyst than it does about the system under study. In order to understand and correctly apprehend and analyze what motivated historically and socially contingent social actors, we have to do some work. We have to assess whom social actors regard(ed) themselves to be in socially and historically contingent contexts before we can hope to understand their interests and motivations. Social identities and group interests are co-constituted, and it is this co-constituted "structure of identities and interests" (Wendt 1992, 1999) that is the starting point of our analysis.

In my book, *National Collective Identity*, I developed the argument that

---

*Note that portions of this argument may be found in a different form in: Rodney Bruce Hall. 1999. *National Collective Identity: Social Constructs and International Systems*. New York: Columbia University Press.

there have been several major transitions in the course of European history that have been driven by changes in societal collective identity. This societal collective identity is the self-image, or self-identification, of societies. It is an image of who they consider themselves to be as a society, or a people, in a historically and socially contingent context. Societal collective identity and individual identity are thought to be co-constituted. They are mutually constitutive. Our socially significant individual identities are embedded in social institutions, and the converse is true as well. I am, for example, husband only within the institution of marriage; I am professor only within the institution of the university; and I am a citizen of the state of the United States of America. Specific instances of the institutions of marriage, universities, and states are constituted in part by the roles that I have been assigned and play within these specific institutions.

When society develops new self-images that are mismatched to the dominant institutional forms of collective action—that is, the institutions by which they are ruled—a legitimation crisis may result in social transformation, rather than the reproduction of these institutions. I have argued elsewhere, following Habermas, that a "legitimation crisis" results in a society when powerful societal members "feel their social identity threatened." In response they revise their "interpretive system" to correct the group identity and "through this group identity assert their own self-identity" (Habermas 1975: 3–4). The prior institutional forms of collective action are demolished, and reconstructed in a fashion strongly influenced by the new, prevailing forms of societal (collective) self-identification. This constitutes historical transformation of the international system, from one form to another. Identities and interests are co-constituted, and it is this co-constituted "structure of identities and interests" (Wendt 1992, 1999) that is the starting point of our analysis.

I argue that changes in co-constituted individual and collective identity result in changes in the legitimating principles of global and domestic social order, and consequent changes in the institutional forms of collective action, through which that identity is expressed to other societies. The norms, rules, and principles of social interaction within, and between, these new institutional forms of collective action are developed by social actors through practice to accommodate the new institutional structure. This new structure manifests the new societal identity and system change.

The institutional forms of collective action are historically contingent modes of social organization. Historically, society has been organized into different institutional forms, which serve, at different times, the needs of different societies that construct them. These forms have always strongly reflected prevailing and historically contingent concepts of the legitimate relationship of the individual member of society to the prevailing conception of legitimate authority. For example, lordship was a legitimate form of authority in feudal Europe, thus fiefs were constructed to institutionalize the relationship between lord and vassal. Similarly, absolute monarchy, in which the king was thought to hold authority to rule directly from God, was a legitimate form of authority in eighteenth-century Europe, thus the territorial-sovereign state was constructed to institutionalize his unmediated sovereignty over the peoples within the territory that he administered. National self-determination of a sovereign people united into a community of shared language, ethnicity, culture, or history has more recently become an accepted form of legitimate authority. Thus the nation-state has been constructed to institutionalize these communal affiliations, and to serve them with an institutional form that can manifest to the world the social action that this form of collective identity seeks to express.

Thus the institutional forms of collective action change with prevailing, historically contingent conceptions of societal collective identity. *Significantly, that which constitutes an appropriate institutional vehicle through which society may take social action is strongly conditioned by what form of polity the society considers itself to be.* A society that rejects lordship as an agency of legitimate authority cannot employ the institution of vassalage to take social action. A society that regards itself as a historically continuous nation, constituted by the ancient common bloodlines of the *Volk*, cannot take the social action it wishes to take, and it cannot express its self-understanding through social action consistent with this understanding, through the institution of a polyglot territorial-sovereign state. I will elaborate by outlining the relationships among three historically contingent forms of social collective identity that have informed equally historically contingent notions of state sovereignty in the context of modern European history. In each case I will elaborate on the consequences of the resulting form of "sovereign identity" for domestic social orders and their institutionalization. The three orders I will describe are what I term the "dynastic-sovereign" or "Augsburg" order, beginning circa 1555, the "territorial-sovereign" or "Westphalian" order beginning in 1648, and the "national-sovereign" or "nation-state" order, beginning as early as the American and French Revolutions, but certainly consolidated in the European context by 1870.

Collective Identity and Early-Modern Dynastic Sovereignty: The Augsburg System

Collective identity in the early-modern era was characterized at the popular level by the confessional hegemony of the prince, and one's social status within a hieratic social order. Confessional hegemony is simply an artifact of

the Christian sectarianism that characterized the period. The religious ideas
(or "confession") of the ruling prince circumscribed the permissible range of
religious confession and practice of his subjects of all social orders. Domestically, one's social status, generally but not always determined by birth, had
a strong effect on collective substate social self-understandings and roles.

A strongly dynastic principle of authority legitimated the state in the early
modern era. The ideational (for Durkheim, sacral) baggage of the medieval-
feudal theocratic order was carried over into the early modern era. From the
onset of the Protestant Reformation in the early sixteenth century through the
end of the Thirty Years' War in the mid-seventeenth century, rulers were principally identified in terms of their Catholic or Protestant religious confessional
status, and their subjects were decidedly expected to conform to the confessional status of the prince. This may well have lead to a large number of very
quick conversions by the nobility during the Reformation period, due to the
chronic unrest that tended to result when the masses of people became reform-
minded much faster than did their prince (Strauss 1988: 194–215). This was to
become a familiar pattern in the urban German Reformation.

Following a generation for the reproduction of Reformed ecclesial institutions, and providing there had been adequate penetration by a given early
modern state into the daily life of society, individuals would generally identify themselves as the subject of a prince with a given confessional status. In
Germany, where state penetration of society was particularly strong, confessional status was likely to be an attribute that was constitutive of individual
self-identification. In many post-Reformation German-speaking states, quite
energetic measures were taken by Protestant German princes to ensure that
the Reformed faith was being taught and internalized in the far reaches of
their realms. This often involved visitations by an entourage of clerics and
state officials, elaborate examinations of parochial clerics and catechists, and
the transcriptions and archiving of highly detailed protocols of the examinations (Strauss 1978: chaps. 8, 9, and 12). Religious confessional identity was
a primary source of personal identity for any mature and reflective early-
modern European in a period so dominated by religious conflict. This status
was constitutive of their collective identity as well, and the collective status
of subjects of their Protestant or Catholic prince was often an extension of
this individual identity.

Of course, Christian factional or confessional status was not the only component of early modern collective identity. Self-identification with an ethnic
and a linguistic community were also present, but these sources of difference were more diffuse components of collective identity as the societies of
the period were fragmented into many subdivisions of dialect due to the
fragmented topography and difficulties of travel and communications.

The fundamental orientation of each toward the person of the prince, and particularly toward his confessional status within the Christian faith, was principally constitutive of the collective identities and legitimating principles of the domestic social order that grew up around the Augsburg system. These new social identities led to new, domestic sociopolitical principles and norms. Previously, during the medieval-feudal theocratic order, individuals had regarded themselves as generic subjects of Christendom, subject to both the secular, temporal authority of a lord and a king, and the spiritual authority of the Church and the papacy (Hall 1997). During the Reformation they had acquired a more particularistic, factional collective identity. Even in the medieval period from the inception of the Carolingian Empire (800 A.D.) to the late medieval period when Strayer (1970) suggests that the outlines of the modern territorial state could be clearly discerned (circa 1300 A.D.), the institution of kingship increasingly had become secularized, and its legitimacy separated from the legitimating principles provided by the political theology of the Church. Kantorowicz (1957) provides a monumental study of how the particulars of the political theology of divine ordination changed significantly, between the tenth and early sixteenth centuries, with respect to the specific qualities that the king's anointing was thought to have conferred upon him. The sacrality of the anointed king was significantly downgraded over the centuries from what Kantorowicz has referred to as an early "Christ-centered kingship," to a "law-centered" kingship, to a "man-centered" kingship. Where ties to Rome had been cut, the spiritual authority of the papacy had been thoroughly supplanted by that of a "national" Church that professed one of the rapidly proliferating variants of a reformed faith.

Significantly, the Reformation and its adaptation by many European princes had created the intersocietal norm of dynastic sovereignty in the principalities and free states that adopted Protestantism. Rome could be freely and willfully ignored without fear of domestic retribution, or even domestic sullenness, in these newly created Protestant states. The prince could take any action that pleased him with respect to domestic and interstate affairs without fear of excommunication, the interdict or the ban, or at least without fear of any serious consequences of these papal penalties, which he was likely to already have suffered in any case. Quite often this involved no suffering at all in the domestic political arena, as a Protestant prince in the German states in particular had as likely as not adopted Protestantism completely instrumentally, because his people had done so in the giddy and disorderly years of the 1520s. A papal sanction might even enhance the domestic standing of such a prince under such circumstances. A norm of what we might call "dynastic self-determination" then developed, at least among the Protestant princes.

In the immediate aftermath of the Reformation, domestic nontoleration of religious difference appears to have emerged as a norm. Disastrous civil and interstate wars of religion were fought among Catholic and Protestant princes of the Holy Roman Empire. The introduction, by way of Geneva, of Calvinism in the French "Huguenot crescent" had resulted in the conversion of up to ten percent of the population of sixteenth-century France to Protestantism. Catholic monarchs ruling regions that included areas where the Reformed faith had been introduced had initially, invariably reacted to repress these religious identities, from Hapsburg Austria and Germany, to Valois France (Ladurie 1994). These civil, violent, religious conflicts had run on into decades and thereby exhausted both sides, and as the lengthiness and savagery of these wars had made it clear to Catholic dynasts, who were reluctant to accept this result, that Protestant collective identity could not be put down by force of arms. The Hapsburg Holy Roman Emperor and the last Valois and early Bourbon dynasts converted the norms of intolerance to principles of toleration of religious confessional distinctions of the principalities within their realms. This norm-shift bolstered the integrity and peace of their states. Significantly, what had originated as a domestic norm of toleration was to take on the characteristics of a positive right in the seventeenth century (Greengrass 1987: 69).

The internecine French Wars of Religion had thus ended with just such a toleration edict, the 1598 Edict of Nantes. But in Germany, the 1555 Peace of Augsburg had left a tenuous political consensus for mutual toleration of neighboring principalities populated by people of another faith. This consensus did not develop into a principle of mutual toleration of religious difference between societies, or within many societies. Thus the Augsburg norms were ineffective both domestically and internationally in pacifying societies composed of religious-based social collective identity, incapable of serving as a long-term basis for stable, domestic, and interstate social order. Religious identity, in the Augsburg system, continued to be highly and aggressively constitutive of societal collective identity.

Collective Identity and Westphalian Territorial Sovereignty

Though the systemic transformation was hardly abrupt, and the Westphalian settlement of the Thirty Years' War cannot be said to have immediately ushered in a new international system, a shift in the constitution of the state and the norms of sovereignty and of interaction between states did slowly develop to an extent to which we can speak of a system transition. Subsequent to the Westphalian Settlement, the confessional status of the prince continued to have constitutive consequences for individual self-identification. The reproduction of both reformed and unreformed ecclesiastical institutions had continued energetically from the time of the Reformation. Religious identity and confessional status had been dissipated as primary sources of both domestic and interstate conflict with the secular Westphalian settlement, and the general European exhaustion at the end of the wars of religion.

Religious identity continued to be constitutive of individual self-identification, however, in domestic society, but this had less conflictual domestic consequences as the internationally, post-Westphalian "secular" state penetrated domestic society and strengthened the apparatus of state control. In an international context, religious identity had become deprived of the highly emotive quality required to dehumanize those abroad with a different religious identity. Decoupling of the confessional status of a foreign power from the issue of that power's status as a sovereign power was an innovation that was formulated by societal elites, and then slowly adopted by their subjects. Monarchy had acquired a sovereign status that was in no way altered by the individual monarch's confessional status. For the first time since the Reformation, the individual would identify with the prince and his state, and defend him and it in the absence of a confessional motivation, because the emancipation of the notion of monarchy from the confessional status of the prince rendered the individual free to experience a filial loyalty to the prince, and a cultural affinity to the prince's lands and peoples. Both the prince's legitimacy and the state's sovereignty had now been emancipated from the issue of individual or collective confessional status. The individual's self-identification now merged with a collective identity and institution that was no longer hegemonically dependent upon confessional status.

War exhaustion and military stalemate had settled the great religious issues that had stirred up the passion of the European masses for three or four generations and had generated the Westphalia settlement. Seventeenth-century European rulers now largely settled down to focus their attention on their state-building projects within their own borders. For the next century and a half, from the Westphalian settlement to the French Revolution, the agency of the European masses that had been so evident in their mobilization to religious causes from 1525 to 1648, would be supplanted by the agency of the developing state. This new, transconfessional legitimacy of the prince and his state was generated juridically by an interstate treaty (thus a legal arrangement), but was to have domestic consequences, as we shall see below.

The most novel and important principles of international interaction that were inaugurated by the Westphalian settlement were the principles of *autonomy* (each state would be recognized as an autonomous actor in its foreign and domestic relations) and that of *equality* (each state and its prince or representatives would be treated as equivalent actors in their rights and obligations in their relations with one another) (Osiander 1994: 77–89). Once the principles of international autonomy and sovereign equality among states and princes had been created, the faith of the ruler of the state became incidental to the legitimacy of his rule, internationally and domestically. Societal collective identity began to coalesce around an expanding state in the absence of politically salient confessional cleavages. Popular passions, lacking religious fervor to give them impetus, lost their significance in affairs that were external to domestic society, which significantly blunted the poisonous rigor of domestic discord. The belief systems of the sovereign, and political and societal elites, specifically "the nobility, the military leaders, churchmen, members of parliament (where parliaments existed)" (Luard 1987: 346), swelled in political salience relative to the belief systems of the common people. International conflict rarely involved any conflict of faiths in the post-Westphalian system, and where it engendered in domestic conflict, it could be quickly suppressed by the state without much fear of intervention by foreign co-religionists. Evan Luard suggests that international policy was determined by the uniquely secular post-Westphalian legitimating principle "the interest of the state: *raison d'état,*" which also prevailed domestically (348).

But this did not happen all at once. Osiander argues, for example, that much more than the 1648 Westphalian settlement of the Thirty Years' War, it was the early eighteenth century Peace of Utrecht ending the War of Spanish Succession that "confirmed the fact that the European system was essentially made up of self-determining actors, none of which were entitled to dictate to the others" (Osiander 1994: 120). The consequent territorial-sovereign "structure of identities and interests" (see Wendt 1992) enabled the territorial-sovereign state to continue to increase its penetration in domestic society various forms of absolutist rule developed in many areas of Europe. Significant innovations in the composition of armed forces followed as ideationally secure monarchies moved to develop the means to effectively and perpetually secure themselves physically from external threats. Even in the absence of the ideologically mobilizing power of nationalism, eighteenth-century states had moved quickly to develop the technical, administrative capacity to ensure the stability of their finances and developed mechanisms to ensure the steady flow of specie to the coffers of the crown. The development of professional standing armies was one of the most significant consequences of this enhanced extractive capacity of the state. Throughout the Thirty Years' War, monarchs had to be content to have access to small armed forces (and then only in time of war), which they had been constrained to lease on an ad hoc basis from private military contractors. They had often been required to raise large sums of money quickly, and at high rates of interest. As the absolutist territorial-sovereign state developed and penetrated society, monarchs would no longer be content with this arrangement. The increasing capacity of the state to extract surpluses from domestic society had allowed the territorial-sovereign state to provision and pay relatively large armed forces in peacetime. Eighteenth century monarchs generally availed themselves of the opportunity to create these forces.

The officer corps provided an outlet for the energies of the scion of the domestic nobility, and the wise absolutist made certain they felt comfortable and appreciated there. Some foreign mercenaries could be obtained, but much of the rank and file had to be recruited or otherwise pressed into service adventurers from the riffraff of domestic society (Black 1990: 315–321).

In this sense, as societal collective identity had solidified around the state, however entangled this state might be with a dynasty, this emerging collective identity permitted the growth and societal penetration of the state to increase dramatically the state's extractive capacity. This extractive capacity furnished the state with powerful standing armed forces. This territorial-sovereign collective identity had not yet, however, generated the capability to mobilize the emotive connection of the subject to the state such that life and limb would be offered willingly by those who served. Certainly the societal emotive response to the "sacrality" of legitimate authority studied by Durkheim had evinced itself in allegiance to the crown. Yet the vast majority of those within domestic society were pleased to pursue profit with their own peaceful professions. They were content to watch the crown fight its wars with armies composed of foreigner mercenaries, alien exiles, haughty domestic nobles, and ne'er-do-well adventurers. This lack of enthusiasm for martial patriotic valor was exacerbated by the fact that access to a military career that could lead to any substantial rank or privilege was the perquisite of the aristocracy in absolutist Europe.

While societal collective identity might cohere at the inter-societal level around a dynasty and a state identified with the dynasty (e.g., the Bourbons, Hapsburgs, Hohenzollerns, or Romanovs) societal collective identity at the level of domestic society was still badly fragmented by de facto legal inequality among members of European society prior to the later emergence of national collective identity. Domestic social relations were characterized by conditions of legal inequality, as exemplified by the estates system in France. Under these conditions, the emerging urban and rural bourgeoisie might well consent to pay their taxes to crown and state, but would not yet themselves do the fighting (Woloch 1994: 383–387). The urban and rural poor at this time could not be induced to believe that they had any stake whatever in society, or much stake in the success of the regime that ruled it. Absolutist eighteenth-century European regimes thus tended to view the non-noble segments of their societies as docile and compliant providers of the resources required for the maintenance of the state.

Internal Dimensions of Territorial Sovereignty:
The Eighteenth Century Domestic Social Order

Let us examine the domestic consequences of Westphalian territorial sovereignty. The Westphalian doctrines of "divine right" sovereignty and *raison d'etat* provided effective weapons to the monarchy in its domestic struggle for power with the lesser nobility. Divine right sovereignty had granted the power of life and death over all who were "subject" to his sovereignty. Friedrich Wilhelm of Prussia could well claim "[w]e are king and master and we do as we please" (Luard 1992: 103). The eighteenth-century monarchs experienced some limits on their freedom of action due to continued, though diminished, privileges and pressures of the lesser nobility. But their sovereignty entitled them to authority over the state so substantial that it necessarily obscured the distinction between the state and the dynasty. Their state-building projects had left them with "supreme legitimate power over the people residing within their borders" as well a monopolies of coercion (the legal use of armed force), taxation (collection and expenditure), administration (command of the institutions of public life and the bureaucracy that served at the pleasure of the crown), and lawmaking (control of the agenda of public policy and legal jurisprudence) (Woloch 1982: 4). This territorial-sovereign structure of identities and interests helped to structure social orders and relations among all classes of domestic society.

Social Identity and the Peasantry

This process of progression from feudal norms of heteronomy and of feudal diffusion of political power had proceeded with greater speed in the west of Europe than in the East. In central and eastern Europe, and particularly Russia, the rural nobility retained more discretion in the administration of their lands and in the governance and discipline of the peasantry within them. The peasant was bound with significant obligations to provide labor services on the land attached to the *demense*, by the tie of serfdom. He was denied legal freedom to leave or change his occupation or even to travel without the permission of the noble. Tenure of his land could in practice be forfeited for serious offenses, defined at the discretion of the lord.

The peasantry, particularly in eastern Europe and Russia, were effectively reduced by legal measures to the status of chattel (Woloch 1982: 61–63). The more pronounced feudal residues of the central and eastern European states limited the penetration of the crown and its state into vast tracts of rural society in the countries where its strength held. A rural peasant in such circumstances was much more likely to self-identify as a steward and servant of his local noble than as a subject of the crown. The local lord retained control of the particulars of the peasant's personal circumstances. The quantity of labor he performed, the dues and taxes he paid, the woman he was permitted to marry, the rents he paid on his lands, the materials from which he was permitted to construct a meager dwelling, and the number of flogging stripes he bore upon his back were determined entirely by his local "lord," not his "sovereign."

The rigid social control and grinding poverty of such conditions generation-to-generation had afflicted the peasantry with the attitude of traditionalism. Thus the aspirations of the bulk of the peasantry were of necessity quite modest, generally oriented toward provision of subsistence for the family. Peasant communal norms of submissiveness to authority and acceptance of social immobility developed. With eyes fixed so firmly on the ground, the primary sources of peasant self-identification were entirely local: the manor (or *chateau*), the parish, the village or commune, and the family. The "interests" of the peasant derived from these identity commitments and featured maintenance of subsistence for the family, avoiding the wrath of the seigneur, and the cultivation of a ragged respectability in social intercourse with peers.

Social Identity and the Nobility and Bourgeoisie

A spectrum of noble elites vied for distinction and patronage in eighteenth-century, territorial-sovereign domestic society. But the century saw little of the social mobility that was to characterize the nineteenth, and none at all in many regions. Noble birth was required, and meritocracy was scarcely yet envisioned. Generally the landed aristocracy sat at the summit of the social pyramid. The wealthy urban nobility and clerics followed. A group of nobles with titles and no wealth clung to the trappings of nobility throughout the century (Woloch 1982: 79–81).

The aristocratic class cultivated its own system of values that quite intentionally radically distinguished itself from either the merchant or the emerging bourgeois classes, and even further from the resigned traditionalism of the peasantry. Class identity was primarily constitutive of the self-identification of the aristocracy and was derived directly from their social role as extensions of the territorial sovereign. To buttress this class identity as nascent capitalist production relations emerged on the continent, the nobility—especially the French nobility—cultivated a passionate disdain for what they denigrated as the "money-grubbing activities" of the "vulgar rich." The landed estates and attendant seignorial rights to rents and dues accruing from this proprietorship assured them of income. They consciously developed as a hereditary, profligate class of conspicuous consumers. They heaped scorn on the bourgeois virtue of frugality that had engendered the accumulation of the fortunes of the "commercial nobility," whom (except in England) they loathed and ridiculed for daring to seek social acceptability among them. In counterpoint to the pretensions of this "commercial nobility" of the "vulgar rich" they proudly identified themselves as a "military nobility" of ancient lineage in the service of the crown and "state." In this and countless other ways, they staked their claim to belong to a race apart (Woloch 1982: 82). As a consequence of their persistent exclusion from the society of the aristocracy, the wealthy bourgeoisie identified more strongly with the state and crown, which particularly in France would ennoble them for a stiff fee, to the revulsion of the landed aristocracy.

The urban nobility prospered in roughly twenty cities on the continent with populations exceeding 100,000. The urban nobility, who generally lacked landed estates, relied more directly on the patronage of the crown for the maintenance of their wealth and position. *The sovereignty of the crown constituted the core of both their political and economic systems of accounting.* Extravagant and opulent lifestyles, huge expenditures prodigal, wasteful and lavish social engagements were often financed by short-term debts. Both the debts and the expenditures were regarded as short-term investments in their social and economic futures. The highest level of visibility was highly rewarded in the system of royal patronage that they relied upon for everything. The higher their visibility, the more "sinecures, pensions, and favorable marriage alliances they could obtain for their children" (Woloch 1982: 92).

Especially in France, the aristocracy had squandered their resistance to the absolutist state for the mere trappings of power, and for lifestyles of idle and purposeless opulence. Except for "the nobility of the robe" who served a residual role as judges and magistrates, the Bourbons had stripped the French nobility of real, political power. The crown spoon-fed the nobility on patronage and pageantry in its stead. Consider the fate of the court nobles. French absolutism, the penultimate expression of territorial-sovereignty, had reduced these to a purely ornamental function. Their function was to enhance the status of the Bourbon kings by their presence, by their attendance to the king's whims. Territorial-sovereign absolutism had induced them to exchange their ancient power and authority for this "unproductive, even dissipated existence" (Woloch 1982: 92). Liah Greenfeld describes the dilemma of the court noble as so dire that the "proud nobles were indeed reduced to the position of children. Denied all independence and treated without respect, they were expending their pent-up energies in intriguing against each other and for the attentions of the ruler whose supreme power over them they no longer dared to contest" (Greenfeld 1992: 138).

A result was the humiliation of the French aristocracy and their consequent alienation from the regime. The primary identity commitment of the bulk of the French nobility under such humiliating circumstances was with their class, rather than with the *roi* or the *patrie*. Regional variations in this absolutist territorial-sovereign structure of identities and interests generated variations in intersocietal class relations across Europe. I will illustrate this briefly with some excursions into the Prussian and English cases.

Social Identity Excursions: Prussian Absolutism and Prussian Noble Militarism

The absolute sovereignty of the Prussian kings over domestic matters was similarly unconstrained. Friedrich the Great (ruled 1740–1786) set the tone as the consummate Prussian autocrat. He exercised an intensely personal rule over the Prussian state, as had his father, Friedrich Wilhelm I, who "directed the state in person, all threads came together in his hand" (Palmer 1973: 53). The Prussian kings held a disdainful view of the potentialities of the common classes. In the eyes of the Hohenzollerns, their limited capabilities required their firm supervision by the Prussian nobility. Thus they insisted that strict preservation of the privileges of military command remain in the hands of the Prussian nobility. A Prussian of low birth could expect no social mobility whatever throughout the century. Over time, service in the bureaucracy became a preserve of the nobility as well (Woloch 1982: 89–90).

As a fortunate byproduct of their severe autocracy, Prussian kings resolved the problem of "how to subdue the nobility without earning their enmity and without creating severe social instability" (Woloch 1982: 86–87)—by setting them apart as a military class *de facto* as well as *de jure*. There were no Prussian sales of military titles to wealthy bourgeois, as in France. In this manner the Prussian kings consistently managed to instill a firm identification of the Prussian aristocracy as domestic and international guardians of the Prussian state in fact as well as in name. In this way the Prussian kings provided opportunities for attainment of the fundamental motivating factors of the Prussian nobility that the Bourbon variant had denied the French nobility; namely their "honor, class-consciousness, glory, or ambition" (Palmer 1973: 50).

While they valued patriotism, the Prussian monarchy certainly did not expect it from the common classes. Obedience alone was both prized and expected from the common Prussian, be they soldier or civilian, and was a virtue prized above patriotism in the lower classes. The self-identifications and self-understandings of the masses of common people were fundamentally of no consequence to their absolutist rulers, so long as they produced and obeyed. As a consequence of absolutist identity, the territorial-sovereign notion of "interest" in this context was structured such that "[a] 'good people' was one which obeyed the laws, and paid its taxes, and was loyal to the reigning house; it need have no sense of its own identity as a people, or unity as a nation, or responsibility for public affairs, or obligation to put forth a supreme effort in war" (Palmer 1973: 50).

The peasantry, in any event, was overwhelmingly preoccupied with the pursuit of subsistence. The lower bourgeoisie was engaged in the pursuit of mastership as artisans and master craftsmen. The primary identity commitment of these was occupational. They pursued a very limited social mobility in that the best journeymen might set themselves up as a master. Attainment of the status of master was a cherished badge of citizenship, denoting honorable social status and considerable economic privilege to guilded masters. Masters enjoyed a modicum of moral respectability. As the century progressed, masters increasingly became capitalists and proprietors, with hope of much more (Woloch 1982: 95–98). But bourgeois enfranchisement with expanded political rights was to be realized only in France in the eighteen century, and quite late. Journeyman artisans lacking proprietorship over their means of production increasingly fell to the status of proletarians as their masters simply salaried them.

Social Identity Excursions: The English Whig Oligarchy

A significant exception to this absolutist form of sovereignty had developed in England, however, where "Whiggism" had triumphed in the "Glorious Revolution" to put an end to Stuart theories of the divine right of kings (Trevelyan 1965: 70–92). A Protestant constitutional monarchy had been restored with the Hanoverian succession. The English monarch's power was circumscribed by a power-sharing arrangement with Parliament, but this was no figurehead crown, as its government ministers retained the power to dispense patronage and sinecures to ensure working majorities for its policies in Parliament (Black 1991). Thus absolutism in England had been held at bay by regicide and Protestant ideology. Hanoverian English suffrage strongly resembled a corporate or group privilege, rather than a universal franchise. Suffrage was "almost a form of property, whose exercise was expected to bring some direct benefit" (Woloch 1982: 30–1). The leading family in the area had the privilege of nominating a candidate for parliament; thus many seats "seemed almost hereditary with sons replacing their fathers as the generations passed" such that on the eve of the Seven Years' War, three quarters of the 1761 Parliament was composed of men whose ancestors had served in the House (Woloch 1982: 33).

The Whig oligarchy dominated English politics in the eighteenth century and successfully opposed Tory demands for a more democratic political order. Whig ideology preached the inherent instability of a democratic form of government in which political equality was granted to all, independent of birth and particularly property. Their doctrines defended both the notion of limited monarchy and the responsibilities (and privileges) of the aristocracy. They rejected Tory theories of popular sovereignty and Stuart notions of absolute monarchy alike, and favored a program that ensured a constitutional monarchy, permitted them to exercise (and profit from) an oligarchic form of territorial-sovereignty. These doctrines ensured the reproduction of the social preconditions for the exercise of oligarchic sovereignty; Protestant succession, the rule of law, and not by accident the defense of property against encroachments by the crown or the commons alike (Dickinson 1981: 29–36).

Thus England's government appears, more than any other eighteenth-century arrangement, to bear the strongest resemblance to Marx's description of capitalist government as the "executive committee of the bourgeoisie" with the exception that it was conspicuously led by a small landed aristocracy. Unless one was bourgeois—a noble or a wealthy merchant—one's franchise was extremely limited. Yet the self-identification of England as a Protestant nation, from at least the end of the sixteenth century (Greenfeld 1992), had created a vehicle for social mobility for at least a portion of the masses that had been unknown on the continent (with the exception of the United Provinces). This had engendered a sense of national feeling that extended at least to those well enough educated to benefit from this "nobility." The ideal of a sovereign people, however narrowly the "people" might be in practice defined, had deep roots in the history of English social collective identity. This notion enjoyed significant credence among the common people in Hanoverian England. This was to have significant consequences for the early emergence of national collective identity in England relatively early, as well as for England's behavior as an eighteenth-century territorial-sovereign power.

National-Sovereign Identity

Having discussed the consequences of a territorial-sovereign structure of identities and interest, I now move to the development and consequences of the national-sovereign structure of identities and interests that resulted in the final transition in the international system to be discussed in this chapter. Recall that we have seen that the rampant absolutism of the French monarchy had deprived the French nobility of their ancient class identity as quasi-feudal legislators and rulers of the French nation. They recognized the crown's penchant for ennoblement of wealthy bourgeois as a more direct threat to the status and legitimacy conferred upon them by their ancient bloodlines. This slur constituted an adequate injury to redirect their class identification with the French crown and state into a primary allegiance to other members of their class. Thus the French nobility had begun to redefine and reorganize itself to construct a new, firmer basis for its identity and status to meet the twin threats of the absolutist tendencies of the crown, and the incursions of the wealthy bourgeois class into its ranks (Greenfeld 1992: 145–188).

As the "virtue" that nobility based upon blood lineage would not provide a sturdy bastion to halt encroachment on their privileges, the French aristocracy would apply their wealth and leisure to the creation of a new barrier against bourgeois incursions. Thus, "[i]n the eighteenth century the [French] aristocracy appropriated education as a quality peculiar to it. It redefined itself as a cultural elite. . . . Schooling became a necessary condition for success in high society. . . . The importance of the Court decreased proportionately. . . . Talent became a ground for ennoblement. Money could buy nobility, but it could not buy social acceptance"(Greenfeld 1992: 148–149). Thus the newly educated aristocracy of birth became augmented with an "aristocracy of merit." Intellectuals who were "cultivated" by their aristocratic patrons formed an affinity with their patrons. Rousseau provided the message when he wrote, "'[t]he best possible government . . . is an aristocracy.' But in an aristocracy of merit '. . . the wisest should govern the many'" (Greenfeld 1992: 175; Ritter and Bondanella 1988).

But it was neither the Rousseauian vision of the sovereignty of the state, lodged in the general will, nor elite or mass alienation from the atomizing capitalism of the vulgar rich, that alone provided the ideological basis of an emerging French nationalism in the French aristocracy. The sources of French nationalism, as it emerged in puerile form in the middle of the eighteenth century, were by no means purely internal to French domestic society.

As the eighteenth century progressed, the early "Anglophilia" of the French intellectual elite evinced in Montesquieu's admiration of the English constitution, articulated in *L'Esprit des Lois*, "gradually gave way to Anglophobia" (Greenfeld 1992: 178). The remarkable decline of French stature and fortune on the international stage after the death of Louis XIV, and humiliating defeat at the hands of the British in the Seven Years' War, had contributed to a vehement *ressentiment* of Britain among the French elite. In this context, "*ressentiment* refers to a psychological state resulting from suppressed feelings of envy and hatred (existential envy) and the impossibility of satisfying these feelings" (15).

Greenfeld's application of the concept of *ressentiment* to the notion of the legitimation crisis developed by Habermas is indispensable in understanding the cognitive origins of national collective identity. Without directly invoking Habermas, her argument strongly reflects his in arguing that "[t]he adoption of a new, national identity is precipitated by a regrouping within or change in the position of influential social groups . . . which creates among them an incentive to search for and, given the availability, adopt a new identity" (Greenfeld 1992: 16).

But why does this new identity crystallize as national identity? At the close of the eighteenth century, French intellectuals and nobility saw much to fear and despise in Britain. They had been mortified by the results of the Seven Years' War, and pined for vengeance against the British. The loathing of the French intellectuals, noble or not, of the *bourgeoisie vulgaire* had led them, with the assistance of the work of Mably, to despise Britain as "[a] capitalist society, a nation that was unjust, avaricious, venal, corrupt, and dominated by commercial interests . . . [thus] . . . no fit model for France"(Greenfeld 1992: 180).

Thus the thrust of Greenfeld's argument is that the revolution would never have been possible without (1) the disaffection of the nobility, (2) their move toward reconstituting themselves as a cultural elite in the face of their political irrelevance on the absolutist state, and (3) the ideology of national collective identity, which sprang from the resulting French Enlightenment, and from *ressentiment* of Great Britain, the principle rival of France. Note that all of these factors are either internal or external artifacts of the territorial-sovereign structure of identities and interests that engender the absolutist state. The ideology of nationalism had sprung from the French nobility and the intellectual elite, not from the bourgeoisie, who later appropriated the revolution. Greenfeld makes it clear that she regards the French bourgeoisie as scarcely being in a position to conceptualize, let alone create and execute, a social revolution. She says the French bourgeoisie "consisted of a middling sort of people, smart enough to recognize a good opportunity. The elite forged and armed the middle classes with weapons it had not much use for itself" (1992: 186).

It is not my intention in this discussion to advocate the adoption of Greenfeld's explanation of the development of the notion of national-sovereign identity in France over competing explanations. Greenfeld clearly takes pains to refute the contentions of theorists as diverse as the Marxist, Barrington Moore; the structuralist, Theda Skocpol; and the French aristocrat de Tocqueville that the French Revolution was a bourgeois revolution (Moore 1966: 40–110; Skocpol 1979: 174–180; de Tocqueville 1955). But there is little documentary evidence provided by the pens of the contemporary French bourgeoisie of the existence of a French, bourgeois class identity. Michael Mann's recent persuasive explanation contains elements of all of these explanations, in his neo-Weberian, multicausal IEMP model (Mann 1993: 1–22).

> Classes were not 'pure' but also were defined by ideological, military, and political forces. The Revolution *became* bourgeois and national, less from the logic of development from feudal to capitalist modes of production than from state militarism (generating fiscal difficulties), from its failure to institutionalize relations between warring elites and parties, and from the expansion of discursive ideological infrastructures carrying principled alternatives. (1993: 167).

What I should like the reader to take away from this brief development of the Revolution and the French national-sovereign identity that resulted from it is an understanding that: (1) The legitimation crisis that spawned the Revolution had sources which were both internal to and external to French society. (2) The sources of this legitimation crisis were cognitive and material, ideational (agential) and structural. (3) Those who argue that the crisis of legitimacy of the *ancien regime* might be explained largely with recourse to sources internal to French domestic society must contend with the fact that the development of the specifically national-sovereign identity of the new regime cannot be explained without reference to factors external to domestic society, such as competition with England. Finally, (4) the power of the French bourgeoisie and the idea of the French nation arose simultaneously.

French nationalism and French nationhood did not arise as a necessary consequence of a remorseless "socialization" mechanism, weeding out dysfunctional modes of state organization with the obdurate purpose of an automaton. France did not shed absolutism to defeat Great Britain, or to become America. France developed national-sovereign identity because the territorial-sovereign identity of the absolutist Bourbon monarchy had become, through external defeat, internal fiscal crisis, and domestic exclusivity, too shabby an overcoat to clothe the talent, energy, and ambition of the self-aware people of all classes that the territorial-sovereign state had misused. Yet it was a specifically national-sovereign identity that emerged from the dynamic and unpredictable interplay of social and political agency and structure required to delegitimate and topple a political regime, and in this case, a social order as well. National-sovereign collective identity may not have been *the cause* of the Revolution, but it was clearly a consequence of the Revolution, and of the subsequent reaction of the crowned heads of Europe to the more than figurative decapitation of one of their own.

Capitalism, Old Regime Liberalism, and Legitimation Crisis

The period between the Congress of Vienna and the Revolution of 1848 was a time of rapid social and economic change throughout much of Europe, and not least in what was to become Germany. All of this rapid change portended a new legitimation crisis of the old regime, which had been reconstituted and propped up with the brace of monarchical legitimacy. Rapidly, society moved into new patterns of socioeconomic relations, which existing institutional arrangements could only obstruct. Social identities were of ancient classes, and stations of life were being rapidly destroyed and reconstructed and, as my theoretical developments suggest, institutional forms of collective action and governance were increasingly incapable of manifesting the newly emerging social identities of broad tracts of the European populace.

The period saw rapid growth in population. The population in Prussia alone increased 87 percent between 1816 and 1865 and was attended by massive migration from the country to the cities, and between rural areas as well (Sheehan 1989: 458). Over a quarter of Prussia's population was to be found in towns with populations greater than 2,000 inhabitants by this date. These patterns were repeated throughout the German-speaking states of Central Europe in this period.

As the cities were experiencing rapid population growth and the incursions of market forces into the familiar patterns of ancient guild privilege, the state began to increasingly take an interest in municipal affairs, and urban autonomy was rapidly eroded by both state and economic forces. The cities now became mere administrative units of the state. The guilds also steadily lost power to the states' regulatory power, and the guilds were soon mere "economic associations rather than expressions of corporate identity and instruments of social control" (Sheehan 1989: 487–492). Proprietorship began to replace residence or guild or corporate privilege as the means of acquiring citizenship in a municipality. As Sheehan argues: "by making property the sole criterion for active citizenship, the Prussian law cut away the special rights, privileges, and liberties with which cities had once determined who could belong and who could not" (491). The combined influences of state and market penetration of urban society had significant implications for urban identity commitments. Both of these forces were integrative in the sense that they reduced the insularity of municipalities and demolished the particularistic attributes of their local power structures. They were also constitutive of new forms of identity in as much as they attended a redefinition of citizenship as a commodity acquired with the acquisition of capital.

Rural social relations were no less transitional in this period. Land reform in Central Europe proceeded at a pace negotiated between noble resistance

and the inexorable state penetration into traditional rural life. Peasant emancipation developed sufficiently to slowly evince a change from the ancient
"personal *Herrschaft* to state authority" in the countryside (Sheehan 1989:
473). Noble resistance was intense in Central Europe and the state was forced
to compromise continuously at the expense of the peasantry. When Prussian
land reform finally came, the elimination of personal servitude of the peasantry came with it, but noble claims to compensation resulted in the conversion of these services to cash payments. Now while the peasant had the legal
right to purchase land, very few could afford to do it. Landowners quickly
converted to hired labor and the short-term result was roughly equivalent to
the result of mass migration from the rural areas to the cities, namely a "growing population of landless agricultural laborers, who were now totally at the
mercy of the market" (474–475).

One permanent and quite progressive change had occurred in this process, however. While the landed nobility retained enormous wealth, power
and privilege, the social basis of this power had changed. The power and
prestige of the Central European "German" nobility no longer "flowed from
their pedigree and person, but few could doubt that their power and privilege
depended on the state." They were thus "transformed from an autonomous
Stand into a regional elite" and as a result "the *Standesherren* struggled to
define a position between sovereignty and citizenship . . . nobility was [now]
seen as a temporary inhibition to economic progress and social emancipation, the doomed residue of a declining order" (Sheehan 1989: 481–483).

Noble class identity remained intact in Central Europe during this period
nonetheless. Sheehan notes that the *Herren* survived the demise of the
Herrschaft so well that an 1833 visitor to Prussia wrote home that society
was well divided into "the vons and the non-vons," and this was so precisely
because of the relationship of the "vons" to the monarch, who remained "the
state's symbolic center and ultimate source of authority" (505). Even so, *the
status of the German nobility was increasingly mediated through the authority of the state.* The status of the German nobility was now a claim, and no
longer an institutional fact that recalled only long-standing tradition to substantiate it. This status now had to be defended. It was no longer constitutive
of the social order. As Sheehan reminds us of this period, their "status became what Weber would call an effective claim . . . [which] . . . is not a
condition of a possession or a fact of life; a claim must be made, it requires
action and can be granted or ignored" (505–506).

Under the new conditions of social and economic life, in which the function of the extraction of societal resources was increasingly privatized and
one's political standing was increasingly juridically predicated on effective
proprietorship, the claim of the nobility to social status was likely to be ig-

nored if the claimant lacked wealth and property, and to be granted if the claimant possessed these. In the absence of property, office (another commodity now mediated through the state) helped buttress effective claims to social status of many of the less well-to-do among the German nobility.

The army was the traditional forum for the claimant to social status in the German states to make their claim effective through the acquisition of office. The vaunted reforms of the Prussian army of which Posen has recently written—in making his case that nationalism was cultivated by states to enhance the effectiveness of their armed forces—had not taken in Prussian society (Posen 1993: 95–99). While, in the initial enthusiasm for reform at the conclusion of the Napoleonic Wars, nobles had constituted a "bare majority" of officers in the Prussian army in 1818, only 14 percent of Prussian officers above the rank of colonel lacked a "von" in their name by 1860 (Sheehan 1989: 507). Posen acknowledges a period of "reaction" that was felt in the Prussian armed forces between 1815 and 1870. Yet he argues that "*Landwehr* officers were chosen from the local elite and included many members of the middle class" (Posen 1993: 103). How many? Either Posen overstates this case or, the more likely, the *Landwehr* was so small a component of the armed forces that Prussia actually relied upon for its defense that the bourgeois component of the *Landwehr* officer corps dissolves into insignificance when these forces are aggregated with the regular army. If Sheehan's statistics are reliable, there were very few non-noble officers in the Prussian army at midcentury.

What is most important from this discussion, for our purposes, is that the new social landscape, molded increasingly by the forces of capital and of the state, had great causal significance for the reconstitution of social identities within European society. In the German case, state penetration and the increasing reliance of the nobility on office rather than noble title to buttress a claim to social status had slowly transformed this class identity into corporate identity. The titled soldier was "likely to be an officer first and an aristocrat second . . . both the army and the bureaucracy [another noble preserve] developed their own ethos and corporate identities" (Sheehan 1989: 508). While this may be taken as evidence of the "uneven" nature of German modernization, inasmuch as noble elites helped the crown to preserve traditional values and institutions, it is also clearly the case that power, wealth, and status no longer coincided as they had in the past. A noble title certainly enhanced the prospects and chances of an aspirant to these social tools, but the nobleman was no longer excused from the burden of competing with "non-vons" for what had once been his birthright. In this sense, the nineteenth-century German nobility "were a product of their age, not a residue of pre-modern times" (1989: 508).

The British were well ahead of Central Europe in this process. In spite of the serious economic deprivation felt in the country in the aftermath of the war and the violent and repressive measures taken to suppress reaction to it, the British people had been alienated by the Jacobin terror, and associated extreme democratic views with the regime of the erstwhile French enemy. This tendency insulated British political institutions from serious revolutionary threats during this period. Michael Mann refers to the period from 1815 to 1832 in Britain as a period of "reform, not revolution" (Mann 1993: 120–129). While governments of the German-speaking states on the continent were accommodating the rising urban bourgeoisie with citizenship based on proprietorship, and penetrating rural society by accommodating the peasantry with legal emancipation and subordinating the rural nobility to the state, the British state was making a series of accommodating moves of its own. As Mann describes the bargain, in England, "[t]he petite bourgeoisie had a property stake in the nation. It should no longer be excluded—provided it broke with the 'populace.' So . . . the rulers looked to detach the petite bourgeoisie from the mob. . . . Property—whatever its source, lineage, or patronage—was to rule the nation . . . the state had changed from particularism and segmentalism, centered on the king in Parliament, to universalism, centered on a capitalist class-nation" (1993: 125).

This pattern of slowly but inexorably enfranchising increasingly more humble and less substantial possessors of capital as a means to ensure domestic stability occurred more slowly on the continent, but may be seen as a pattern characteristic of the century. Most often these maneuvers were not intentional nation-building projects, but tactical concessions designed to permit a ruling class still committed to a territorial-sovereign structure of identity and interests to hold on to power. When these tactical concessions did not come quickly enough for the peoples whom state penetration, and the civil associational networks required for the development of capitalist production relations, had imbued with a nascent "national" collective identity, troubles came and upheaval followed.

And so trouble came to Central Europe by midcentury. The trouble was the culmination of what Mann suggests were the four great "crystallizations" of society resulting in capitalism, militarism, liberalism, and nationalism, which had all been institutionalized in the half century between 1770 and 1830 or so. And thus Mann is at pains to point out that "classes and nations rose together, structured by all four sources of social power" (1993: 214). They had also seen the "growing involvement of the state in social life—as tax collector and policy-maker, educator and employer, regulator and patron" (Sheehan 1989: 588). Thus the steady increase of popular interest in public affairs in the ensuing decades is not surprising. The period witnessed the growth of civil society. The state-as-educator had enhanced discursive literacy and created a demand for more political news in the press. As a logical consequence of increasing state penetration into society, people developed an increasing self-identification with the state, and with the political process. "Slowly . . . Germans created the intellectual systems and associational networks upon which participatory politics could be based. As a result, the character of public life was fundamentally altered" (1989: 589).

1848 and After: Citizenship and Sovereignty and Nationalism

But in German Central Europe, the conservative social residue that attended the nobility's retention of social status, through the acquisition of state office, had attenuated the move toward nearly unlimited social mobility through the acquisition of capital, as had occurred in Britain, where peerages were readily created for those with the price of entry. The Hanoverian rulers of Britain had acceded to a quasi-constitutional rule of a capitalist nation and prized above all other qualities in the men they recruited to head their governments the capacity to balance the ledgers of the government. The dynastic rulers of Prussia and Austria had not come to their thrones with the understanding that they would subordinate their sovereignty to a constitution. They might buy off the peasantry at the expense of their nobility, and increase noble dependence on the crown for the status left to them in the bargain, but they would not accede to the limitations of their sovereignty and power by any constitutional device without dire exigency. This attitude had lent German society a conservative cast residual of the old order, and it pervaded social and institutional domestic life.

Thus as capitalism transformed economic life and created a German bourgeoisie, this bourgeoisie lacked both the courage of its convictions required for the advancement of bold claims of its own and the fear of lower orders required to encourage it to advance claims on behalf of these orders to fuller participation in civil and political life. The German bourgeoisie was a very ideologically and politically timid class relative to its British counterpart. Here we have some evidence with which to credit the claim Mann has made that, contrary to what Marx believed and argued, class organization does not emerge directly from the relations of production. The bourgeoisie are "more likely to choose segmental than class organization. . . . Political organization by classes also has specifically political causes involving the institutional particularities of states" (Mann 1993: 211). Thus when the consequences of militarism and emerging capitalism raise the ire of the petite bourgeoisie and laboring masses "[these masses] claimed civil citizenship to freely protest political economy, and when protest was ineffective, they demanded political citizenship" (211). But unlike the British case, the protesting classes found no allies in their claims in the German bourgeoisie. Not yet in any case. German liberalism during this period was limited franchise liberalism. Many German liberals, who were themselves in a minority position in their countries, did not wish to extend the franchise to wage laborers, apprentices, small farmers, or shopkeepers, let alone women or servants. German bourgeois liberalism was very insecure indeed. No Rousseauian vision of the general will pervaded it, therefore no governmental responsibility to accede to the wishes of the general will was implied (Sheehan 1989: 599–600). In order to rectify this situation, the common people were required to voice their protest in much more emphatic terms than had been required for these classes to gain civil and political citizenship in Britain. Their voice may be heard in the events attending the Revolution of 1848.

Radical liberal opinion demanded universal suffrage, an armed domestic militia, the equalization of educational opportunity, reform of the tax system, abolition of residual social privilege, and structural transformation of the civil service to enhance the possibilities of its service as a vehicle of upward mobility. The steady and stubborn refusal of governments to move on this agenda swelled the ranks of the opposition in the climate of insecurity engendered by rapid economic change during the period. By the 1840s the opposition included, according to one sympathetic contemporary, "everyone with talent, all free and independent spirits, in short, the entire third estate" (Sheehan 1989: 635–637). Yet these disaffected persons constituted only a small minority of the populace, until economic recession deepened the crisis. According to Hagan Schulze, "[t]his multiform national opposition received its explosive charge from the growing impoverishment of the society and economy" (Schulze 1991: 68).

But while economic distress is easy enough to identify as an impulse to social protest, upheaval, and even revolution, why did the 1848 revolution manifest itself as a nationalist movement and result in nationalist demands? One reason was that the intellectual energy behind the 1848 revolution was, unlike the French Revolution's, in large measure provided by the German bourgeoisie. Eighteen forty-eight came at a time when "nationalism was an expression of *bürgerlich* . . . emancipation . . . an ideology of modernization" (Winkler 1993: 182). The creation of an all-German state was desired, among other reasons, because the national state was seen at this time as an essential precondition for economic modernization and competitiveness by the bourgeois classes. But the timidity of the German bourgeoisie squandered the short-term fruits of 1848. This pan-German national collective identity was not to be consolidated until the close of the Franco-Prussian War, when events engineered by Bismarck induced the princes of the German-speaking states of Central Europe (less

Hapsburg Austria) to offer the imperial Crown of a pan-German Second Reich to the Prussian King. (For a detailed analysis, see chapter 7 of Hall [1999].)

German national collective identity had, in Bismarck's eyes, been fleshed out with the institutional form that best suited it, and this was the imperial form. In my own view, German national collective identity could have never developed into its modern form, something very close to the form that it had developed by 1871, without the events following the Revolution of 1848. Without the experience of participatory politics, however limited that franchise might have been, that had permitted the German people within their various states to feel some stake in the policies of the governments of their monarchs, their "German" collective identity would likely have been forever subordinated to particularistic political identities developed around their particularistic relationships with their princes. Without the maintenance of that franchise and its creeping extension to ensure the participation of the people in the society and state consistent with the requirements of rampant capitalism, the people would likely have never been sufficiently politically aware for their budding self-identification as "Germans" to contain the meanings that it did for them by this date. And, of course, certainly without their shared experience of victory (Anderson 1983: 187–203) *qua* Germans over a powerful French foe which had historically oriented its policy toward ensuring their continued political disunity, German national collective identity could never have crystallized (to borrow from the lexicon of Michael Mann 1993) with the potency that it clearly did at this time.

Yet German institutional history had been, for a thousand reasons—many of these dating back to the Reformation period—both particularistic and distinctly feudal. The strength of the feudal residue in German Central Europe by 1871 was such that it would be difficult to envision German national collective identity adopting a different institutional form with which to manifest its agency to the world than that of the long lost German Empire. Germany now had its Second Reich, and Bismarck correctly observed that it suited Germany in 1871 in a fashion that would not at all suit German national collective identity today. Bismarck had written, immediately upon the promulgation of the Second Reich:

> For German patriotism to be active and effective, it needs as a rule to be dependent upon a dynasty. Independent of a dynasty, it rarely comes to a rising point. . . . The German's love of the fatherland has need of a prince on whom he can concentrate his attachment. Suppose that all the German dynasties were suddenly deposed, there would then be no likelihood of German national sentiment sufficient to hold all the Germans together amid the friction of European politics. (quoted in Eyck 1968: 183–184)

Table 4.1

Distinctions Between Territorial and National Sovereign Order

Territorial-sovereign order	National-sovereign order
Absolutism (*L'Etat c'est moi*)	Liberal or communitarian national government
Monopoly of coercion / taxation / administration / legislation to sovereign via dependent nobility	Monopoly of coercion / taxation / administration negotiated with national-sovereign entity
Hieratic / hereditary privileged order	Privilege competes with capital
Parochial peasant self-identification	Mass self-identification with national community
Social immobility	Social mobility (bourgeois meritocracy)
Aristocrat self-identification proportional to degree of domestic absolutism —French identification with noble class —Prussian identification with state (military class) —English Whig identification with Crown / Nation	Franchise extended to ever lower socioeconomic strata —eudaemonic state —mass participation in projects of state —elite accessibility —elite concern with public opinion

Note the manner in which this passage invokes the causal and constitutive linkages between co-constituted individual and collective identities, the legitimating principles of domestic and global social orders, and the derivative institutional forms of collective action. Durkheim's emotive identification with the "fatherland," his "organic solidarity of dissimilar individuals" is depicted here (Durkheim 1953). Similarly the Habermassian, Kratochwillian, Weberian formulations of a theoretical construct oriented toward the individual's valuation of "duty" to legitimate social authority is illustrated in Bismarck's assertion of the dependence of German patriotism upon a prince (Bloom 1990; Kratochwil 1989; Weber 1964; and Hall 1999: 34–39). The institutional form of collective action suitable to manifest pan-German nationalism was understood intuitively by Bismarck to be a consequence of the particularities of co-constituted individual and pan-German national collective identity.

The historical particularities of German history had, then, ultimately proved to present a series of institutional facts which guided German national collective identity into an institutional form that is entirely consistent with our knowledge of the functioning of such facts. They provided a context in which the new game of German national-state formation took on concrete meaning (Kratochwil 1988: 271).

Conclusions

Many of the salient issues I have discussed can be summarized in Table 4.1. Table 4.1 focuses, as I have focused in the chapter, on the distinctions between territorial-sovereign and national-sovereign domestic social and institutional arrangements resulting in different notions of sovereignty arising from historically continent variations in collective societal self-identification. An interesting project for the future (and the subject of a future book) might see the application of this approach to discovering the outlines of a post-national-sovereign order.

Bibliography

Anderson, Benedict. 1983. *Imagined Communities: Reflections on the Origins and Spread of Nationalism*. London: Verso.

Black, Jeremy. 1990. *Eighteenth Century Europe 1700–1789*. New York: St. Martin's Press.

———. 1991. "Chatham Revisited," *History Today* 41 (August): 34–39.

Bloom, William. 1990. *Personal Identity, National Identity and International Relations*. Cambridge, UK: Cambridge University Press.

de Tocqueville, Alexis. 1955. *The Old Regime and the French Revolution*. New York: Doubleday.

Dickinson, H.T. 1981. "Whiggism in the Eighteenth Century." In *The Whig Ascendancy: Colloquies on Hanoverian England*, ed. John Cannon, 28–50. New York: St. Martin's Press.

Durkheim, Emile. 1953. *Sociology and Philosopy*, trans. D.R. Pocock. New York: Free Press.

Eyck, Eric. 1968. *Bismarck and the German Empire*. New York: Norton.

Greenfeld, Liah. 1992. *Nationalism: Five Roads to Modernity*. Cambridge, MA: Harvard University Press.

Greengrass, Mark. 1987. *The French Reformation*. Oxford: Basil Blackwell.

Habermas, Jürgen. 1975. *Legitimation Crisis*, trans. Thomas McCarthy. Boston: Beacon Press.

Hall, Rodney Bruce. 1997. "Moral Authority as a Power Resource." *International Organization* 51: 591–622.

———. 1999. *National Collective Identity: Social Constructs and International Systems*. New York: Columbia University Press.

Kantorowicz, Ernst. 1957. *The King's Two Bodies: A Study in Medieval Political Theology*. Princeton: Princeton University Press.

Kratochwil, Friedrich. 1988. "Regimes, Interpretation and the 'Science' of Politics: A Reappraisal." *Millennium: Journal of International Relations* 17: 263–284.

———. 1989. *Rules, Norms and Decisions: On the Conditions of Practical and Legal Reasoning in International Relations and Domestic Affairs*. Cambridge, UK: Cambridge University Press.

Ladurie, Emannuel Le Roy. 1994. *The Royal French State 1460–1610*, trans. Juliet Vale. London: Blackwell.

Luard, Evan. 1987. *War in International Society: A Study in International Sociology.* New Haven: Yale University Press.

———. 1992. T*he Balance of Power: The System of International Relations, 1648– 1815.* New York: St. Martin's Press.

Mann, Michael. 1993. *The Sources of Social Power, Volume II: The Rise of Classes and Nation-States, 1760–1914.* Cambridge, UK: Cambridge University Press.

Moore, Barrington. 1966. *The Social Origins of Dictatorship and Democracy.* Boston: Beacon Press.

Osiander, Andreas. 1994. *The States System of Europe, 1640–1990: Peacemaking and the Conditions of International Stability.* Oxford: Clarendon Press.

Palmer, R. R. 1973. "Frederick the Great, Guibert, Bülow: From Dynastic to National War." In *Makers of Modern Strategy: Military Thought From Machiavelli to Hitler,* ed. Edward Mead Earle, 49–74. Princeton: Princeton University Press.

Posen, Barry R. 1993. "Nationalism, the Mass Army, and Military Power." *International Security* 18: 80–124.

Ritter, Alan and Julia Conaway Bondanella, eds. 1988. *Rousseau's Political Writings,* trans. Julia Conaway Bondanella. New York: Norton.

Schulze, Hagen. 1991. *The Course of German Nationalism: From Frederick the Great to Bismarck, 1763–1867.* Cambridge, UK: Cambridge University Press.

Sheehan, James J. 1989. *German History 1770–1866.* Oxford: Clarendon Press.

Skocpol, Theda. 1979. *States and Social Revolutions: A Comparative Analysis of France, Russia, and China.* Cambridge, UK: Cambridge University Press.

Strauss, Gerald. 1978. *Luther's House of Learning: Indoctrination of the Young in the German Reformation.* Baltimore: Johns Hopkins University Press.

———. 1988. "The Reformation and its Public in the Age of Orthodoxy." In *The German People and the Reformation,* ed. R. Po-Chia Hsia, 194–215. Ithaca: Cornell University Press.

Strayer, Joseph. 1970. *On the Medieval Origins of the Modern State.* Princeton: Princeton University Press.

Trevelyan, G.M. 1965. *The English Revolution 1688–1689.* New York: Oxford University Press.

Weber, Max. 1964. *The Theory of Social and Economic Organization,* trans. A.M. Henderson and Talcott Parsons. London: Collier-Macmillan.

Wendt, Alexander. 1992. "Anarchy is What States Make of It: The Social Construction of Power Politics." *International Organization* 46: 391–425.

———. 1999. *Social Theory of International Politics.* Cambridge, UK: Cambridge University Press.

Winkler, Heinrich August. 1993. "Nationalism and Nation-State in Germany." In *The National Question in Europe in Historical Context,* ed. M. Teich and R. Porter, 181–195. Cambridge, UK: Cambridge University Press.

Woloch, Isser. 1982. *Eighteenth-Century Europe: Tradition and Progress 1715–1789.* New York: Norton.

———. 1994. *The New Regime: Transformations of the French Civic Order, 1789– 1820.* New York: Norton.

Part II
Case Studies

5

The Role of the State in Ethnic Conflict: A Constructivist Reassessment

Virginia Q. Tilley

In the post-cold war era, the startling surge of ethnic conflicts has prompted a burst of attention by social scientists. Taken individually, each conflict requires close study for its unique qualities, such as its deeper history, immediate precipitating economic and political stresses, diverse ideas and goals within competing groups, policy implications, and so forth. Such studies are the forte of comparative politics (CP), especially in the area studies, where interdisciplinarity enables theoretically holistic and multivariate approaches. But the sheer number of these conflicts also raises a central theoretical conundrum for many comparativists: that the modern state system, and the civic-nationalist political order it embraces or promises, has so dramatically failed to mediate and defuse ethnic conflicts over time, as several schools of thought (liberal, Marxist, neoclassical economics) once believed it would do. Worse, such conflicts seem to have increased in frequency, and lost no significant degree of intensity, dampening enthusiasm for claims that they are mere holdovers, imminently obsolete. In response, some scholars have argued that we missed something about ethnicity: that ethnic sentiments run deeper, and their politics are more complex, than was thought. I have supported that view elsewhere (Tilley 1997). But I suggest that we have also missed something about the state: that the state itself, as the framing institution of the domestic ethnic arena, is complicit in ethnic conflict in ways generally unrecognized.

No clearer illustration of the conundrum can be offered than the wave of new mobilizations in Latin America by indigenous peoples. When these movements surfaced afresh on the radar screen of social scientists, in the late 1980s and the 1990s, most scholars found them a startling and unconvincing phenomenon. For one thing, a hegemonic Latin American claim had shaped CP assumptions that, while certainly deeply fractured by class, the heavily miscegenated populations of Latin American nations at least enjoyed relative ethnic and racial harmony. For another, my own conversations with colleagues have suggested that many comparativists—perhaps laboring under an iconographic spear-fishing imagery of Amazonian peoples like the Yanomami—had unreflectively understood "indigenous peoples" either as microminorities or as "closed corporate communities," culturally obsolete in a ruthlessly modernizing and globalizing world.

Diverse theoretical perspectives had therefore uniformly considered "Indian-ness" to be politically irrelevant to the major national challenges and transitions of the region. The region's Marxist theorists, leftist movements, and left-leaning researchers had, lip service aside, largely considered indigenous ethnicity as epiphenomenal to class: the "Indian" identity was merely a sordid legacy of colonialism and early-republican racial-caste exploitation, aggravating class fractionalism, and properly to be erased through rural-proletarian solidarity (e.g., Quijano Obregón 1967). Liberal analyses, where they paid attention to indigenous communities at all, had lamented their economic marginalization and pushed for remedial measures oriented toward their better assimilation into the nation. The democratization and "transitology" canon had ignored them altogether, conflating them into de-ethnicized "peasantries" (e.g., contributions to the volumes edited by Collier 1979; O'Donnell and Schmitter 1986; Diamond, Linz, and Lipset 1989). All these schools had, implicitly or explicitly, understood the best interests of "Indians" to lie in their more complete absorption into state-centric national politics, whether through democratic reforms or socialist-revolutionary projects.

A decade later, the supposedly obsolete "Indian" category has reemerged, with armed mass uprisings of national importance in several Latin American countries (Mexico, Colombia, Ecuador, Peru), with prodigious political force in others (Guatemala, Nicaragua, Panama, Bolivia, Chile). It has obtained significant territories as autonomy zones in several countries (Nicaragua, Costa Rica, Panama, Venezuela, Colombia, Ecuador, Brazil) and is startling the national press with new initiatives in most of the rest (Honduras, El Salvador, Argentina). All this activity has forced new efforts by social scientists to explain the apparent "resurgence" or "reemergence" of indigenous ethnic politics. Anthropologists and sociologists have provided an array of new case studies of indigenous movements, often under the theoretical rubric of "new social movements" (e.g., Findji 1992). In one of these rare CP studies, Donna Lee Van Cott has recognized the difficulty that indigenous politics presents to questions of sovereignty (1995) but has focused primarily on how such questions are being negotiated through state-centric measures such as constitutional reforms to protect cultural rights (2000). Franke Wilmer (1993) and Alison Brysk (2000) have focused more on changing "external" conditions: for example, an ethnic pluralist international human rights climate that has provided new incentives for ethnic politics and new allies for indigenous peoples, and the globalization of telecommunications which has permitted transnational networking among formerly isolated groups. All these discussions provide valuable insights into the changing political conditions which have permitted indigenous movements to gain new voice and influence in national politics.

Yet a certain bias is embedded in the CP studies which impedes their analysis of indigenous movements: indeed, it is the same bias that formerly marginalized recognition and study of indigenous politics within the discipline. That bias is the prior, usually tacit premise that the nation-state is the fundamental normative framework for political order, and that the territorial state demarcates the nation. In other words, they uncritically adopt the frame of sovereignty, a concept that privileges the state within a normative ontology in which indigenous peoples are innately nonsovereign: "ethnic groups" or perhaps "racial formations." Indigenous politics are then understood through theory and method normally brought to bear on ethnic and racial conflict in, say, the United States, decolonized sub-Saharan Africa, or post-Soviet Central Asia.

The tacit acceptance of the nation-state as the naturalized and normative frame for considering the politics of indigenous peoples shapes their study in powerful ways. As Karena Shaw (2001) has pointed out in her trenchant critique of international relations (IR) theory, the theoretical privileging of sovereignty sets up the study of groups like indigenous peoples in particular terms: "marginal" relative to what is "central." Within these terms, their "reinclusion"—however generous the motive—reinforces the very presumptions that generated their exclusion:

> In other words, because international relations necessarily assumes the ontology of sovereignty as its precondition, and because indigenous peoples function within discourses of sovereignty as the determination and marking of margins, any invocation of them necessarily reproduces the terms of their exclusion: by arguing that they "should be" included, their exclusion from what international relations "really" is is reinforced. Further, this invocation of difference, this play at the margins, even the graceful and generous gesture to include all, function to reinforce the centrality/identity of the center. The "center"—in this case international relations—is reinstated as the central and dominant discourse, that which authorizes, that which is universal or at least universalizable, that which matters. The terms of inclusion or exclusion thus remain those of the center.

Shaw's critique extends easily to mainstream CP, and helps us consider how and why CP theory and method have so extensively failed to grasp the unique qualities and political trajectories of indigenous politics. First, reflecting the uncritical acceptance of the nation-state frame noted by Jackson and Nexon in this volume, mainstream CP has approached indigenous politics as "internal" matters relative to the (reified) state boundary. The "state" is considered in its domestic manifestation: as "government"—a complex of institutions, perhaps captured by a particular ethnic or multiethnic elite, but innately neutral, and certainly a political given. Networking among indigenous peoples physically located in different states is therefore "transnational"; their alliances with "external" actors (like human rights organizations) are understood through such concepts as "boomerang effects" (Keck and Sikkink 1998). These theoretical devices are insightful tools for grasping key features of indigenous politics. But they also incorporate a crippling weakness: they remove from interrogation how the state itself—the principle of territorial sovereignty, constructed and naturalized through a fluid and evolving discourse of "statehood"—has also created and sustained "indigeneity" as a particular ethno-racial formation (and as a category of ethnic conflict), and, especially, how indigenous politics contest that categorization. An IR perspective may quickly reveal this distinctive feature (Brysk 2000). But most CP studies miss the essential metaconflictive quality of indigenous movements—their contestation of their own definition by various authoritative discourses—that so profoundly shape their political strategies, determine their alliances, and underlie their surprising tenacity.

Second, the nation-state frame composes indigenous peoples as discrete populations whose study can be effectively bounded by the state territory: For example, we find references to "Brazilian," "Ecuadorean," "Peruvian," and "Mexican" indigenous peoples. Although granted a positivist gloss through attached statistics (census data and the like), such groupings are essentially imagined, a cognitive by-product of hegemonic ideas about the state-as-given. This device obviates certain crucial questions: for example, whether "Ecuadorean" or "Peruvian" are meanings relevant to the indigenous peoples physically located in those states (or how and when those meanings came to be relevant); or whether "indigenous" is defined the same way by all participants, including the census authority; or whether culturally diverse indigenous peoples within a given state perceive or experience any common political or material conditions; or whether data on "Brazilian" and "Mexican" indigenous peoples are usefully comparable—that is, whether their populations have anything in common at all beyond their colonial and postcolonial construction as "Indians." Problems with quantified data on ethnicity are not unique to indigenous peoples, as David Laitin's (2001) devastating critique of the ELF (Ethno-Linguistic Fractionalization) database illustrates. Yet the case of indigenous peoples adds an additional pitfall: that the authority of statist statistics also feeds into policy making in ways that confuse and obscure salient issues. For example, to manipulate data on "Ecuadorean" indigenous peoples implicitly reinforces their conceptual placement within the "Ecuadorean" nation, and so posits political solutions to the "Indian problem" within the frame of "Ecuadorean" politics (e.g., that "Ecuador" itself is a problem, a construct challenged by the indigenous movement, is occluded through such methods. For "Ecuador" is not a "nation" in the sense that its entire territorial population desires to be under one government (Crain 1990). Nor is "Ecuador" simply a political reality, of necessary importance to indigenous peoples who must deal with the state's authority. "Ecuador" is also a normative discourse that constructs indigenous peoples as a particular kind of ethno-racial formation in ways that enhance and confirm state power (Conaie 1989; Macas 1992).

Thus the *state* frame, by situating indigenous peoples within the more complex *nation-state* frame, establishes the values and meanings brought to bear on indigenous peoples' issues ("closed corporate community," "oppressed sector," "marginalized"). The same effect establishes the range of imaginable and principled (state-centric) goals for resolving related conflicts: for example, economic integration, bilingual education, voter registration campaigns. Even if deliberately detached from historical value-laden concepts ("backward," "primitive," "wards of the state"), indigenous peoples are nevertheless reinforced in a strategic ontology of world politics that determines their nonsovereign political type ("ethnic group," "racial labor caste," "peasantry") and so their political-theoretical mapping ("peripheral," "closed," "social movement").

It is precisely these mappings that indigenous peoples' movements challenge. For all their diversity (which I do not wish to diminish), the politics of indigenous peoples can usefully be generalized as being distinguished precisely by their constestation of the nation-state *frame* itself, which supports the host of attached values and meanings that determine their own political experience (Anaya 1996; Brysk 2000; Shaw 2001). Their challenge to that frame indeed explains otherwise confusing juxtapositions in their platforms and alliances: for example, their relation to the nation and to nationalism. As noted, indigenous movements challenge the very precept of the nation-state. They also invoke elements of classic, late-nineteenth century nationalism, particularly through invoking the right to self-determination. Yet they also sustain what some observers have called a "postmodern" rejection of the statist frame normally attached to nationalism. On one hand, their platforms invoke tropes of conquest, of illegitimate rule by Others, of deprivation by racial others of formerly held land rights—all familiar to decolonization discourses in, say, Africa. On the other hand, indigenous platforms show a consistent aversion to outright secession and independent state formation, concerned rather to renegotiate their relationship to existing governments—or rather, the terms of sovereignty so closely guarded by governments. Thus indigenous politics typically seek not greater incorporation into the state's central governing system but rather greater distance from the state, often through territorial autonomy and varying degrees of self-rule, which require some transfer of sovereignty from the state. Yet they do not seek statehood as it is presently understood. Rather, they critique and challenge the very precepts that posit such stark dichotomies (state/nonstate, sovereign/nonsovereign), even as they challenge their positioning as "marginal" to what is "central." In doing so, they challenge the state, the nation, and the international ontology itself (again, see Shaw 2001).

The case of indigenous peoples is invoked here not to propose some special importance to their conflicts, or to privilege their study relative to others. Rather, the indigenous angle of vision—"looking awry" at the state, so to speak (Zizek 2000: 11)—reveals elements of the state normally not visible, yet significant to ethnic politics and conflict more broadly. The deliberate challenge of indigenous peoples to the nation-state formula—that is, discourses of nationhood, statehood, and their fusion—suggests that the state has certain kinds of influences in constructing the domestic ethnic environment.

To explore these influences, we cannot understand "state" merely as government. IR theory helps us consider the state in other lights: as a framing condition and interested actor in itself, conceptually distinct from the government. From a constructivist IR perspective, the state is a fluid complex of evolving international rules and norms; in realist and neorealist views, states manifest as unitary actors with identities, interests, and survival imperatives of their own. I suggest that these qualities of states translate into government institutional design and into state-elite perspectives in ways directly relevant to the domestic ethnic *environment*: the multivariate ethnic perceptions, interests, and values that shape ethnopolitical opportunities and constraints at the local level. The substance of this chapter, therefore, is a close theoretical exploration of how the state functions in these ways, in which conflicts involving indigenous peoples and other ethnicities will be cited as illustrations.

Ethnic Dimensions of the Modern State

To suggest that viewing the modern state in light of IR theory will reveal the state's ethnic biases may inspire skepticism from both comparativists and IR scholars. Certainly from a neorealist perspective—in which states are mere units, identical in kind and differentiated only by the degrees of power they command (Waltz 1979)—anything *less* ethnic could hardly be imagined. Even from a liberal (society of states) perspective, the suggestion of an ethnic bias to the state may seem misplaced or even prejudicial. Liberal theorists have held for some time that, because state elites and nationalisms today seem to reflect the world's full ethnic and racial gamut, the modern state has become a universally adaptable (ethnically neutral, cosmopolitan) apparatus (e.g., Pye 1962). To the "English school," the modern international system (its institutions, laws, norms) is clearly understood as the cosmopolitan product of state negotiations (Bull 1977; Watson 1992).

As constructivist IR theory has already been discussed by Daniel Green in this volume's introduction, a quick brush will suffice here to set up the discussion. Realist, neorealist, and liberal IR theory all understand the international system as being composed of states, which generate that system (understood variously as power balances, rules, institutions, and/or regimes) through their interactions (conflicts, rivalries, alliances, negotiations, relative capacities, and economic exchange). In this sense, modern states are analogous to Lockean political individuals, which have matured or appeared on the international stage as autonomous entities and interacted or joined into a community by forming a set of rules or codes for their interactions. In this understanding, the state—whatever form it takes—is ontologically prior to the system. By contrast, constructivist approaches understand that the modern state and the international system are co-constituted. In this view, the state itself is the conceptual, normative, and juridical creation of evolving international rules and norms which, in turn, states develop and sustain through practice (e.g., Wendt 1987, 1992; Biersteker and Weber 1996). These rules and norms establish the state's juridical personality and provide the evolving standards or criteria for a state's recognition by other states, yet continue to evolve as they are contested and renegotiated by states. All these schools allows us to identify ethnic biases embedded in the international system.

First, recent work on the international system's institutional demands has improved our understanding of its impact on the state's institutional design. For most comparativists, it is no groundbreaking claim to point out that the basic design of states, all over the world, traces historically to the hegemonic impact of European imperialism. Especially since the sixteenth century, peoples, kingdoms, empires, confederations, and now-lost forms of governance encountered Europe's (evolving) standards for admission to the Family of Nations under the (figurative and literal) guns of European mercantilism and colonialism. Systems of governance that did not match Europe's institutional criteria were not granted recognition by European imperial powers, and were considered legitimate targets for conquest or control. Gerrit Gong (1986) has described the cultural biases that imbued European diplomacy and jurisprudence in this hegemonic process as forming a "Standard of Civilization" which undergirded diplomatic admission to the Family of Nations. Certainly European rigidity about such matters was adjusted as needed; the military capacity of a non-European power to repel European conquest might inspire greater latitude or special dispensations regarding cultural diversity . . . for a while. But as international trade demanded ever more complex financial and juridical arrangements, the terms of European recognition entailed increasingly elaborate standards for the institutional design of government— even their physical attributes: rectangular (and preferably Greco-Roman) stone buildings and the like.

Hence nationalist politicians and intellectuals who wished to avoid such takeover undertook vigorous reform programs to meet Europe's narrowing criteria: Japan's Meiji Restoration is one of the better-known successful examples of such an urgent project, but similar anxious climates surrounded late-nineteenth century Latin American efforts to modernize state institutions and economies. Sometimes called "socialization" in IR literature, this global convergence was inspired not only by military considerations but also by elites' sincere admiration of European accomplishments, especially Europe's formidable economic productivity, technology, and legal systems (Ikenberry and Kupchan 1990). But few local political leaders in non-European regions enjoyed significant options in the matter. The emerging state template was not a pure European export, being itself born partly of imperial-peripheral dialectics, but given sheer power considerations (political and economic), European (and eventually U.S.) interests clearly guided its design.

The modern state today therefore represents a convergence by the entire world to a fairly rigid template, a process that has weeded out alternatives. The template has translated international norms into domestic norms important to ethnic conflict in three interdependent dimensions: institutional, ontological, and normative.

Institutional

To sustain their standing as international actors (and to avoid invasion or seizure), all states today must maintain at least the basic institutional approximation of an international presence. Statehood requires, at a minimum, some kind of central policy voice, diplomatic corps, customs authority, border security, and, for most of the past century, a central bank or other currency and exchange authority. Without such institutions, a state cannot even manifest, let alone function effectively, on the international stage. But those institutions that constitute the state as an international actor cannot be of any autonomous domestic design. To function as required, they must abide by the international standards and codes that guide their interaction with other states. Clearly such vital (internationally compulsory) state institutions as a diplomatic corps and currency authority must adopt the international rules that govern their respective domains of international activity if they are to serve state interests with the minimal success necessary to even a formal semblance of sovereignty (Jackson and Rosberg 1982). Globalization of finance and production has vastly increased these demands. For the vast majority of states, which have little (or only token) say in making the rules and standards governing these activities, this onus constitutes an externally imposed set of obligations regarding the state's institutional design and performance.

Hence the *vector* effect: in adopting practices and norms necessary to meet international standards, state institutions translate a package of externally authored norms and procedures into the domestic institutions and agendas of government and the political arena (see, e.g., Finnemore 1996). This (compulsive or strongly favored) institutional compatibility also imports certain behavioral and procedural standards into the design—and staff recruitment—of governing institutions in states everywhere. The vector effect can be seen most clearly through historical studies of decolonization (in the Middle East, Africa, India, and southeast Asia), which reveal the institutions of the independent state to be direct European creations, little altered in design or function (or pomp) after independence. If some state bureaucracies fail to meet such standards, their performance is defined as relative success or failure; as Basil Davidson (1992) has pointed out, other models—for example, some of the governing forms of precolonial Africa—are no longer an option. The worrisome phenomenon acknowledged in the IR literature as "state failure" reflects this rigidity.

The vector effect can contribute to ethnic conflict in several ways. First, it contributes to determining which groups assume and retain state power. The state's elite or dominant group may well have gained that dominance in the first place because it was best positioned to emulate international standards for state governance: especially, by sustaining the conditions favorable to European ("first world") trade. Although superficially not concerned with ethnicity, such standards nevertheless incorporate a bias because they exclude incompatible cultural systems: for example, consensus-based decision making among many native peoples, which may mandate an *absence* of centralized authority; or nomadic territorial usufruct, a norm toward which states are notoriously hostile. Sometimes political elites retooled or recomposed themselves to match European criteria: again, successful examples include the Meiji reformers. Where Meiji-style initiative or capacity was lacking, elites were invented and cultivated by Europeans to take state power: for example, now famously, the Tutsi of Rwanda; less famously but no less poignantly, the now-princely families of the United Arab Emirates. But whatever their unique histories, the ascent of such elites to control of state governments was contingent on their (promised) compliance with Europe's institutional demands. That constraint discriminated against, or outright excluded, those groups less well positioned or motivated to make the shift (e.g., nomadic chieftain groups).

Second, the vector effect has a continuing effect in aggravating ethnic discrimination in domestic politics and governance: for example, access by ethnic nonelite groups to government employment, and even mass democratic access to the political system. Obvious biases in civil service include language and education requirements—which, again, are often tied to international interests such as the country's continued links to the former hegemon, which incorporates into government the need for fluency in the colonial language. Less obvious but more profound are biases derived from broader socialization to the behavioral norms of the state bureaucracy, an assimilation burden notorious for its discriminatory effects, and often manipulated by dominant groups to their own advantage. In CP studies, such political discrimination and institutional bias are normally treated as products of local prejudices, or of insufficient resource distribution to neglected groups. But the vector effect suggests that such biases trace not solely to the prejudices of the state's dominant ethnic group. Rather, they are informed also by the international standards that partly determine the government's internal design and performance—and, as noted above, may well have determined who would *be* the state's dominant ethnic group.

Finally, by constraining the design and flexibility of state institutions, the vector effect renders government biases ethnically "sticky," irrespective of the state elite's motives. Although most institutions can accommodate ethnic diversity to some extent, particularly if it is culturally insubstantial, it is an old political saw that no bureaucracy is infinitely flexible to *cultural* diversity: that is, differences in basic shared meanings, values, and behaviors that can render a minority individual's normal behavior incompatible with, or even abrasive to, majority sensibilities and social norms. Examples of such differences include concepts of time; of hierarchy and reciprocity; of dignity and "face"; or the sensitive ways that people develop confidence in each other, and express humor, respect, and courtesy. Such subtle yet profound social issues are vital concerns in bureaucratic hiring because they are essential to effective leadership, communication, and teamwork. For this reason, bureaucrats typically select and train their staff with these factors heavily in mind: hence, the "team player," the "nice guy," or "our sort." Cas Sunstein (1991) has pointed out that such embedded practices are notorious for their racially discriminatory effects, even if such effects are unintended. Thus all bureaucracies must sustain some kind of cultural framework, and, whatever it is, that framework structurally limits the bureaucracy's capacity to embrace others, in proportion to their degree of difference. But relevant to our inquiry here is that a state's bureaucratic culture, and its flexibility toward others, is limited also by the vector effect: international norms that contribute to the state's domestic bureaucratic design.

As noted above, liberal critics of the above arguments might protest that, although the colonial history is undeniable, today the criteria for statehood are ethnically impartial, and the state's design itself is "universal," because any group can assume state power if it masters the (supposedly ethnically neutral) skills of state governance. This argument presumes a universal and impartial quality to the modern state, now viewed askance by many, and is basically an assimilation argument; yet it merits attention. In its light, my charge of an ethnic bias to the modern state might even seem prejudiced, if it implies that some cultures or ethnicities are intrinsically incapable of state governance. No such implication is intended; cultures are fluid and flexible, and no group is culturally frozen. Nor would I argue (as some do) that social-institutional adaptation of a people's political system to changing international conditions—even Eurocentric adaptation—is, by definition, cultural "loss."

Still, sustained in this objection is the acknowledgement that it is precisely cultural fluidity—that is, change—that is often required of groups. The change required may be great or small (although the broader social impact of any governmental redesign is often surprisingly profound, again as the Meiji Restoration demonstrated). But the greater the change required by groups, the less successful the effort is likely to be: The dilemma of hunter-gatherer peoples like the Yanomami or the Namibian San suggests this problem most dramatically, but a spectrum of cultural difference is differentially implicated. Moreover, assimilation may be unwelcome on political grounds, especially if it promises to change too profoundly the ways that the group sustains its own cohesion: that is, its social-institutional character, including its internal political norms. For many indigenous peoples, to take on the full apparatus of modern statehood would be to create new forms of power incompatible with the group's social mechanisms of political authority, and perhaps to assume the onus of activities deemed antithetical to group values, such as border policing. Avoiding statehood can therefore be a matter of political integrity, attached to ethnic survival: for example, the Kuna autonomy region in Panama, in which the Kuna sustain their own distinct indigenous political system, reflects a strategy built around this objection. To use an analogy not as anachronistic as we might like it to be (especially in Latin America and the Anglophone settler-colonial societies), the goal of most indigenous peoples is not to become "white" (here, in a cultural sense) but to reject the need to become "white."

Ontological

A second problem with the above claim of state universalism is that it reflects an optimism based on a logical slip-up, because it traces the formation of international society backward from those states now present on the international stage, whose elites and governments were ultimately "socialized." Obscured through this perspective is that "socialization" historically also weeded out or demoted a myriad of rival or alternative political systems, partly through simple force but also through a device more subtle: their *redefinition*, through a complementary ontology of nonsovereign formations. Sociopolitical formations that lost or lacked the required fixtures of statehood—again, obvious examples include nomadic peoples—are today granted no international personality or, crucially, sovereignty. Most powerfully, and feeding into the frustrations of such excluded groups, the exclusivity of state sovereignty has naturalized in modern political thought and philosophy, obtaining a self-evident and uncontroversial quality even as it has become embedded in international law. Thus the politics of indigenous peoples necessarily engages not just the state's authority but the logics by which their own loss of territorial control, and their incorporation as "domestic" matters under the sole authority of the territorial state, is rendered seemingly natural, inevitable, and even appropriate to relevant authorities (including social scientists).

A dramatic illustration of how this ontology formed and naturalized is the gradual deterioration in international standing of Native American peoples in the United States, between the sixteenth and nineteenth centuries. In the first two centuries of European settlement in North America, European criteria for "nationhood" were still quite broad. European legal thought had yet to rank a wide range of ideas about kingdoms, principalities, and non-European political systems into a clear hierarchy of legal standing; nomadic hunters were considered nonsovereign, but even "savages" *qua* savages were not understood to lack sovereign rights (Vattel [1758] 1916). For the British, Dutch, and French pursuing settlement and trade in North America, several native peoples manifested as "nations" by the contemporary standards of European diplomacy: most famously, the Iroquois Confederation in the Northeast, and the "Five Civilized Tribes" of the Southeast. Treaties and diplomacy between European states and such peoples were explicitly pursued, according to European chronicles, within the Law of Nations (Berman 1992).

But as Europe's increasingly elaborate criteria for admission into the Family of Nations translated through advancing settler colonialism, the Native Peoples gradually slipped out of the "nations" category. Widening disparities of military strength do not entirely explain this shift, for in 1776, the

Iroquois Confederation was still the equal of U.S. military forces. Yet the United States Constitution (Article 1, section 8) set "Indian Tribes" in a separate category, which, although clearly external to the United States, was vaguely apart from other "foreign nations." By the 1830s, although still formidable military powers in the West, "Indians" as a category were formally considered to have lost their sovereign claims to any territory in the United States. Native Americans' former "nation" status survived only in its diminution in U.S. federal law as "domestic dependent nations," a condition explicitly understood as being comparable to that of a child or ward, a minor for whom the federal government was guardian. (On this formula, see *Cherokee Nation* v. *State of Georgia*, 30 U.S. [5 Pet.] 1 [1831]). But more strikingly, by the late nineteenth century, American Indian peoples were determined in U.S. federal law *never to have been nations.* Earlier recognition of their sovereignty was recast as cynical ploys to pacify the natives and facilitate white settlement (*Cherokee Nation* v. *Southern Kan. Ry.*, 135 U.S. 641 [1890], 654). The idea that "savages" *intrinsically* lacked—*and had always lacked*—all sovereign rights became the only reasonable idea. Disagreement—alternative views once propounded vigorously not only by native Americans but also by their advocates in the U.S. Congress and elsewhere—came to seem strained or even fanciful. As a consequence, present-day claims by native American peoples to "nation" status (e.g., the "First Nations" formula prominent in Canada) now often seem, to nonspecialists, contrived and instrumental: an innovative adoption of an inappropriate category to gain its political benefits.

Normative

The complex of ideas through which the native American peoples were reclassified as intrinsically ineligible for "nation" status also illustrates the normative dimension of the selection process: those complementary ideas and values that give the current typology its self-evident character as well as its seeming moral force. In any society, new ideas must find consonance with an existing ideational and ideological terrain. Incremental change to that terrain, new ideas filtering into societal norms, brings strains that are typically reconciled through public debate (Sikkink 1991; Adler 1991). And indeed, the definitional shifts about Indian sovereignty summarized above were made with considerable European and later U.S. Congressional disagreement and debate about the humanity, rationality, and sovereign rights of the native Americans nations, and about the legal and moral standing of non-European peoples generally. Whatever their pragmatic utility in providing juridical mechanisms and military rationales for advancing white settlement and extending U.S. sovereignty, public discourse about Indians also had to accord with a complex of evolving concepts about morality, Christian values, human dignity and worth, and an understanding of how these cherished principles were properly to be codified in social organization, industry, commerce, art, and law. The full moral and cognitive consonance that these ideas carried for European settler colonialism, at both elite and popular levels, was not gained from their utility to the "Indian question" alone. Rather, their cognitive force regarding Indians—their ability to seem natural, rational, or simply inevitable—derived from their consonance with a larger body of thought about such staple normative issues as race, progress, modernity, justice, rationality, and the righteousness of the civilizing mission. That very broad complex of ideas and values was, of course, part of the above-mentioned Standard of Civilization, which, again, constituted a standard that aspiring state elites the world over became (necessarily) anxious to match. The interplay of these ideas with romanticized nationalisms completed the affective and moral order of the nation-state.

From the above discussion, we can proceed to consider how international norms inform state elite policies toward ethnic diversity and conflict, and can even affect the construction of ethnic identities themselves.

International Norms and Domestic Ethnic Logics

In comparativist studies of ethnic identity and conflict, it has become commonplace to treat ethnic identities not as given but as socially constructed: historically fluid, with contested boundaries, often dependent on context. In any deep historical study of ethnic identities, we find that the criteria for membership change over time, reflecting ethnicity's adaptive and contingent nature. Of course, ethnopoliticians also sometimes invent, "reconstruct," or adapt existing ethnic profiles to support particular claims for group rights or privileges, leading some theorists to treat ethnic identities entirely as instruments of politics. But ethnic identities are not entirely malleable by the ambitious ethno-architect (Smith 1991). While they are fluid, they are not infinitely so; they are attached to myriad social experiences, collective memories, and norms, which carry their own logics and inertia. Political claims may also embed in popular consciousness, shaping social perceptions of ethnic identities (and altering political behavior). Accordingly, most analyses of ethnic identities assume that ethnic identities are socially constructed by their constituencies even while debating the extent to which they are also the tools of instrumental politics and/or "primordial" in the Geertzian sense (i.e., deriving from deeper cultural traits or meaning systems).

Moreover, ethnic identities are dialectics. While constructed internally by group experience and in public and nationalist discourse steered by artists, intellectuals, and politicians, they are also "imagined" by other groups, who may generate differing or even contradictory definitions. Such definitions are often explicitly political. For example, a dominant ethnic group, controlling the government, may try to define a secessionist or insurrectionary ethnic group as intrinsically "backward" and therefore unqualified to assert grievances. Or a state elite may even deny a group's existence as a discrete group altogether; René Lemarchand (1994) has traced such a strategy by the Tutsi elite in Burundi, regarding the Hutu. The subordinated group will then consider that derogatory and/or politically disempowering discourse in constructing some counter-discourse. For example, ladino (non-Indian) society in Guatemala generally understands "Indian" to be an ethnic identity of the peasantry. Thus, viewing a Mayan Indian who has gained a university degree and seeks to represent indigenous interests to the government, many ladinos will deny that person's legitimacy as an ethnic spokesperson because she is no longer "Indian." The Mayan response, of course, is to reject the conflation of "Indian" and "peasant": Hence, one reason for celebrating ancient Mayan art and civilization is to reassert the capacity of "Mayan" to embrace a full range of class strata (Warren 1998).

Significant here is that the state's international interests can contribute to such dialectics. As noted above, for many states, not only prestige but their very ability to resist conquest has depended on presenting a "civilized" aspect on the European model—a project "ethnic" in itself. For this reason, state elites are sensitive to any domestic ethnic formation that might erode the state's "civilized" claim—again, on European terms. Hence, historically, we have seen considerable tension and debate among state elites in Latin America about their "backward" peoples, and a disownment (as vanishing, already vanished, stubbornly ignorant, irrational, or otherwise ignorable) of any "primitive" elements in the nation. Such concerns have translated into clumped policies ranging from deliberate political marginalization to the abduction and forced adoption of children, to population transfer, to forced assimilation in schools, many of which have left a legacy of bitter resentments and resistance among groups so targeted.

Thus the state template translates international norms into "standards" that inform state elite perceptions and values regarding ethnic diversity and even the social construction of ethnic identities themselves. By contributing to how ethnic identities are understood and valued (as beneficial or detrimental to state interests), state interests further help to establish the domestic criteria by which state policy toward ethnic diversity is guided. Such ethnic constructions are not, however, developed in isolation. The larger context is the cognitive terrain of nation-building, in which, again, we can identify neglected contributions by the state.

The Onus of National Unity

Nation-building and nationalism are familiar subjects for comparativists, who usually study them for their complex domestic dimensions. Nation-building is of course infamous for inspiring ethnic conflict of the most violent forms: from Turkey's expulsion and genocide of the Armenians in 1918 to the Nazi Holocaust to Iraqi attacks on the Kurds in the 1990s. In recent decades, Anthony Smith (1986) and others have extensively explored the *ethnie* of nationalism, and journals like *Ethnic and Racial Studies* and *National Identity* have been assembling a rich body of comparative case studies addressing ethnic questions in nationalist thought.

But nation-building is also a Janus-faced state project in the more IR sense developed here. First, to varying degrees, both the state's domestic hegemony and its international security rest partly on nationalism, because popular cooperation with military service and tax revenues is crucial to its capacity in both concerns: For this reason, Crawford Young (1994) has called these needs state "imperatives." Second, the international standing of the modern state rests partly on its ability to manifest as a "nation-state"— that is, to represent a population bound together, at a minimum, by the common will to live under one government. A hasty qualifier is necessary here: Of course, many states lack domestic unity, and the international community can be notoriously unconcerned with such lack. Indeed, quite a few states rest heavily on international recognition to override their glaring lack of domestic cohesion (Jackson and Rosberg 1982); today, Somalia stands out presently as a diplomatic fiction. But for the great majority of states, the *diplomatic claim* of unity remains key, because that claim underlies the essential diplomatic premise that the state government has the right to represent its territory's population in international forums and, conversely, that it can secure its population's compliance with the state's international treaties and international law. In most IR literature, the "unitary" character of states in these basic senses is indeed assumed, and a presumption (often extraordinarily uncritical) of true underlying national unity is often tacitly attached (spilling over, most glaringly, into naïve analyses of "national" economic development strategies). If domestic national divisions (including ethnopolitical schisms) are sufficiently severe to imply a significant lack of consensus about the fundamental national integrity of a state, the state may appear internationally as an illegitimate voice, unqualified to make decisions for its population and perhaps incapable of enforcing them (as did, for example, South Africa in the last years of apartheid).

These external exigencies add to domestic concerns about national unity by constituting an additional, structural pressure on state elites to claim national integration even when it does not exist. Accordingly, internal ethnic divisions which gain sufficient international attention actually to threaten the state's image as a unified nation will impel state elites (who otherwise might be uninspired to care) to seek some "solution": for example, rhetorical denials that ethnic divisions are sufficiently serious to require action, or even that the group exists as a coherent "group" at all. Because they are promoted by state spokespeople, and perhaps by a complementary nationalist intelligentsia, such claims filter back into the domestic ethnic environment as claims of ethnic accord: for example, as mentioned in the introduction and discussed more fully below, in the hegemonic, pan-Latin American denial that ethnicity and race still have political salience. But such tactics tend to leave conflicts festering, subsumed only superficially by the national ideology and prone to erupt when conditions are favorable (Scott 1990). Indeed, many of the "new" conflicts we see today represent such reemergences, surprising more to those who had uncritically accepted state-nationalist claims of ethnic harmony than to those observers closer to conditions on the ground.

Thus state-driven claims about national unity feed into nationalist discourse. But further, nationalism in its more ethnic sense—the weaving of mythologized histories, language, religion, festivals, and emblematic traditions—is also a Janus-faced state project, because construction of the national identity in public discourse is also informed by what kind of "identity" is advantageous to the state's external posture. This linkage brings us to consider the state from a more realist IR perspective, as an "actor" in the international system.

State Identity Politics

Today, thanks to advancing constructivist IR theory, it is no new assertion to point out that states form identities (e.g., Katzenstein 1996). Yet basic realist concerns inspire such projects. Facing the intrinsic "security dilemma" of the anarchic international system, a state may form an identity to stabilize its alliances with other states, or to consolidate an antihegemonic posture, or to craft its membership in a security community defined as sharing some kind of deep commonality. Such an identity may be built on any concept or set of principles. For example, in the post-cold war period, an identification with liberal economic policy and democracy has helped some former Soviet states to reorient and solidify their alliances toward western Europe and the United States.

Such identities go beyond mere policy choices because they are less malleable; once linked ideologically to the state's intrinsic character, and embedded in the national consciousness, they help to stabilize a domestic governmental orientation toward a particular foreign policy and to overarch the vagaries and swings of domestic politics. In the international arena, state identities help to glue over any temporary differences of interest, reassuring allies of long-term commitment. Indeed, a state identity even compels a government to hold to a particular foreign policy, again because of both their domestic embeddedness and the longer term international obligations they accrue. But most significantly to our concerns here, such *state* identities are constructed not solely from domestic nationalist thought, consensus or experience. They are heavily influenced by state elites' interpretations of the state's external needs and conditions, such as the state's structural position in the cold war bipolar system, or its best options for security and trade alliances (Wendt 1994).

When such state identities are conceptually linked to ideas about the nation's culture, or when the state's international identity is tied to transnational ethnic elements like race, language, or religion, state identities become more explicitly "ethnic." (The emphasis is suggested because, although successfully anthropomorphized for certain purposes as Wendt (1999) argues, states are not, in fact, human beings; they are fictions, and so cannot have ethnic experiences of their own.) Such identities build alliances out of some (purportedly) shared cultural values and collective history; hence "Latin American," "African," and "Arab" states are all identities to which are ascribed various cultural traits and values, propounded (in various evolving and contested ideological formulations) to establish an "organic" regional solidarity after decolonization.

Significant here is that, as a strategic foreign relations maneuver, a state's "ethnic" identity is inspired and driven by the state's external environment. Therefore, as the identity forms (or changes) to accord with that environment, it may diverge from the actual ethnic demographics of the state's population. Of course, a state's "ethnic" identity must have some consonance with its domestic constituency or it will fail to resonate sufficiently to engage the desired popular and foreign response. But an "ethnic" identity may represent only a majority of the population, or the politically dominant sector. For this reason, it may actually render a digressive ethnic minority (or even a majority) problematic to state interests in new ways. For example, in the 1960s, Algeria sought to consolidate an "Arab" state identity to accord with then-current ideas about Arab nationalism, an "imagined community" extensively debated among Arab state intellectuals and political leaderships and conceptually central to the formation of the Arab League as a security community. But the project recast the (non-Arab) Berber population as corrosive to the "Arabness" of the nation. Newly vigorous "Arabization" (forced assimilation) projects ensued, triggering major Berber resistance (Stone).

Australia offers another illustration. From its independence, Australia was anxious to sustain its close ties to Britain despite its vast distance from the metropole and its own geographic location in an "Asian" cultural zone. One related state measure was the "white Australia" policy, which prohibited non-white immigration (Kane 1997). Another measure was ethnocidal and sometimes genocidal policies toward the continent's Aboriginal people, policies certainly fed by domestic land competition and general racist thought but also by the Standard of Civilization and by an anxiety to confirm Australia's unity and legitimacy by utterly eradicating Aboriginal sovereignty (Stokes 1997). But the state's external interests changed, and the domestic ethnic environment was impacted accordingly. Since the 1970s, Australia has confronted an economically booming "Asia-Pacific" and has tried to reaffirm its natural membership in the "Asian" region (Hudson and Stokes 1997). The country's historical "white" identity was now an embarrassment: Hence, the state modified its "white-only" immigration laws to permit more Asian immigration, and retooled its national ideology to emphasize its Aborigine "roots" (a famous manifestation of the project was the lavish "Dreamtime" sequence introducing the 1998 Olympics). Growing popular consensus supporting such shifts also reflects a local dialectic with the new international human rights climate (in a sense, a new Standard of Civilization), which rejects racism and celebrates "diversity." The impact on domestic ethnic politics have been direct: for "Asians," a small surge of immigration; for Aborigines, some narrow political openings for political activism and representation at the state level, and some cautious yet significant accommodations by the state, especially regarding Aboriginal land claims. Yet these measures have also triggered a white-racial-nationalist backlash, emblemized by the "One Nation" party led by Pauline Hanson.

State identity politics may even contribute to how state elites define the very existence of ethnic and racial groups: for example, the state-led conceptual dissolution of "Indian" as a racial identity in Latin America. Around the turn of the twentieth century, nationalist intellectuals throughout Latin America debated and developed a new racial doctrine, *mestizaje*: the proposition that the diverse races of Latin America had, over the centuries, interbred and come to constitute a single melded Race (the *mestizo*). In the writing of nationalists like Manuel Gamio ([1916] 1960), *mestizaje* partly reflected domestic concerns: sincere liberal efforts to overcome the deep racial schisms that seemed so obviously to impede their countries' economic and social development. Rapidly disseminated into public discourse, partly through public celebrations such as the annual Day of the Race (*Dia de la Raza*, the equivalent of Columbus Day), *mestizaje* has since become a much-celebrated component of the "Latin American" identity (Stabb 1959; Knight 1990; Hale 1996; Mallon 1996).

But *mestizaje* was also a foreign policy device to counter European scientific racism, then attached to imperialism. In the late nineteenth century, social Darwinism and the new social sciences had been enlisted by German, French, and English intellectuals to explain European imperial gains and U.S. hemispheric hegemony as driven by their populations' "white" or "Anglo-Saxon" racial superiority. Thus nationalist intellectuals like José Vascòncelos (1989a, 1989b) promoted *mestizaje* as an anti-imperial counter-discourse, designed to redignify less-than-white Latin America as a region, and to propose an innate commonality among the region's states that would grant moral and cognitive authority to their forming a security community to resist European and U.S. imperialism.

Yet in affirming universal racial mixing as fundamental to a pan-"Latin American" identity, *mestizaje* implicitly rejected any persistent racial or ethnic politics that might belie that claim. Further, *mestizaje* jelled (predictably enough) around the mestizo core to which most intellectuals belonged: the mostly European ("Latin") mixture characteristic of the upper classes in the dominant society (Masferrer 1961). Hence nonwhite groups that retained too distinct a racial profile—Chinese, blacks, "Indians"—became problematic afresh, because they undermined the one-race claim so integral to state discourses of national and regional unity. Since the "backwardness" of indigenous cultures also eroded "Latin" America's claim to "civilization," they were doubly unwelcome. The consequence for the Chinese was intensifying Sinophobia and a series of pogroms; the consequence for Afro-Latinos has been the persistence of antiblack racism almost entirely unchallenged in popular thought or public debate. The consequence for the indigenous peoples has varied with their importance to the labor force: sometimes ethnic cleansing; sometimes deliberate neglect; more rarely, assimilative (and repressive) state-led policies, designed to "uplift" and assimilate them but ultimately to eradicate them as distinct ethno-racial groups. Yet this ongoing racial hierarchy is denied through *mestizaje*'s one-race claim, and state complicity is that hierarchy is rendered a nonquestion. Thus the "Latin American" identity discourse, designed partly for international consumption, contributes powerfully to normative ideas in the domestic ethnic arena: undefining "Indians," and so rendering their politics anachronistic.

Conclusion

Although a distinct form of ethnic conflict for reasons discussed here, the politics of indigenous peoples illuminates dimensions of the state that are of broader import to CP studies of ethnic conflict. The "state" is not merely "government": It is an international institution, a complex of rules and norms generated by international society, obtaining an entity-like presence in international law and politics. All these dimensions contribute to creating a hegemonic discourse of the nation-state as the normative order for politics, and therefore the principal site for ethnic conflict. More subtly, they can also contribute to that arena's particular ethnic *environment*: that is, the body of salient ideas about ethnicity and race, and about specific groups, that shapes and constrains the political options deemed viable and reasonable within the arena of national politics. The state's external concerns reflect inward into this environment to affect elite and nationalist thought about ethnicity and race, the political significance of ethnic diversity, and the meanings and values attached to specific groups. Countervailing ethnic discourses also emerge in this environment, raising alternative images, meanings, and ontologies. The local ethnic environment cannot be fully appreciated, then, without attention to the state's role.

To conclude, I offer two quick observations about the implications of this argument for CP methodology. First, I do not argue that the state's role will always be equally significant, but that it routinely be considered to determine whether and to what extent it is significant. Moreover, the state's role clearly varies in each case, not simply from state to state but from group to group. Each group may signify differently to state identity politics, and may differently engage, or fail to engage, with government institutions. Therefore, to establish the experience of one group does not establish state's overall ethnic effects. For example, a politically successful ethnic group does not necessarily signal potential success for other groups, because the relation of those other groups to state interests may not be the same. For this reason, studies of ethnic conflict must address the state's role carefully, on a case-by-case basis.

Second, I submit that considering the state's role is vital to prescribing public policy. If the above discussion is well founded, simply strengthening the state (as government) may actually aggravate ethnic tensions arising from the vector effect. Similarly, increasing government capacity may allow state elites more forcefully to pursue the domestic ethnic logics derived from state identity politics, with grim implications for any groups manifesting as contradicting or undermining the state's external profile. Stronger states may indeed permit more effective governance; yet given state complicity in the domestic ethnic environment, other adaptations may also be necessary to ensure that "strength" does not equate with "capacity to repress."

To sum up, if the important dimensions of the state laid out here are even partially valid, studies of ethnic conflict that omit consideration of the state's role are likely incomplete. I suggest that, in future, studies that take the boundary of the state as the boundary of the study, and that ignore the state itself, will be defended rather than assumed.

Bibliography

Adler, Emanuel. 1991. "Cognitive Evolution: A Dynamic Approach for the Study of International Relations and Their Progress." In *Progress in Postwar International Relations*, ed. Emanuel Adler and Beverly Crawford, 43–88. New York: Columbia University Press.

Anaya, S. James. 1996. *Indigenous Peoples in International Law*. New York: Oxford University Press.

Berman, Howard R. 1992. "Perspectives on American Indian Sovereignty and International Law, 1600–1776." In *Exiled in the Land of the Free: Democracy, Indian Nations, and the U.S. Constitution*, ed. Oren Lyons et al., 125–188. Santa Fe, NM: Clear Light Publishers.

Biersteker, Thomas, and Cynthia Weber, eds. 1996. *State Sovereignty as Social Contract*. Cambridge, UK: Cambridge University Press.

Brysk, Alison. 2000. *From Tribal Village to Global Village: Indian Rights and International Relations in Latin America*. Stanford: Stanford University Press.

Bull, Hedley. 1977. *The Anarchical Society*. New York: Columbia University Press.

Collier, David, ed. 1979. *The New Authoritarianism in Latin America*. Princeton: Princeton University Press.

Conaie. 1989. *Las Nacionalidades Indígenas en el Ecuador: Nuestro Proceso Organizativo*. Quito, Ecuador: Abya-Yala.

Crain, Mary. 1990. "The Social Construction of National Identity in Highland Ecuador." *Anthropological Quarterly* 63: 43–59.

Davidson, Basil. 1992. *The Black Man's Burden: Africa and the Curse of the Nation-State*. New York: Times Books.

Diamond, Larry, Juan J. Linz, and Seymour Martin Lipset, eds. 1989. *Democracy in Developing Countries: Latin America*. Boulder: Lynne Reiner.

Findji, Maria Teresa. 1992. "From Resistance to Social Movement: The Indigenous Authorities Movement in Columbia." In *The Making of Social Movements in Latin America: Identity, Strategy, and Democracy*, ed. Arturo Escobar and Sonia E. Alvarez, 112–133. Boulder: Westview Press.

Finnemore, Martha. 1996. *National Interests in International Society*. Ithaca: Cornell University Press.

Gamio, Manuel. [1916] 1960. *Forjando Patria*. Mexico: Editorial Porrúa.

Gong, Gerrit. 1986. *The Standard of "Civilization" in International Society*. Oxford: Clarendon Press.

Hale, Charles R. 1996. "*Mestizaje*, Hybridity, and the Cultural Politics of Difference in Post-Revolutionary Central America." *Journal of Latin American Anthropology* 2(1): 35–61.

Hudson, Wayne and Geoffrey Stokes. 1997. "Australia and Asia: Place, Determinism and National Identities." In *The Politics of Identity in Australia*, ed. Geoffrey Stokes, 145–157. Cambridge, UK: Cambridge University Press.

Ikenberry, G. John, and Charles Kupchan. 1990. "Socialization and Hegemonic Power." *International Organization* 44: 283–315.

Jackson, Robert, and Carl Rosberg. 1982. "Why Africa's Weak States Persist: The Juridical and Empirical in Statehood" *World Politics* 25: 1–24.

Kane, John. 1997. "Racialism and Democracy: The Legacy of White Australia." In *The Politics of Identity in Australia*, ed. Geoffrey Stokes, 117–131. Cambridge, UK: Cambridge University Press.

Katzenstein, Peter. 1996. *The Culture of National Security*. New York: Columbia University Press.

Keck, Margaret and Kathryn Sikkink. 1998. *Activists Beyond Borders: Advocacy Networks in International Politics*. Ithaca: Cornell University Press.

Knight, Alan. 1990. "Racism, Revolution and *Indigenismo*: Mexico, 1910–1940." In *The Idea of Race in Latin America, 1870–1940*, ed. Richard Graham, 71–113. Austin: University of Texas Press.

Laitin, David. 2001. "The Implications of Constructivism for Constructing Ethnic Fractionalization Indices." In *Symposium: Cumulative Findings in the Study of Ethnic Politics*, ed. Kanchan Chandra, 13–17. American Political Science Association—Comparative Politics section newsletter (Winter).

Lemarchand, René. 1994. *Burundi: Ethnocide as Discourse and Practice*. Cambridge: Cambridge University Press.

Macas, Luis. 1992. "El Levantamiento Indígena Visto por sus Protagonistas." In *Indios: Una Reflexión sobre el Levantamiento Indígena de 1990*, ed. Diego Cornejo Menacho, 17–36. Quito, Ecuador: Abya-Yala, ILDIS.

Mallon, Florencia E. 1996. "Constructing *Mestizaje* in Latin America: Authenticity, Marginality, and Gender in the Claiming of Ethnic Identities." *Journal of Latin American Anthropology*, 2, no. 1.

Masferrer, Alberto. 1961. *Paginas Escogidas*. San Salvador: Ministerio de Educación, Departamento Editorial.

O'Donnell, Guillermo and Philippe C. Schmitter. 1986. *Transitions from Authoritarian Rule: Tentative Conclusions About Uncertain Democracies*, vol. 4. Baltimore: Johns Hopkins University Press.

Pye, Lucien. 1962. *Politics, Personality and Nation Building: Burma's Search for Identity*. New Haven: Yale University Press.

Quijano Obregón, Aníbal. 1967. "Contemporary Peasant Movements." In *Elites in Latin America*, ed. Seymour Martin Lipset and Aldo Solari, 301–340. New York: Oxford University Press.

Scott, James. 1990. *Domination and the Arts of Resistance: Hidden Transcripts*. New Haven: Yale University Press.

Shaw, Karena. 2001. "Indigeneity and the International: Repoliticizing Decolonization." Unpublished paper, International Studies Association Annual Meeting, Chicago, IL.

Sikkink, Kathryn. 1991. *Ideas and Institutions: Developmentalism in Brazil and Argentina*. Ithaca: Cornell University Press.

Smith, Anthony. 1991. "The Nation: Invented, Imagined, Reconstructed?" *Millennium: Journal of International Studies* 20: 353–368.

———. 1986. *The Ethnic Origin of Nations*. London: Blackwell.

Stabb, Martin S. 1959. "Indigenism and Racism in Mexican Thought: 1857–1911." *Journal of Inter-American Studies* 1: 405–424.

Stokes, Geoffrey. 1997. "Citizenship and Aboriginality: Two Conceptions of Identity in Aboriginal Political Thought." In *The Politics of Identity in Australia*, ed. Geoffrey Stokes, 158–171. Cambridge, UK: Cambridge University Press.

Sunstein, Cas. 1991. "Why Markets Don't Stop Discrimination." *Social Philosophy and Policy* 8(2): 22–37.

Tilley, Virginia. 1997. "Terms of the Debate: Untangling Language about Ethnicity and Ethnic Movements." *Ethnic and Racial Studies* 29(3): 497–522.

Van Cott, Donna Lee. 1995. "Indigenous Peoples and Democracy: Issues for Policymakers." In *Indigenous Peoples and Democracy in Latin America*, ed. Donna Lee Van Cott, 1–27. New York: Inter-American Dialogue.

———. 2000. *The Friendly Liquidation of the Past: The Politics of Diversity in Latin America*. Pittsburgh: Pittsburgh University Press.

Vasconcelos, José. [1925] 1989a. "La Raza Cósmica." In *José Vasconcelos*, ed. Justina Sarabia. Madrid: Ediciones de Cultura Hispánica.

———. [1926] 1989b. "Indología." In *José Vasconcelos*, ed. Justina Sarabia. Madrid: Ediciones de Cultura Hispánica.

Vattel, Emer de. [1758] 1916. *The Law of Nations, or, the Principles of Natural Law*, trans. C. Fenwick. Reprinted, Washington, DC: Carnegie Institute.

Waltz, Kenneth. 1979. *Theory of International Politics*. Boston: Addison-Wesley.

Warren, Kay B. 1998. *Indigenous Movements and Their Critics: Pan-Maya Activism in Guatemala*. Princeton: Princeton University Press.

Watson, Adam. 1992. *The Evolution of International Society*. London: Routledge.

Wendt, Alexander. 1987. "The Agent-Structure Problem in International Relations Theory." *International Organization* 88: 384–396.

———. 1992. "Anarchy Is What States Make of It: The Social Construction of Power Politics." *International Organization* 46: 391–425.

———. 1994. "Collective Identity Formation and the International State." *American Political Science Review* 88: 384–396.

———. 1999. *Social Theory of International Politics*. Cambridge, UK: Cambridge University Press.

Wilmer, Franke. 1993. *The Indigenous Voice in World Politics: Since Time Immemorial*. Newbury Park, CA: Sage.

Young, Crawford. 1994. *The African Colonial State in Comparative Perspective*. New Haven: Yale University Press.

Zizek, Slavoj. 2000. *An Introduction to Jacques Lacan through Popular Culture*. Cambridge, MA: MIT Press.

6

Transnational Flows, Legitimacy, and Syncretic Democracy in Benin

Bruce A. Magnusson

Introduction

Case studies of democratization tend to focus primarily on internal factors and processes (within the territorial and institutional realm of the state), relegating external factors and processes to positions of exogenous influence. This conceptual predisposition can mislead us in our understanding of what democratization is and how it works, and it provides an especially treacherous framework for understanding institutional development and democratic legitimacy. We have to be concerned about how the external is internalized, and how exogenous factors and processes are "endogenized" into forms that may look quite different as a result of their encounter with "the local." In order to get at how this works, constructivism provides promising tools for understanding the local development of democratic institutions whose form may appear to be universal, but whose legitimacy is dependent on how external ideas and norms articulate with particular contexts.[1] It can help explain how countries with new democratic regimes become democratic, how new regimes become legitimate, and how external ideas and norms become internalized as part of a network of boundary-crossing institutions and understandings constituting a democratic identity.

In Africa, democracy is a discursive framework within which transnational ideas and institutions encounter the power of local norms and institutions in particularly profound ways. The "modern-traditional" dichotomy has retained a particularly deep resonance in postcolonial Africa such that many people live it rather self-consciously, understanding which institutions, activities, and causal relationships are considered "modern," and which are considered "traditional."[2] Both are lived simultaneously, much as large portions of the world live the globalization-localization dichotomy simultaneously, but often much less self-consciously. Most of our attention has been aimed at how the "modern" or the "global" has transformed "tradition" or the "local." We are disturbed, sometimes appalled, and often resigned about the inevitability of these transformations or little evolutions. Less visible are the more subversive, but just as important effects of the local or traditional on the modern or the global. The underlying assumption of this dichotomization is that the modern and the global are external (usually Western) and that Africa is primordially traditional and local (Ferguson 1997). What is hidden in these assumptions is the articulation of ideas with historical context and present realities. What is being lived every day is not just the assault of external values on primordial (and therefore somehow legitimate) culture and systems of governance, but change and adaptation and struggle. The result is not simply the replication of received ideas, but nuance and transformation and even new ideas and institutional forms.

We hear a variety of claims that Western institutions (such as democracy) imposed willy-nilly on African countries will not work; that Africa has not achieved the level of economic development necessary to sustain democracy; or that the ethnic configurations of African countries are unsuitable for competitive politics. Alternatively, those with more flexible understandings of democracy ask us to consider institutional structures developed from African understandings of culture and society and power; that authentic African democracies might look very different from Western democracies; and that democracy might not even require multiple political parties. Responses to these claims vary. While few would support the notion that any outsider should "impose" democracy on a country, it is arguable that most contemporary democratic blueprints are derived from Western experience, thereby undervaluing historically African forms of democratic governance. In fact, critics such as George Ayittey would claim that democracy in its Western form is alien to Africa only because self-interested military and economic elites have made it so—that the aversion to multiparty politics serves only the interests of the ruling political class who have the power to define what is African and what is not. According to this view, what the people want is democracy and freedom and human rights and they should not have to settle for anything less just because they are African.[3]

While often sterile and circular, these debates do go to the heart of democratic legitimacy in Africa, pointing to its importance as political strategy. Because legitimacy has important internal and external dimensions, especially in weak states, for a democratic regime to hold a legitimate claim on national power, it must respond to both internal and external claims on that legitimacy and rearticulate the murky boundaries between realms of democratic knowledge. The process of democratization and its legitimation in Africa (and elsewhere) is an ongoing syncretic political process involving transformative encounters with transnational flows of ideas, culture, and people within fluid historical and political contexts.

It is important to keep in mind that what looks like normative and institutional isomorphism is not just an outcome, but a political strategy aimed at resolving certain key tensions in postcolonial (and post–cold war) Africa.[4] I will examine this claim more closely with respect to these tensions at the heart of many political debates in the decade old democracy in Benin, the vanguard of "national conference democracy" in Africa, and one of the most successful.[5]

- Representation (Competition and consensus define the parameters of representative politics, particularly in an ethnically diverse society.)
- National Identity (What does it mean to be Beninois and non-Beninois in a country at the center of transnational trade and culture with ties across borders as well as to a broader francophone community? Is there a Beninois nation?)
- Security and Insecurity (What are the tradeoffs between domestic order and human rights in a fragile new democracy in an unfriendly regional neighborhood?)

These tensions do not operate in isolation from each other. Rather, they operate in a complex interrelationship. Issues of representation within the state are deeply connected to issues of national identity and economic security in the regional context of West Africa. Security issues, too, are cross-cut by internal representation of ethnic, regional, and economic interests, and the representation of the nation vis-à-vis world society. In each of these domains, something new has emerged in Benin that is not explained by the simple internal-external dichotomy, but rather by the work (the practice) involved in the articulation of ideas, norms, and context among communities within the territorial state and across territorial lines.

Dimensions of Legitimacy

I have defined legitimacy elsewhere as being an exceptionally fluid concept having both internal and external dimensions (Magnusson 1997). It is the internal dimension of political legitimacy that has been elaborated traditionally by political philosophers and social scientists. But, because judgments by external actors (states, multilateral institutions, transnational nongovernmental organizations, multinational corporations) regarding the internal governance of weak states weigh more and more importantly on internal decision making, the external dimension of legitimacy and its articulation with the internal deserves serious attention. More and more, developing countries face a set of "accreditation standards" in order to benefit from the array of international and transnational resources accruing to "legitimately governed" states. Typically, these standards include scales specifying degrees of democracy, compliance with human rights norms, and levels of corruption. Compliance with macroeconomic and financial policy conditions set by the IMF and the World Bank has been one determinant of external financial support for African countries since the 1980s. Requirements regarding regime type, compliance with international standards of governance and the internal relationship between leaders and citizens is relatively new to the post–cold war period. The key point here is that this international and transnational attention to issues of internal governance creates the basis for a political strategy as the importance of these issues as internal resources for political contestation and legitimacy increases.[6]

Conceptually, legitimacy has normative, procedural, and performance components with both external and internal dimensions. These three components of legitimacy apply to both its external and internal dimensions. Nevertheless, they will articulate differently in different contexts, and their relative importance both internally and externally is likely to differ dramatically. For example, the pursuit of a normative political goal (such as "national unity") may not supersede the manner in which it is pursued (procedure) or the fact that it may have been achieved (performance). How a legitimating political goal is achieved may be as important normatively as its actual achievement, and that kind of evaluation is carried out not just internally, but also by relevant external actors such as other states, international organizations, and nongovernmental organizations (Magnusson 1997.)[7] In Africa, legitimacy is particularly crucial for democratic survival, attached as it has come to be in the 1990s with the protection of human rights, individual and community security, and the control of official and unofficial corruption. Nigeria's first two democratic regimes and their relatively popular overthrow by the military are cases in point, as are the more recent military coups in Niger, Gambia, and Côte d'Ivoire (Joseph 1987).

Transnational Flows and Syncretic Democracy

Transnational flows of ideas, culture, and people can both support and threaten fragile and vulnerable new democratic regimes. They are also intimately connected to legitimacy. The institutions of weak states are constructed out of encounters with these transnational flows in order to protect against them, to incorporate them, or to accommodate them. With an apt environmental analogy, Virginia Tilley describes how ideas about ethnicity "can move through continents and societies like great changes of weather. Local ethnic arenas engage with such currents in ways peculiar to their unique circumstances, but can never be entirely isolated or insulated from them" (Tilley 1998a). The "climatic" changes in the international system following the cold war blew a front of economic and political liberalism across Africa when alternative support networks from the eastern bloc disappeared and the West became more interested in nurturing democracy and free markets than in building dikes against communist influence. This "liberal moment" is characterized by concerns for self-determination, universal human rights, the rearticulation of sovereignty, and a democracy norm (Green 2000).

In a vivid image, Ali Mazrui describes an Africa trapped in "two contradictory prison-houses—one incorrigibly and rigidly *national* and the other irresistibly *transnational*. One is the prison-house of the sovereign state, a fortress of political and military sovereignty. The other is the prison-house of capitalism, compulsively transnational and constantly mocking the very principle of national sovereignty" (Mazrui 1984: 289). As Virginia Tilley illustrates, though, the sovereign state, rather than being "rigidly national," is also "irresistibly transnational" as a template that carries with it the discipline of an imagined set of structural and behavioral attributes conforming to international standards and operating requirements (Tilley 1998b.)[8] To describe the sovereign state in Africa as rigidly national ignores the very physical fact of cross-border ethnic, religious, and economic relationships which have survived both the nineteenth century partition and the postcolonial maintenance of territorial boundaries. These relationships have changed because of borders, but the relationships still exist and have become important economic, cultural, and political resources.[9]

Democracy, too, has acquired the aura of a template regime being "imposed" (like development strategies) as a condition for international aid and support. Opinions differ on whether it is possible or desirable to import it as a regime type. Is it "imposition"? Do elections cause ethnic conflict? Isn't a viable middle class (or other prerequisites) necessary for the success of democracy over the long term? These kinds of questions bound the issue of democratization in a way that ignores domestic, grassroots mobilization for democratic reform and for a rearticulated institutional relationship between the governed and those who govern. Labeling democracy "a western imposition" also does disservice to the possibilities of local reinterpretations of what is democratic, who is to be represented and how, and what expectations flow from the democratization project. Templates, in other words, may not always be as rigid as their purveyors and critics would like to think.[10] But, we cannot understand the character of the transnational dimensions of domestic politics without understanding that translation, reinterpretation, resistance, and opposition with respect to transnational ideas and norms is a necessary part of legitimating normative and institutional change at the domestic level.

Democratization in Benin provides an interesting case for how institutions are constructed out of the encounters between transnational templates and local practice and norms. As a weak and economically poor country in an authoritarian "neighborhood" in West Africa, it is particularly vulnerable to transnational economic and political currents.[11] The limits of competitive party politics, the definition of national "Beninois" identity, and the construction of new meanings of security are all illustrative of how the transnational articulates with internal politics and ideas in Benin for a particularly rich gloss on the idea of democracy. A competitive, multiparty democracy coexists with an extra-constitutional, policy-generating system of sectoral *états-generaux*. National identity becomes bound up in being democratic and different (from Nigeria and Togo and Rwanda, and France). Democracy generates new debates about the role of French culture in Beninois identity prompting a reinvigoration of Beninois history, culture, and languages. Insecurity takes on new and different hues with political openness. The police have not yet assumed the role of the protector of individuals and democracy rather than the arbitrary enforcers of authoritarian will. Crime has increased along with neighborhood "protection" societies. Refugees threaten with each new political crisis in Togo and Nigeria. Transnational criminal networks infiltrate a less secure countryside.

Aside from the formal institutions of democracy—the executive, the judiciary, and the National Assembly—that are operative in Benin, other emerging institutions take on a more syncretic cast, complementing the "normal" operatives of government with structures that fill in the gaps between "borrowed" institutional formulas and local practices. These syncretic institutions are developing as integral elements in the democratization project in Benin, as necessary to the maintenance of democracy and domestic peace as elections and parliamentary debate. They have emerged in response to institutional borrowings from abroad, from threats permeating national borders, and from the continued political, economic, and cultural penetration from France. While some of this syncretic response is formalized and even institutionalized, much of it exists in the less formal public realm of debate and local practice.

Benin: The Context

Since Dahomey (now Benin) gained its independence in 1960 (and before), the country has been crippled by an intractable three-stranded political conundrum. All postcolonial regimes have had to reconcile a tripartite, ethno-regional political rivalry; a north-south cultural divide marked by economic and political inequities; and a resource-poor economy unable to absorb its large educated (and mostly southern) elite.[12]

Between 1960 and 1972, Dahomey experienced six military coups and seven constitutions. The 1972 coup by Mathieu Kerekou developed into a military-led Marxist-Leninist dictatorship by 1974 that lasted until the civil-ian rebellion of 1989 and the 1990 National Conference that organized the transition to multiparty democracy. During this thirty-year period, a wide variety of regime types and electoral systems were employed to try to re-solve the political conundrum of politicized ethnicity, regionalism, economic inequity, and a politically vocal and underemployed urban elite.[13]

With independence in 1960, multiparty representation came to an abrupt end. Foreseeing only a triple ethnicity-region-party deadlock or even civil war if the system of multimember districts decided under plurality rules were to continue, independence brought with it a plurality-based electoral system with one national district—guaranteeing one-party rule in the name of na-tional unity. The winner-take-all stakes of such a system, combined with declining economic performance and continual austerity programs, led to dangerous levels of ethnic and civil unrest, and eventually to a long series of military coups d'état (Decalo 1990).

In addition to fiddling with electoral systems, each new regime attempted other constitutional power-sharing formulae to mitigate the deadlock and conflict inherent in the sociopolitical configuration of the country. By 1970, Dahomey had tried presidential systems, a two-headed executive, cabinet government, and the French system of divided powers between president and prime minister. All were ended by military coups following austerity measures that generated social unrest and ethno-regional political mobiliza-tion. Finally, in 1970, elections were abandoned, and the three regional lead-ers agreed on a consociational arrangement with a rotating presidency within a three-member executive council, with mutual veto rules and the equitable distribution of jobs, services, and goods. Following a peaceful handover of power to the second member of the executive council in 1972, the military overthrew the government for the last time, inaugurating the eighteen-year Kerekou regime.

The Kerekou regime deliberately set out to redefine the nation in such a way as to eliminate the sources of political instability. The leadership of the ethno-regional patronage networks was decapitated (figuratively) and these networks were integrated into a highly centralized system of political and economic patronage under the guise of Marxist democratic centralism. The politically powerful labor and student unions were silenced with the benificence of a nationalized economy that created hundreds of state-owned enterprises—and jobs. The oil boom of the 1970s in Nigeria lubricated Benin's ubiquitous informal economy, as well as the state-owned sectors, and the global flow of petrodollars ensured increased investment (although not the quality of the investments). Ideologically, the enemy of the nation (state) was externalized into the neocolonial beast, as foreign (i.e., French) assets were nationalized.

The externalization of national threat served as pretext for the securitization of the new regime. Critics were jailed, tortured, and occasionally killed. Ethnicity and religion as political mobilizers were demonized as handmaidens to imperialist neocolonialism. Traditional religious practices, a major marker of ethnicity and region, and their adherents were repressed as feudalistic threats to the revolution. Nation-building was authoritarian and brutal. Revolutionary unity in the struggle against imperialism and neocolonialism defined (officially) the Beninois nation.[14] State-building was the beneficiary. By the 1980s, two-thirds of the country's salaried employees worked for the state.

The 1979 and 1984 Revolutionary National Assemblies, the first "parliaments" since 1964, were elected by occupational and social class categories, although individual candidates were vetted by the single national party, the Peoples' Revolutionary Party of Benin. Regionalism and ethnicity were outlawed as political mobilizing categories. The regime itself, in its desire to rid the country of ethno-regional disorder, undertook rather deliberate efforts to divide the spoils of the state with a rather high level of ethno-regional sensitivity. Ironically, Kerekou (a northerner) was so concerned about avoiding ethnic favoritism that his own northern region was virtually ignored developmentally during his eighteen years in power—in stark contrast to the prevailing practices in Togo and Nigeria.

By 1988–89, the state was bankrupt, drained of resources by huge salary bills (paying for workers in bankrupt public enterprises) and debt—a victim of the expansionist state and the nation-building tactics of inclusion, centralized patronage, and a state-centric ideology. The state was unable to meet salary payments for six months at a time, and the state-owned commercial bank (the only commercial bank) had been looted by the profligate cronyism of the state elites, destroying whatever tacit support the regime enjoyed in the informal sector of the economy. When first the unions and then the civil service went on strike, the state ground to a halt and, for all intents and purposes, utterly collapsed.

Without going into detail about the February 1990 National Conference, it was a unique and risky venture in trying to establish a new national consensus about how to organize power and institutions in Benin. While certainly external pressures (France, the World Bank) moved the conference forward as an appropriate mechanism for resolving national differences, its organization and the way it functioned was a surprise to the ruling military and ideological elites, neighboring dictatorships (which soon found themselves called to account at similar national meetings), and the people. When delegates forced a vote to declare the sovereignty of National Conference decisions, no one knew that the military would decide to remain in the barracks, or that President Kerekou would trade effective power for a transitional, but empty, presidency. Certainly, the Ceaucescu lesson was still fresh. But the will to peacefully and systematically dismantle an entrenched dictatorship via a representative national conference was a revolutionary development carried live on the radio for other West African leaders to contemplate. Its success caused shockwaves that emboldened other populations in the region to seize control of the "liberal moment" (Boulaga 1993; Decalo 1997; Magnusson 1997).

Regime institutions work together as an integrated whole, but they are not isolated, either, from a global framework of understanding about what a regime is and how it is supposed to act. The values of democracy, while not globally homogenous, do carry transnational weight. It is not, though, particularly useful to discuss, for example, the advantages and disadvantages of particular types of electoral systems without reference to historical context or to other institutions—the memory of important social and economic cleavages; the strength of the presidency; presidential versus parliamentary institutions; the existence and effectiveness of a constitutional court. Institutions are created with some purpose in mind, often to solve problems that are local rather than universal. These aspects of Benin's democratic system have been discussed elsewhere (Magnusson 1997, 1999). Rather, in the final part of this paper, I will discuss three defining tensions of Benin's democratic experiment, their transnational dimensions, and the syncretic nature of resulting institutions. Tensions regarding the mode of representation, national identity referents, and new security problems can begin to illuminate how institutions are constructed not simply out of local materials or borrowed ideas, but out of a productive confrontation between them—sometimes salutary for legitimacy and sometimes not.

Representation: Competition and Consensus

The formal institution of representation is the National Assembly. The process of selecting a legitimate form of representation has been at times highly technical, sometimes deeply populist, and always fraught with larger questions about national identity and subnational attachments, and security. While on a certain level, the borrowing from "western" ideas about representation has been explicit—proportional, multimember districts versus plurality single-member districts—this discussion, while extremely important, is supplemented on a variety of levels by the creation of other kinds of extraconstitutional institutions.

The most interesting efforts to manage competing claims of representation have been national consultations, a formula that achieved its apogee in the 1990 National Conference. Ranging from semi-institutionalized advisory bodies to large ad hoc meetings to air grievances or to formulate policy, leaders have employed variations of this form of participatory representation since the early 1960s (Magnusson 1991). Following the National Conference, this mode of representative policy making is an innovation in democratic governance in Africa worth paying attention to.

Since the National Conference, a series of sectoral "estates-general" meetings have been convened to help formulate policy—or to at least provide policy guidance—for education, territorial administration, the military, the judiciary, health, and most importantly for the national economy. Each of these meetings of the estates-general is representative in a quite different way than the National Assembly. In addition to the professionals and government representatives of each sector, these meetings ensure representation by important groups in civil society—religious leaders, women's groups, youth groups, traditional leaders, labor, business, community development associations, and other nongovernment organizations (NGOs). These corporatist representatives are composed internally of representatives from each region of the country, guaranteeing a combination of territorial and functional representation. The influence of these meetings on actual policy has varied.

The estates-general of education and territorial administration—the first two to be held—were effective in forcing major changes in official government policy. The proceedings and conclusions of most of these meetings have been published. While government often resists implementing the policies as amended, the failure to do so becomes a source of public political debate. The institutionalization of this "other branch" of government provides an additional check on the powers of the president and the National Assembly, as well as satisfying a deeply felt need for broader categories of representation in government. In addition, it provides the government in power with a needed resource to legitimate its policy agenda in a context in which party coalitions in the National Assembly (and the cabinet) are extremely fragile.

The estates-general provide a form of representation for group interests that is internally legitimate, and which one finds in communities all over Benin and elsewhere. Representatives of youth, women, and elders, as well as the relevant "intellectuals," usually have a role in community governance, as well as in the governance of local equivalents of health, education, and welfare structures. In Benin, the "template" representative institutions provide an historically necessary mechanism for providing a guaranteed means of access to the state for ethnic and regional communities, but have been less successful as a key locus of state policy making. Ethnic and regional interests are crucial in legitimating policy, but other kinds of representative institutions such as the estates-general (extraconstitutional as they may be) have provided the kind of functional expertise necessary for building cross-party (ethnic, regional) policy consensus. These mechanisms have also been extremely important in the broader process of constructing a national identity linked to democratic politics.

National Identity

One of the most striking aspects of identity in Benin, in addition to its rich ethnic diversity and the multiplicity of religious traditions, is the negative identity of being "not Nigerian." Coupled with an increasing tendency to question the institutions binding Benin to the community of *francophonie*, the task of defining a national identity and the role of subnational attachments within that identity is still in full bloom. It has been nourished by the new democratic openness to ethnic, religious, and cultural freedom of expression, and is tied inextricably to both ideas about representation (who is to be represented and what does that tell us about who we are?) and to ideas about security (who and what are to be secured? and against whom or what?). On a civic level, the Beninois take great pride in having set a continental standard for toppling authoritarian regimes via a national conference. It is viewed popularly as their own political innovation derived from African-based norms of political governance, even though the resemblance to the revolutionary French estates-general is more than striking. It is something that sets Benin apart even from the much more powerful and wealthy Nigeria to the east. Its success in deposing the dictator sets it apart from Togo to the west, and its apparent consolidation sets it apart from the failures of Niger to the north, and Togo to the west. Benin is self-consciously a democratic island in a sea of authoritarian neighbors, or in the case of Obasanjo's Nigeria, of tenuous democracy.

The "transnationalized" character of Beninois society is increasingly evident in public debates over what it means to be Beninois. Although often a debate confined to the elites, it is often localized (and vocalized) in particularly revealing ways. In a heated debate over a simmering ethnically based conflict over the choice of a new capital in a new regional subdivision proposed by the Estates-General for Territorial Administration, one commentator reflected on the political meaning of ethnic and national attachments:

> Who am I if I was born in Djougou [Atacora Region] of a father born in Atakpame [Togo] and a mother born in Savalou, but spending most of her life in Tchetti, in Bohicon [Zou Region] and in Porto-Novo [Oueme Region]? What nationality or ethnicity should my children claim, one born in Abidjan [Côte d'Ivoire], another in Saint-Ouen near Paris, and the third born in Jos, Nigeria, all of them born of a Togolese mother born in Niamey [Niger]? Will my children be called upon to decide how to vote based having lived in Cotonou for the past few years?[15]

The Beninois nation is not an endogenously reproduced entity. Relationships through marriage, work, travel, and especially small-scale business, cross borders haphazardly. In other words, the broader context of "being" Beninois is not confined to the territorial boundaries of the country, nor is the context within which ethnic competition and disputes are resolved, as we see below.

The proposed decentralization reforms in 1993–94 caused numerous small-scale and localized disputes based on ethnicity. This was a period in which the Rwandan genocide was being reported daily on the radio. The leadership of these regions called for calm by reminding the population of the consequences of uncontrolled ethnic competition.

> [We] reject all alliances based on ethnocentrism for the choice of the capitals of our new departments. In this respect, and drawing lessons from the situations in Burundi, Rwanda, Croatia, Serbia, and Bosnia-Herzegovina, we invite the population of Zou-Nord to stay calm and to keep their serenity in the face of divisive efforts based on tribalism.[16]

It was not unusual to hear the disputes of daily life in Cotonou resolved by making reference to Rwanda during this period of time. The stakes of even personal conflict were imagined in terms of what identity-based frameworks could lead to with what were terrifyingly real examples from thousands of miles away in central Africa or in Europe. Rather than imagining themselves immune to such a descent into total bloodletting, the Beninois knew from averted civil wars in the 1960s, as well as from the experience of Nigeria on their eastern border, how very possible such an outcome was.

The democratic regime and civil society groups have made concerted efforts to create institutional mechanisms to short-circuit such conflicts. Aside from proportional representation in the National Assembly, these have included the creation of an Association of Traditional Kings bringing together for the first time the traditional leaders of the country for periodic consultations, as well as the equally important Association of Traditional Medical Practitioners, many of whom have important religious functions in their communities. While these organizations do not prevent serious interpersonal conflict, it is an effort to govern disputes by organizational norms and rules. The government has, on occasion, involved itself in mediation efforts within these groups.

On a much more elite level and a product of intellectuals in Benin, the cultural influence of France is also under assault in the reformulation of Beninois identity. Instigated as much by the "betrayal" of the CFA franc devaluation in 1994 as by the prospect of hosting the 1995 Francophone Summit, the cultural and intellectual relationship to the French language and its cultural institutions became a matter for a burgeoning critical reexamination. Guy Midiohouán, for example, in a book on the subject published a year before the summit complains that the use of the prefix "franco- has become our castrator, our first reality, the beating heart of our cultures, the living source of our energies, the sublime crucible of our identities. . . . We must become conscious that in Africa we are first and foremost, not francophones as they seek to convince us, but Africans" (Midiohouán 1994).

In contrast, multiple intellectual projects are recreating the history of Benin's precolonial and colonial past. Often in the form of low-cost pamphlets, the glories of past heroes, military, and religious figures are being reinvigorated in order to reappropriate an authentic past. These often recall past conflicts among the kingdoms of what is present-day Benin, as well as muckraking into the deep wells of regional-historical silence that characterized the Kerekou regime of 1972–90.[17] But they too become an object of wider debate about historical objectivity, authentic history, and the "dangers" of dredging up old conflicts and rivalries.

At a more popular level, "traditional" religious practices and festivals have found new legitimacy in democratic Benin. The priests are present at state events, and the government supports the reflowering of local traditions and religions for the first time since they were suppressed by the colonial state—a "tradition" that continued and intensified during the postcolonial period, culminating in President Kerekou's war against "feudalism" in the 1970s and 1980s.

It is difficult to separate this cultural renaissance in Benin from the focus on legitimate institutional representation and the experimentation with syncretic forms of democracy. The revitalization of systems of knowledge and history, along with a reconsideration of Benin's role in the world and its claim of establishing a genuinely African democracy, are not unrelated. The articulation of the "authentic" with existing templates of governance will be an ongoing process fueled by both international and domestic understandings of democracy, as well as the particular security concerns of a transitional regime in a volatile neighborhood.

Security: Domestic Order and Human Rights

Benin's curious relationship with Nigeria provokes a particularly striking identity response closely tied to security issues. Simultaneously market (and source of wealth) and mighty monolith with twenty times the population of Benin, Nigeria and the Nigerian border is a daily presence in the life of Benin. For Benin, Nigeria evokes images of chaos, disorder, and criminality. In contrast, the Beninois speak of their own relatively peaceful and nonviolent characteristics as a society. Even their military coups have been relatively bloodless.

As in many new democracies, crime has increased dramatically since the fall of authoritarianism. When dictators fall, their police often remain. One of the most intractable problems in new democracies has been how to reform the apparatus of state security. Police and soldiers trained to protect the government from the people are suddenly required to protect the people from each other and from the government. This "security transition" is not an easy one (witness Russia, El Salvador, and South Africa) (Magnusson 2001).

Ordinary Beninois blame both Nigeria and democracy for the increase in crime, although sometimes refugees from Togo are the target of blame. Criminals are often assumed to be Nigerians, and Nigerians are often assumed to be criminals. While it is true that Nigerian criminal networks (especially those tied to drugs and money laundering) have infiltrated Benin, the personal fear is curious given the deep cross-border family, ethnic, religious, and economic relationships that exist.

While providing a fair measure of communal security and communal access to the state, democracy has failed so far to provide a level of security at the personal and community level that people imagine existed during the military dictatorship. Simultaneously remembering the excesses of arbitrary imprisonment and torture, the nostalgia is certainly not unconditional. But the police and security forces have failed to legitimize themselves as protectors. More often, they are viewed as impotent or simply corrupt. As neighborhood crime has increased in the cities and banditry has increased in the countryside, people have created new forms of security that fall somewhere on a continuum between vigilantism and "neighborhood watch."

Realizing that this security gap is a real threat to democratic consolidation, the government has officially authorized the operations of local security organizations. Some of these are related to local religious traditions in which nighttime security is maintained by the masques of male secret societies. Some of them are more "modern" equivalents, resembling neighborhood watch groups that occasionally become protection rackets allied with corrupt local police. In northern regions, it is the male youth that are traditionally responsible for maintaining community security, and this mechanism too has been officially sanctioned by the state during the past few years.[18]

This rapid and rather radical de facto devolution of some security and policing responsibilities to communities and local systems of authority obviously reduces the reach of the central state. In some cases, it has created new levels of insecurity that the state is unable to control. In other cases, particularly where local religious practices are invoked, the nature of community control has induced demonstrations by other religious communities, as well as by women, for whom these practices are often particularly onerous. Human rights activists in Benin have actively deplored this situation, but in many cases, the daily trade-off is between the possible abuses of local security groups and the high levels of insecurity from crime. These solutions to government incapacity may be of a more transitional nature until the state's security and police forces are trained in the completely different functions of policing a democracy.

Conclusion: Transnationalism, Syncretic Democracy, and Legitimacy

A poor, vulnerable, institutionally weak country such as Benin is almost by definition buffeted by external norms, ideas, and threats. Yet, the emerging institutions which glue together the democratic regime in Benin are quite distinct from the received ideas from abroad. How is it that Benin has fashioned syncretic responses to international norms of democracy, ideas about the role of nation and subnational identity, and new domestic and external security threats? It has been stated that what is involved in these evolving institutions is an articulation of norms and ideas from abroad with local norms and practices. Rather than being a system of government legitimated and legitimate solely with respect to external agents of change, internal processes of legitimacy required the adaptation of western democratic institutions to the internal norms and practices that help them function in ways that resonate internally and induce consent (estates-general). At the same time, the demand for democracy in Benin was generated internally as a response to the illegitimacy of the kinds of authoritarianism the West had taken for granted in Africa, and the increasing power of international norms transnationally.

Democratic legitimacy in Benin requires the recognition of subnational identities while reconstructing a territorial national identity. The legitimacy of negotiated norms and rules is at stake in the success they have in providing the framework within which multiple affective communities must coexist without threatening either the territorial unity of the country or democracy itself. The development of rules for representation is taking place not only in the context of the learning involved from Benin's past failures in this regard, but in the global context of the negative examples of Rwanda and Yugoslavia. On normative, procedural, and performance levels, democratic Benin seems to have done quite well in walking the tightrope of national unity and cultural pluralism. Democracy also seems to be facilitating a reexamination of Beninois national identity with respect to its internal ethnic and regional divisions, with respect to its place in West Africa, and with the former colonial power.

The most troubling problem Benin faces in terms of democratic legitimacy and the search for internally legitimate institutions is that of personal and community security. No good formula has been found to replace an illegitimate security and police force. Local solutions antagonize different groups within communities; without supervision and regulation, local security groups are highly susceptible to criminalization themselves. Human rights norms are all too easily sacrificed to public order. On the other hand, what is considered threatening to people is no longer their own state; rather, threat has been externalized to its neighbors in a way that may be useful in terms of developing a cohesive national identity and defusing internal conflict, but has the potential of causing future trouble transnationally.

Notes

1. See chapter 1 of this volume by Dan Green.

2. This dichotomy should in no way suggest static understandings of what is traditional or modern. People see and talk about "tradition" changing as much as they see and talk about "the modern" changing.

3. The argument that democracy is unsuitable in Africa has many threads, including the modernization literature of the 1960s and some of its more recent derivatives, such as Przeworski et al. (1996). Also, see Lipset (1960) and Huntington (1991). Huntington's earlier book *Political Order in Changing Societies*, focuses on institutional inadequacies in developing countries that threaten stability. In the 1960s, exponents of the one-party state in Africa included Morgenthau (1961) and Zolberg (1966, 1969). Many politicians including Sekou Toure, Kwame Nkrumah, and more recently presidents Moi and Yuseveni have supported variations of these views. Ayittey (1998) and others including Wole Soyinka, Claude Ake and numerous contemporary politicians have blasted these views as naked political instrumentalism.

4. See Jackson and Rosberg (1982) and Jackson (1990) on external and internal dimensions of the state, which I apply here to legitimacy. With regard to institutional isomorphism as an effect of state socialization in world society, see Martha Finnemore (1996). The idea of institutional isomorphism as a strategy is suggested in Hendrik Spruyt (1994).

5. Benin's National Conference and its transition to democracy has been addressed elsewhere. See Decalo (1997); Heilbrunn (1993, 1994); Magnusson (1997, 1999).

6. On normative and institutional standards, see Finnemore (1996). On the use of external normative interests as internal resources to contest state power and legitimacy, see the discussion of human rights norms in Risse, Ropp, and Sikkink (1999).

7. *Normative legitimacy* refers to the affective attachment to regime norms, rules, and procedures with respect to their moral justification and their adherence to belief systems regarding purpose, behavior, compliance, the distribution of power and benefits, and accountability. . . . *Procedural legitimacy* refers to the attachment to the means by which state, regime, or government purpose is pursued, compliance is exacted, and power and benefits are distributed. . . . *Performance legitimacy* refers to the expectations regarding the effectiveness of the regime in producing or enabling the production and distribution of desired goods and services.

8. This is, of course, also a key insight of the sociological institutionalists regarding institutional isomorphism.

9. When most of a country's crossborder trade is unrecorded (as is Benin's with Nigeria), is it useful to continue to refer to it as "informal international trade" or "smuggling," or is it more accurate to call it "transnational trade?" See Igue and Soule (1992); Miles (1994).

10. For good examples of oppositional and/or transformative practices arising from within the "development template," see Gupta (1997) and Pigg (1997).

11. Benin is surrounded by more or less authoritarian countries, including Togo to the West, and Niger to the north, and the recently democratizing Nigeria to the east. Togo's President Eyadema was able to effectively disembowel the National Conference in Togo leaving his authoritarian regime relatively intact; in Niger, the constitutional regime ushered in by the National Conference was ushered out by the military following an institutional impasse between president and prime minister.

12. As in Nigeria, three regions became associated with three rival political parties and their leaders generating zero-sum political games aimed at capturing the state.

13. For historical detail on regime changes in Dahomey and Benin, see, among others, Allen (1989), Decalo (1990), Glele (1969), and Ronen (1968).

14. Kerekou changed the name of Dahomey in 1974 to the People's Republic of Benin. This was a clear rejection of Dahomean influence over the rest of the country —Dahomey was one of the more important expansionist, precolonial bureaucratic and militarized kingdoms which had warred with neighbors in order to capture slaves to sell for guns. While an insult to the Dahomean Fon groups, it was a liberating name change for much of the rest of the country. Ironically, the Benin Kingdom was centered in what is now Nigeria. Even for the country's name, the leadership crossed state boundaries to kidnap the glory of a neighboring state.

15. Augustin Ainamon, "Pouvons-nous eviter les risques d'un nettoyage ethnique?" *La Nation* (December 3, 1993), p. 5.

16. Comité savalois de suivi de la reforme de l'administration territoriale, "Rejet de toute alliance ethnocentriste," (Cotonou), November 23, 1993.

17. See, for example, the large number of historical pamphlets by Bio Bigou, an historian at the Universite nationale du Benin.

18. *La Nation* (May 26, 1994), p. 8. There are similarities here with the Sungusungu groups in Tanzania. See Abrahams (1989) and Tripp (1997: 12).

Bibliography

Abrahams, Ray. 1989. "Law and Order and the State in the Nyamwezi and Sukuma Area of Tanzania." *Africa* 59: 356–370.

Ainamon, Augustin. 1993. "Pouvons-nous éviter les risques d'un nettoyage ethnique?" *La Nation* (Cotonou: December 3, 1993), p. 5.

Allen, Chris. 1989. "Benin." In *Benin, The Congo, Burkina Faso: Politics, Economics and Society*, ed. Bogdan Szajkowski. New York: Pinter.

Ayittey, George. 1998. *Africa in Chaos*. New York: St. Martin's Press.

Boulaga, F. Eboussi. 1993. *Les Conférences Nationales en Afrique Noire*. Paris: Karthala.

Decalo, Samuel. 1997. "Benin: First of the New Democracies." In *Political Reform in Francophone Africa*, ed. John F. Clark and David E. Gardiner. Boulder: Westview.

————. 1990. *Coups and Army Rule in Africa*. 2nd ed. New Haven: Yale University Press.

Ferguson, James. 1997. "Anthropology and Its Evil Twin: 'Development' in the Constitution of a Discipline." In *International Development and the Social Sciences*, ed. Frederick Cooper and Randall Packard. Berkeley: University of California Press.

Finnemore, Martha. 1996. *National Interest in International Society*. Ithaca: Cornell University Press.

Glele, Maurice Ahahanzo. 1969. *Naissance d'un état noir*. Paris: R. Pichon and R. Durand-Auzias.

Green, Daniel. 2000. "Liberal Moments and Democracy's Durability: Comparing Global Outbreaks of Democracy—1918, 1945, 1989." *Studies in Comparative International Development* 34: 83–120.

Gupta, Akhil. 1997. "Agrarian Populism in the Development of a Modern Nation (India)." In *International Development and the Social Sciences*, ed. Frederick Cooper and Randall Packard. Berkeley: University of California Press.

Heilbrunn, John. 1993. "Social Origins of National Conferences in Benin and Togo." *Journal of Modern African Studies* 31: 277–299.

————. 1994. "Authority, Property, and Politics in Benin and Togo." Ph.D. dissertation, UCLA.

Huntington, Samuel P. 1968. *Political Order in Changing Societies*. New Haven: Yale University Press.

————. 1991. *The Third Wave: Democratization in the Late Twentieth Century*. Norman: University of Oklahoma Press.

Igue, John and Bio Soule. 1992. *L'Etat-entrepot au Bénin: Commerce informel ou solution a la crise?* Paris: Karthala.

Jackson, Robert. 1990. *Quasi-States: Sovereignty, International Relations and the Third World*. Cambridge: Cambridge University Press.

Jackson, Robert, and Carl G. Rosberg. 1982. "Why Africa's Weak States Persist." *World Politics* 35: 1–24.

Joseph, Richard. 1987. *Democracy and Prebendal Politics in Nigeria*. New York: Cambridge University Press

Lipset, Seymour Martin. 1960. *Political Man: The Bases of Politics*. New York: Doubleday.

Magnusson, Bruce. 1991. "Antecedents to Political and Economic Reform in Benin." In *Democratization and Structural Adjustment in Africa in the 1990s*. ed. Lual Deng, Markus Kostner, and Crawford Young. Madison: University of Wisconsin African Studies Program.

————. 1997. "The Politics of Democratic Regime Legitimation in Benin: Institutions, Social Policy, and Security." Ph.D. dissertation, University of Wisconsin–Madison.

————. 1999. "Testing Democracy in Benin." In *State, Conflict, and Democracy in Africa*, ed. Richard Joseph. Boulder: Lynne Rienner.

————. 2001. "Democratization and Domestic Insecurity: Navigating the Transition in Benin." *Comparative Politics* 33: 211–230.

Mazrui, Ali. 1984. "Africa Entrapped: Between the Protestant Ethic and the Legacy of Westphalia." In *The Expansion of International Society*, ed. Hedley Bull and Adam Watson. Oxford: Oxford University Press.

Midiohouán, Guy. 1994. *Du Bon Usage de la Francophonie*. Porto Novo: Editions CNPMS.

Miles, William F.S. 1994. *Hausaland Divided: Colonialism and Independence in Nigeria and Niger*. Ithaca: Cornell University Press.

Morgenthau, Ruth Schacter. 1961. "Single-Party Systems in West Africa." *American Political Science Review* 55(2).

Pigg, Stacey Leigh. 1997. "'Found in Most Traditional Societies': Traditional Medical Practitioners Between Culture and Development." In *International Development and the Social Sciences*, ed. Frederick Cooper and Randall Packard. Berkeley: University of California Press.

Przeworski, Adam, Michael Alvarez, José Antonio Cheibub, and Fernando Limongi. 1996. "What Makes Democracies Endure?" *Journal of Democracy* 7: 39–55.

Risse, Thomas, Stephen C. Ropp, and Kathryn Sikkink, eds. 1999. *The Power of Human Rights: International Norms and Domestic Change*. New York: Cambridge University Press.

Ronen, Dov. 1968. *Dahomey: Between Tradition and Modernity*. Ithaca: Cornell University Press.

Spruyt, Hendrik. 1994. *The Sovereign State and its Competitors*. Princeton: Princeton University Press.

Tilley, Virginia. 1997. "The Terms of the Debate: Untangling Language About Ethnicity and Ethnic Movements." *Ethnic and Racial Studies* 20: 497–522.

————. 1998a. "Crafting the 'Indian-Free' Nation: State Racial Doctrine and Nation-Building in Central America." Paper presented at the Annual Meeting of the American Political Science Association, Boston, Massachusetts.

————. 1998b. "The Ethnic State: The Unseen Origins of Ethnic Conflict." Paper presented at the Northeastern Political Science Association/International Studies Association Meetings, Boston, Massachusetts, November 12–14, 1998.

Tripp, Aili Mari. 1997. *Changing the Rules: The Politics of Liberalization and the Urban Formal Economy in Tanzania*. Berkeley: University of California Press.

Young, Crawford. 1993. "The Dialectics of Cultural Pluralism: Concepts and Reality." In *The Rising Tide of Cultural Pluralism*, ed. Crawford Young. Madison: University of Wisconsin Press.

Zolberg, Aristide. 1966. *Creating Political Order: The Party States of West Africa*. Chicago: Rand McNally.

————. 1969. *One Party Government in the Ivory Coast*. Princeton: Princeton University Press.

7

Trading Culture: Identity and Culture Industry Trade Policy in the United States, Canada, and the European Union

Patricia M. Goff

> *Before radio and television can be businesses, public institutions, or technologies, people must have ideas and hopes about them and seek to implement those ideas and hopes.*[1]
> —Thomas Streeter

In recent years, many scholars of international relations (IR), especially those associated with constructivism, have argued that attention to nonmaterial aspects of world politics—norms and identity especially—gives us a fuller picture of events in the international arena (Campbell 1998; Waever et al. 1993; Wendt 1994; Klotz 1995; Katzenstein 1996; Lapid and Kratochwil 1996). As this discussion advances, new questions are raised about the relationship between norms, identities, and interests and about *how* these various elements influence outcomes, once we've established that, indeed, they do. Empirical research in these areas promises to help us tease out some of these issues.

Perhaps one of the most salient recent examples of identity's influence in world politics is the exclusion of culture industries from the North American Free Trade Agreement (NAFTA) and the exclusion of audiovisual industries from the Uruguay Round General Agreement on Tariffs and Trade (GATT). These trade disputes provide an opportunity to investigate further the nature of the relationship between identity and interest formation. These cases are particularly interesting, I believe, because not only do they demonstrate that identity considerations may provide a compelling explanation of domestic trade policy formation where material interests do not (Goff 2000), but they also show that identity functions even in situations where the pursuit of material interests does seem to point to a compelling explanation of policy choices and it is this aspect that I accentuate in the pages that follow. In other words, analysis of the "cultural exception" in NAFTA and GATT suggests that we need not oppose rationalist explanations to social construction ones.[2] Nor need we assume that social construction explanations can only be introduced as a residual category to solve puzzles that rationalist explanations cannot. Instead, I argue that there is a complex relationship between identity and interests, and both are always in play to varying degrees.[3]

To develop this argument, this chapter proceeds in two parts. First, I briefly examine the role identity played in shaping the stance of the Canadian and European Union (EU) governments regarding culture industries during NAFTA and GATT talks respectively. In so doing, I distinguish three dimensions of identity that come into play in the trade disputes. Next, I show that these dimensions also contribute to the formation of U.S. trade policy toward culture industries. In particular, I contend that the various realms of American cultural policy—arts funding, broadcasting policy, entertainment industry exports—are largely consistent with each other. This convergence is not coincidental; rather it is reflective of "ideas, principles, and norms rooted in the nation's sense of self" (Ruggie 1998: 203).

Such a contention implies that U.S. policies governing these realms are not strictly the culmination of material interest calculations. Rather, these policies, including the stance on culture industries during NAFTA and GATT, are consistent with certain ideas, values, and beliefs prevailing in the United States about appropriate policy in this sector, ideas associated not only with efficient or profitable outcomes, but also with the discourses that reflect and (re)produce the American imagined community. In making this argument, I am not suggesting that we should look to identity *instead of* interests as the explanation of policy outcomes. I am suggesting that material interests often point to a desired outcome, but identity may help us understand the road a given government will take to produce that outcome. Furthermore, many interests are represented in a sector as diverse as the culture industries. That interests compatible with certain dominant identity narratives often prevail suggests a role for identity in trade policy formulation with regard to culture industries.

The fact that my starting point is a set of multilateral trade disputes might suggest that this inquiry has greater relevance for scholars of International Relations (IR) than for comparativists. However, the analysis proceeds in such a way as to situate it firmly in the realm of Constructivist Comparative Politics (CCP), as articulated by Daniel Green in the opening chapter of this volume. While I examine specific negotiating positions taken by the United States, Canada, and the EU in NAFTA and GATT, I do so in order to compare domestic policies, the differences in which became particularly salient in an international forum. In addition, I give sustained attention to American cultural policy, with implicit comparisons with Canadian and European cultural policies providing the context for that analysis.

What aspects of the inquiry take it beyond the realm of CP to CCP? First and foremost is attention to identity and its influence on policy formation. Indeed, my argument turns on the centrality of identity in illuminating national government choices about policy toward culture industries. Second is the effort to "transnationalize" the analysis by dropping the "internal/external barrier between state and international system" (Green, chapter 1 of this volume). Identity narratives shape cultural policy and, by extension, trade policy with regard to culture industries. In so doing, they influence the norms and practices of relevant international institutions, as well as the identities and practices of state counterparts. Furthermore, commitments to international agreements and institutions can place constraints on national governments that can, in turn, shape domestic identities and practices. Ignoring this dynamic would limit our understanding of the manner in which national policies evolve in response not only to developments at the domestic level, but also at the global level.

Part 1

The "Cultural Exception" in NAFTA and GATT:
Canada, France, and the EU

Twice in the last fifteen years, disagreement over the regulation of culture industries[4] has stalled major trade negotiations. During talks leading to the Canada-U.S. Free Trade Agreement[5] (CUSFTA), Canada demanded that film, television and radio broadcasting, periodical and book publishing, and video and sound recording be excluded from the treaty. Despite U.S. opposition, CUSFTA excepts the cultural sector, allowing Canada to continue support measures to domestic cultural producers. The North American Free Trade Agreement,[6] which expands CUSFTA to include Mexico, maintains the so-called cultural exception.

Similarly, in the closing days of Uruguay Round GATT[7] talks, negotiators encountered the road block of culture industries. This time, the EU, led by France, sought the cultural exception for the audiovisual industries, including television, film, and potentially, the internet. Once again, the United States provided strong opposition but, in order to meet the December 1993 U.S. Congressional deadline, the Uruguay Round closed with the audiovisual sector excluded, at least until subsequent World Trade Organization (WTO) talks reopen the question.[8]

The EU and Canada sought the exclusion of culture industries from the trade agreements not merely to protect jobs, as the American negotiators suggested, although this is certainly part of the story. They pursued the cultural exception strategy so as to safeguard the mechanism perceived to be fundamental to a democratic collectivity's ability both to reflect and to (re)constitute collective particularity. Although American officials described the Canadian and European stances as thinly veiled economic protectionism, it is apparent that many European and Canadian officials equate "national culture industries" with identity and "national consciousness" formation, and therefore with the continuity and distinctiveness of political community. This conceptualization of these industries and their potential role has particular relevance in the Canadian and EU contexts where national and supranational collective identity, respectively, are typically viewed as weak. In both Canada and the EU, cultivation of collective identity is linked to broader political goals of consolidating relatively loose federations and negotiating regional, cultural, linguistic, and economic heterogeneity.

Officials in Canada, Europe, and, increasingly, elsewhere, have repeatedly expressed the fear that if government measures designed to assist domestic culture industries are removed—as inclusion of this sector in trade agreements would require—goals associated with identity formation and collective particularity cannot be satisfactorily met. The overwhelming power of U.S. conglomerates would impoverish the domestic offerings because more marginal voices, many of which are presumed to be less profit-driven or profitable, yet valuable for the ideas they explore or the constituencies they engage, would not survive. The range of such voices seems to include broad conceptualizations such as "Canadian music" or "European programming" and narrower notions of "French-Canadian feminist literature" or French "auteur-style film making." While these categories are not unproblematic, efforts to protect them capture a resistance to potential cultural, political, and economic homogenization as well as to a loss of control over the ability to set the terms of national debates and to represent and (re)constitute national narratives in which the priorities and aspirations of a national community (often as defined or interpreted by elites) can be articulated and negotiated. If this cannot be achieved, there is a desire at least to create a space for domestic discourse to occur.

The cultural exception strategy, therefore, has the broader goal of negotiating the cultural implications of economic liberalization. Underlying these trade disputes are definitional struggles, often rendered in terms of stale dichotomous categories: What counts as a commodity to be governed by market forces? What counts as a cultural good, worthy of special protection? As I argue in my conclusion, the answers to these questions (as well as their formulation) may have far-reaching implications for the types of trade policy justifications validated by the emergent World Trade Organization in the culture industry sector specifically and in the services sector more generally.

Critics of the cultural exception strategy argue that identity is fluid and shifting, therefore the Canadian and European governments cannot realistically hope to preserve some already existing, simplistic definition of Canadian or European identity. Indeed, I would argue that it is precisely *because* identity is dynamic and always evolving in response to circumstances that governments endeavor to retain control over what is perceived to be a primary means of identity formation so as to be able to participate in the ongoing work of (re)constructing the (supra)nation and defining its identity. As Hopf (1998) notes, in addition to recognizing that states deploy discursive power, "[h]aving resources that allow oneself to deploy discursive power—the economic and military wherewithal to sustain institutions necessary for the formalized reproduction of social practices—is almost always part of the story as well" (1998:175). Culture industries count among these resources.

As such, this strategy is shot through with concerns about power in the Foucauldian sense. In recent decades, the idea that power is exercised through discourse has become synonymous with Michel Foucault. He contends that "the production of truth is thoroughly imbued with relations of power" (1978: 60) and that the processes of definition, naming, and meaning-making serve the interests of those who control them. Control over discourse is a formidable source of power and discourses must be construed as assets.

> Indeed, it is in discourse that power and knowledge are joined together. And for this very reason, we must conceive discourse as a series of discontinuous segments whose tactical function is neither uniform nor stable. To be more precise, we must not imagine a world of discourse divided between accepted discourse and excluded discourse, or between the dominant discourse and the dominated one; but as a multiplicity of discursive elements that can come into play in various strategies. It is this distribution that we must reconstruct, with the things said and those concealed, the enunciations required and those forbidden, that it comprises; with the variants and different effects—according to who is speaking, his position of power, the institutional context in which he happens to be situated—that it implies. . . . Discourse transmits and produces power; it reinforces it, but also undermines and exposes it, renders it fragile, makes it possible to thwart it. (1978:100–101)

Discursive power has the great advantage of shaping belief systems and patterns of behavior at a fundamental level, thus lessening the need for overtly coercive approaches. Those who exercise discursive power may be more difficult to identify than those who exercise more traditional forms of coercive power. Yet it is arguably the subtlety and pervasiveness of these networks of power that account for their potency.

The Foucauldian approach is innovative when compared to traditional understandings of power in IR and CP theory. These typically equate power with military capacity—armies and weapons arsenals—and economic capacity—size and efficiency of manufacturing sector, level of industrialization, and wealth. It is not surprising that explanations informed by this traditional understanding of power would conclude that the exclusion of culture industries from multilateral trade agreements is nothing more than economic protectionism. The Foucauldian perspective on power, however, opens up another explanation.

> By power, I do not mean "Power" as a group of institutions and mechanisms that ensure the subservience of the citizens of a given state. By power, I do not mean, either, a mode of subjugation which, in contrast to violence, has the form of the rule. Finally, I do not have in mind a general system of domination exerted by one group over another, a system whose effects, through successive derivations, pervade the entire social body. The analysis, made in terms of power, must not assume that the sovereignty of the state, the form of the law, or the over-all unity of a domination are given at the outset; rather, these are only the terminal forms power takes. (1978: 92)

Elsewhere, Foucault ("Truth and Power," 1984) elaborates on his understanding of power:

> [I]t seems to me now that the notion of repression is quite inadequate for capturing what is precisely the productive aspect of power. In defining the effects of power as repression, one adopts a purely juridical conception of such power; one identifies power with a law which says no; power is taken above all as carrying the force of a prohibition. Now I believe that this is a wholly negative, narrow, skeletal conception of power, one which has been curiously widespread. If power were never anything but repressive, if it never did anything but to say no, do you really think one would be brought to obey it? What makes power hold good, what makes it accepted, is simply the fact that it doesn't only weigh on us as a force that says no, but that it traverses and produces things, it induces pleasure, forms knowledge, produces discourse. (60–61)

The idea that discourse can be controlled is abstract. But operationalizing culture industries as one important medium through which discourse circulates shows European and Canadian efforts to avoid inundation by American cultural products to be founded on a recognition of the potent power of meaning-making inherent in culture industries. If a country can exert some control over culture industries as a productive power network, it is in a better position to define truths about collective identity, to accentuate a certain worldview or set of socioeconomic priorities, to influence the foci and terms of public debate, all of which have implications for, among other things, citizen formation and institutional legitimacy.

Of course, government officials favor certain shared meanings over others. Those espoused by mainstream American entertainment products, though often enjoyed by Canadian and European consumers, are not always favored by the governments. Canadian and European officials perceive American cultural products to be infused with American values and to portray American life. Ostensibly in opposition to comparable Canadian and European conceptions, American products cannot cultivate and reinforce the belief systems of other countries. Here it becomes clear that power is at stake in the exclusion of culture industries from GATT and NAFTA—the power to define identities so as to endow Canada, France, and the EU with recognizably distinct cultural and political attributes and the power to determine who gets to speak authoritatively about collective particularity.

How Identity Matters

The trade disputes over culture industries suggest that trade negotiations are yet another contemporary forum in which identity issues are being contested, and in which cultural strategies, instruments, and objectives are increasingly central. While cultural concerns may not play a *greater* role than commercial considerations in the formation of trade policy, ignoring cultural concerns limits our understanding of government choices. But this insight, in turn, opens up another line of questioning, specifically what is the relationship between identity and policy? Of late, the concepts of culture and identity have been invoked by scholars of Constructivist International Relations (CIR) with increasing regularity (Wendt 1994; Katzenstein 1996; Lapid and Kratochwil 1996). But there is no consensus on what these terms mean. Indeed, Canadian, French, and EU officials repeatedly invoked identity and culture to justify their policy position in the trade disputes over culture industries, but it is apparent that they attribute multiple meanings to these terms, meanings that are not mutually exclusive and that, more often than not, overlap. I argue that three dimensions of identity recur in the culture industry trade disputes—the normative, the instrumental, and the pluralist. I explore each below.

In identifying these three dimensions, I am arguing that when Canadian and European officials invoke identity, it can be construed as, in some ways, shorthand for any one or several of these elements, all of which move beyond the traditional notion of national cultural identity. It seems clear that more traditional renderings of identity in terms of ethnic nationalism do not capture the fullness of contemporary notions of identity. Analysis of the Canadian and European perspectives in the culture industry trade disputes provides a window on at least some elements of identity that are influencing world politics, including such things as the means of identity formation, socio-economic and political distinctiveness, and policy legacies.

The fact that the term "identity" can mean so many things is a cause for concern for Brubaker and Cooper (2000), who argue that the term has lost its precision. I persist in using it here because other possible terms would be incomplete. For example, we could certainly carry on our discussion of the cultural exception in terms of principles, norms, practices, ideas, legitimating discourses, organizing or animating principles, and dominant or master narratives. But, as I hope will be apparent below, while these are highly relevant and do figure into my analysis, no one of these terms captures the multiple aspects that Canadian and EU officials invoke when they speak of identity. They are, instead, I believe, components of identity.

The Normative Parameter Dimension

Every country has a unique historical experience that shapes the parameters of political debate and creates policy legacies and patterns. Policy makers do not start with a clean slate; instead, they function within a normative environment in which certain approaches are favored. This contention does not presume consensus among policy makers. Nor does it deny any explicit intentionality, conscious choice, or protection of interests on the part of policy makers. Nevertheless, not all policies are entertained as viable options. Certainly, some policies are ruled out because they are costly or inefficient. But some are ruled out because they contradict assumptions about "how we do things," where "we" can be a national community. Norms are periodically contravened. They evolve in response to historical events, and the prevailing normative environment is one of many factors affecting policy outcomes. Still, we can identify certain normative assumptions that guide policy makers.

In his discussion of the French developmental state, Loriaux (1999) argues that state elites "pursu[e] moral goods whose definition is informed by a certain mythological construction of how the world works and what we can and should accomplish in it" (1999: 253). He goes on to clarify his use of the term "mythological":

> I use it in the everyday sense to denote a conceptual construction of "the world" that may not be entirely accurate but that nevertheless has wide-

spread appeal and influence. It might be thought of as a commonly accepted "misrepresentation." As a commonly accepted misrepresentation,
the myth in social life nourishes routines and habits of thought and action,
just as myths in religious life nourish rituals. Those routines can become so
ingrained in social relations that people lose the urge or even the tempta-
tion to question the myths that legitimate and justify them. (1999: 253)

This argument implies, among other things, that comparison of policy
choices across two or more countries requires much more than identification
of economic interests. Even policy makers embracing the same economic
assumptions may arrive at very different policy choices because these assumptions are filtered through a different set of "myths, rules, and norms
that inform human action" (1999: 252). In addition, this argument recognizes the pursuit of "moral goods," "valued simply because they correspond
to a customary good or social norm that has been constructed historically
within a particular society" (1999: 252).

Loriaux's work on policy makers that have been socialized into a certain
normative framework, in which a set of historically constructed myths "generate and justify routines (secular "rituals") that embed themselves in discursive habits and institutional procedures" (1999: 254), suggests that identity
limits and structures the range of policy choices. I do not take this to mean
that there is an inherently French way of doing things. Instead, such an analysis
suggests that there is a range of policies and approaches that has been favored in France due to such things as its historical development, resource
endowments, and institutional structures. (These policies may, in turn, reinforce these institutional structures). As a result, a certain type of state involvement, for example, has come to be associated with France. This is not
an inevitable or unchanging feature of French political life. But there are
patterns across time and resistance to efforts to alter them.

Therefore, when Canadian or French officials object to the inclusion of
culture industries in the major trade agreements because such a step compromises identity, in part they are objecting to what would amount to a fairly
radical change in the nature and extent of the role the state could play in
cultural life. This includes the threat this would pose to the public broadcasting system in their respective countries and to the cultivation of art house
cinema, especially valued in France. Such a change would have the effect of
inverting what is considered necessary (or possible or desirable) policy and
what is considered unthinkable.[9] To date, state subsidies to the film industry,
for example, are both desirable and possible in the Canadian and European
contexts, although these take various forms. If culture industries were to be
incorporated into the NAFTA and GATT regimes, these policies would be

rendered unthinkable, and not due to a natural progression in policy. Recognizing that resistance to these sorts of abrupt and externally imposed changes can arise from this normative dimension of identity does not deny the economic aspects of the industry in question. Rather, it confirms that there are normative and ideological parameters within which economic interests are pursued.

The Instrumental Dimension

The instrumental dimension of identity presumes that culture industries are carriers of meaning whose value lies not only, or even primarily, in their capacity to make a profit and to entertain. The Canadian and EU position in the trade negotiations sprang, in part, from the assumption that culture industries can play a central role in the construction of political community by providing a forum in which the repertoire of signs, traditions, values, myths, and intersubjective understandings that make up collective identity can be transmitted and debated. Culture industries can, therefore, (re)produce, perpetuate, and/or destabilize certain notions that may influence such things as citizenship formation and institutional legitimacy. There may be an excessive dependence upon culture industries to fulfill this role, which I would argue stems from the imperatives to which contemporary democratic and multicultural entities must conform.

In the past, identity has been fostered in other ways. France provides an interesting model of state effectiveness in creating a national collective identity by using instruments other than culture industries. Weber (1976) asserts, for example, that in the nineteenth century the army became "the school of the fatherland" teaching, among other things, "what it meant to be a French citizen"(1976: 298). The French school system also played an important socializing role. Instructors taught only in French, prohibiting the use of regional languages.

> Teaching French, "our beautiful and noble mother tongue," asserted Ferdinand Buisson, the leading light of Republican education in the 1880's, "is the chief work of the elementary school—a labor of patriotic character." (1976: 311)

The state set national curriculum standards for various subjects in order to cultivate a love of France that would replace regional loyalties. In particular, Weber contends that "[t]here were no better instruments of indoctrination and patriotic conditioning than French history and geography" (1976: 333). Rosanvallon (1990: 108) concurs, noting the following:

> While the goal of teaching is to enlighten the populace and prepare them
> for employment, education also has a directly political intention, that of
> making a disparate mass of individuals into one nation. From Condorcet to
> Jules Ferry and from Mirabeau to Ferdinand Buisson, the same trend has
> been present in all efforts to reform education, that is, the persistent desire to
> create "citizens," meaning individuals prepared for communal living and
> aware of the community in which they are destined to lead their lives. In this
> context it is far easier to understand the origins of this attachment to the
> principle of the public monopoly over education. (Author's translation)[10]

The French state also worked to produce a nation of Frenchmen by dividing French territory into centrally administered departments, imposing a national system of weights and measures, and establishing national holidays.

Much as the French experience suggests that the prospects for identity
formation need not be bleak simply because Americans dominate culture
industries, adopting the past strategies of the French state seems unlikely for
reasons both logistical and philosophical. Obviously, the EU faces great resistance to efforts to designate a "European" language, mostly because this
would, in all probability, be English. Furthermore, the Education Ministers
of the member states are showing no signs of harmonizing curriculum so as
to teach "European history" or "European literature."

Canada faces many of the same obstacles. The country is officially bilingual and any effort to impose English on the population would surely cause
Quebec to secede. In fact, both the federal and provincial governments have
shown a willingness to move in the opposite direction, embracing French as
one of two official languages in 1968. In addition, harmonizing curriculum
is difficult in Canada because the constitution gives jurisdiction over the
education system to the provinces. Neither Canada nor Europe could rely on
the military. Obviously, there is no European army yet. Moreover, in order
for the military to serve identity formation goals in the way the French army
has, mandatory service would be required and the Canadian forces have shown
no inclination to introduce this.

In addition to the fact that these alternative strategies are not viable for
these logistical reasons, emulating the French example of nation-building is
unacceptable on a philosophical and political level. In the current period,
diversity is celebrated. There is heightened awareness of the rights of minority groups. In Canada, multiculturalism is official federal policy, and the
rights of ethnic and other groups are protected by the Charter of Rights and
Freedoms of the Canadian Constitution and by the Multiculturalism Act of
1988. The principles enshrined in these documents are wholly incompatible
with the type of nation-building project mounted by the French state in

previous centuries. Although the EU has no similar documents, the very fact that it is essentially a collection of disparate cultures suggests that it can only be multicultural in nature. Therefore, the governments look to culture industries, spurred by a belief that the media is one of the most potent socializing agents available today, with the potential to have a significant effect on the thinking and behavior of citizens. Partly this taps into Anderson's (1991) argument that these provide shared referents and sources. But this also concerns the content of cultural products and here is where one must question the degree to which this strategy will be effective in the long term.

Ideally, for the purposes of identity formation, cultural products could be infused with certain values by privileging certain stories, themes, or character profiles. But democratic governments can influence the content of a text only in indirect ways. They rely on their citizens to privilege certain perspectives, defining a Canadian or a European good in terms of whether nationals participate in the production process in certain key capacities, but there is no guarantee that this will translate into a work that will contribute to the formation of a certain identity. In part this has to do with the fact that there is no consensus on what a "Canadian film" or a "European novel" is.[11] This has always been difficult to determine because artists are often influenced by their counterparts in other countries.[12] This is increasingly challenging as coproductions and cross-national mergers of culture industry companies become more common.

Even if we could agree on how to define a national cultural product, other issues remain. For example, as Shapiro (2000) argues in his analysis of "world music," cultural products are as likely to disrupt prevailing systems of belief as they are to reinforce them. Furthermore, Feigenbaum (2000) contends that technological innovation, such as satellite transmission and digital compression of programming, as well as electronic transmission of periodical and book text, will render ineffective the measures currently in place to protect and promote domestic cultural products.

Finally, that culture industries play a socializing role is widely accepted, but the nature and extent of this role is at issue. In particular, many question the apparent assumption that a spectator passively receives and internalizes the message(s) of a cultural product. Rejecting the model of the passive spectator ripe for manipulation by savvy producers of cultural products, the Centre for Contemporary Cultural Studies at the University of Birmingham introduced in recent decades an alternative model of a spectator finding meanings that differ from, even repudiate, the one intended by the producer of the text. A film, television program, or novel may (intentionally or inadvertently) attempt to "position" or "inscribe" the receiver. But the receiver need not accept this. At the very least, the possibility of subjective interpretations by audiences must be acknowledged if only because "subjects have histories" (Morley 1980: 166).

> At the moment of textual encounter other discourses are always in play besides those of the particular text in focus—discourses which depend on other discursive formations, brought into play through "the subject's" placing in other practices—cultural, educational, institutional. And these other discourses will set some of the terms in which any particular text is engaged and evaluated. (Morley 1980: 163)

From this perspective, the spectator becomes an active participant, negotiating, even *producing*, the meaning of a given cultural product. Therefore, meaning-making is not confined to the creative process that produces a film or a sound recording. The audience itself participates in the process of meaning-making by receiving the message(s) of the work according to his/her own interpretive tool kit. While a cultural product *may* constitute a viewer/listener/reader, how and to what extent it does so depends, in part, on the receiver.

This body of research certainly calls into question the effectiveness of the cultural exception strategy. Nonetheless, the risk involved in relying on culture industries for identity formation does not obviate the influence on culture industry trade policy of officials' beliefs that it *can* achieve this.

The Pluralist Dimension

The third dimension of identity that is invoked by the Canadians, French, and Europeans in debates about the cultural exception essentially amounts to an effort to preserve a space for domestic discourse. It also captures a desire to promote local culture industries as an emblem of a vibrant cultural community and as a source of a variety of cultural forms. This differs from the instrumental dimension in that there is not a particular set of values or symbols to be reinforced or (re)created. Instead, there is a desire for local voices to be heard, regardless of what they might say, because there is ostensibly an inherent democratic right for members of a national community to participate in the national (and global) conversation via culture industries. Here, the French, the Canadians, and the EU all bemoan the monopoly that the United States has on television programming and film distribution and exhibition in particular, but also in sound recording and periodical and book publishing. The critique, and thus the invocation of identity concerns as a defense, hinges on the notion that only a narrow range of ideas and creative works manages to circulate in industries shot through with commercial philosophy or Hollywood criteria. This perspective is implicit in the statements by French directors who lament the loss of non-Hollywood-style films, even if they themselves experiment with Hollywood approaches. Similarly, Canadian publishers who regret the loss of diversity in publishing as marginal groups who may not capture a broad market fall from the book list in commercial publishing houses also start from this pluralist assumption.

What I have called the normative parameter, the instrumental, and the pluralist dimensions are the three facets of identity that arise in the disputes over culture industry trade policy involving the European Union, the United States, and Canada. These three dimensions do not constitute an exhaustive list of the possible aspects of identity that might come to the fore in all circumstances. This paper has the modest goal of illuminating how identity functions in a particular debate. Only further research can confirm whether these three dimensions are salient for other actors in this sector. In addition, analysis of other sectors will, in all likelihood, identify other dimensions of identity that do not surface in the culture industry disputes.

Part 2

Fighting the "Cultural Exception": the United States

Identity concerns specifically, and nonmaterial concerns more generally, animate Canadian and EU trade policy formation with regard to culture industries. Commercial interests are, of course, also in play here, but consideration of them alone does not give us a full understanding of the cultural exception strategy pursued by Canada and the EU in world trading regime negotiations. If identity influences culture industry trade policy formation in Canada and Europe, what role does it play in the United States? Is it possible that Canadians and Europeans are driven by a combination of cultural and economic goals, while Americans are propelled solely by economic interests? I suspect not, although the nature and extent of the role of identity may be different.

Above I delineated three dimensions of identity that come into play in Canadian, French, and EU culture industry trade policy formation. These dimensions do not manifest themselves identically in the policies of each actor. For example, the normative parameter dimension is particularly relevant for Canadian and French governments because there is a long history of public sector cultural activity. EU policy in this area, however, dates to the early 1980s. There has been little time to establish "European" policy patterns beyond what is advocated in the member states. Therefore, the normative parameter dimension comes into play to a lesser degree, although it is still lurking because there is a sense of a "European" approach to cultural policy making that may not be identical across all the EU member states. Nevertheless, the policies they do each embrace tend to resemble each other much more than they resemble that of the United States.

The instrumental dimension, on the other hand, has enormous relevance for the European Union and Canada, but less for France. The EU has identified audiovisual industry policy as a means to cultivating European identity or consciousness, and thus to moving European integration beyond the realm of economics to sociopolitical unification. Development of European defense, foreign, or social policy must be grounded in a profound commitment to Europe rather than (sometimes selective) participation in European agreements and institutions. This commitment, so the argument goes, must not rest solely with elites or decision makers, but extend to the citizens of the member states.

In Canada, a similar strategy is deployed in an effort to elicit some support for a Canadian imagined community amongst citizens who might otherwise be inclined to identify first with their region (Westerners versus Maritimers, for example) or with their ethnic heritage (Aboriginal peoples, French-speaking Quebecois, unassimilated, first-generation immigrants, and so forth). While the instrumental dimension is not irrelevant to the French policy, it comes into play less at the domestic level because cultivating French identity is not the central political project that it is in the European Union or Canada. American dominance of audiovisual industries might be construed as a greater threat to French *film* culture and identity than it is to French identity generally. Nonetheless, many in France do bemoan the representation of certain values in American cultural products that do not reflect those generally embraced by French citizens. It is important to note that the instrumental dimension is particularly relevant to the culture industry sector. While there are other sectors where this dimension of identity is significant, its influence may be less broadly applicable across sectors than other aspects of identity.

The pluralist dimension of identity is important for the Canadian, French, and EU governments. All three profess a desire to preserve a space for a variety of minority voices and cultural forms. Therefore, in positing that identity influences culture industry trade policy formulation in the United States, I do not suggest that the mix of material and nonmaterial factors is the same as it is in Canada or the EU or elsewhere. Nevertheless, I would argue that the normative parameter dimension in particular, and the instrumental and pluralist dimensions to a lesser degree, shape U.S. policy in this sector.

The United States took the stance of wanting to open up international markets to American products in both NAFTA and GATT negotiations. This is not surprising, given the commercial success that U.S. culture industries enjoy and the general orientation of U.S. trade policy in the post–World War II period. Trade negotiations are, after all, first and foremost about economics and it is easy to assume that the American approach to culture industries—and to their regulation in trade agreements—emanates strictly from their commercial value. Indeed, these industries are big business in the United States. Hollywood is held up as the consummate example of how to generate enormous sums of money through the production, distribution, and exhibition of film and television programs. Not only is Hollywood lucrative in the United States, but entertainment industries rival the aerospace industry as the top U.S. export. Hollywood has discovered that its products sell outside of American borders also and, therefore, resists any efforts by foreign governments or artists that may be perceived as restricting the sale of U.S. entertainment products abroad. The United States does not dominate the recording or magazine and book publishing industries to the same extent, although Canada is treated as an extension of the U.S. market in these industries.

It is not surprising, then, that U.S. negotiators would emphasize the commercial value of American entertainment industries during GATT and NAFTA talks. Because these industries are so lucrative, it is assumed that the American government seeks open trade in this sector to reap the profits that market dominance can bring. But just as an economistic understanding of the European and Canadian cultural exception strategy is incomplete, so is a strictly economistic explanation of American opposition to it. As much as culture industries are highly successful commercial undertakings for Americans, we must move away from economics in order to understand why many American officials *deny the very validity* of the cultural exception strategy. The majority of American culture industry policy makers function in a normative environment that, despite the commercial value of culture industries, does not favor the sorts of communications policies embraced by France, Canada, and the EU. In other words, even though American officials commonly justify their culture industry policy in economic terms, I argue that specific "myths and moral ambitions" also inform the actions of American policy makers.

Because culture industries have great economic importance for the United States, there is reluctance to acknowledge a role for identity in the formation of U.S. trade policy toward this sector. This is especially true if one conceives of identity in traditional, ethno-nationalist terms. Given this, U.S. trade policy in this sector provides a particularly good opportunity to think about identity's role. Therefore, I test the typology of identity dimensions derived from the Canadian and European cases against the American case, knowing that finding identity to be influential in a case for which we ostensibly have an economic explanation would be compelling evidence that identity is not merely a residual factor to be considered only when economic explanations fail.

The Culture of American Cultural Policy

Each country conceives of the value of the arts and culture in different terms. These differences may be small in some cases and larger in others, and no approach is necessarily better than another. Nevertheless, the differences are always significant because they set the boundaries for cultural policy and influence the relationship between government and the arts community. Included here are definitions of cultural and commercial endeavors, conceptualizations of the spectator as citizen or consumer, perceptions about the role of private and public broadcasting, ideas about the state and its role, all of which can be tied to broader notions of sociopolitical and economic practice. Cultural policy in any country is grounded in historical experience and ideological predisposition.

The United States, Canada, and the members of the EU are often grouped together as similar societies with convergent interests. They are affluent Western democracies with highly industrialized, capitalist economies. Yet despite all that these countries have in common, the notion of culture industries that prevails in the United States is fundamentally different from that of the proponents of the cultural exception. These industries are first and foremost a business in the United States, and a very lucrative one at that.

It is even awkward to use the term "culture industry" in discussing the United States. This term surfaces in American academic circles, but in everyday discourse, it is much more common to speak of "entertainment industries" or "show business." This terminological distinction is instructive, if only anecdotally. Americans employ a term that captures a very specific component of what culture industries can do. To entertain is to amuse, to divert, to hold someone's attention in a pleasant way. To entertain does not mean to educate, to inform, or to cultivate identity; however, these may indeed result from an entertaining experience. Speaking of "entertainment industries" rather than "culture industries" removes a certain sociological imperative. Entertainment industries are not expected to fulfill a sociopolitical purpose in the same way that culture industries are. As a result, it is much less controversial when they are commodified and valued for their commercial contribution. There is also a tendency to conceptualize the receiver—reader/listener/viewer—narrowly as "a consumer" rather than more broadly as "a citizen" of a given country and to evaluate the impact of the industries accordingly (Brown 1991). At the international level, it is then much easier to categorize the regulation of these industries as nothing more than a trade issue.

In recent years, Jack Valenti, the president and CEO of the Motion Picture Arts Association (MPAA) and one of the leading American spokespersons fighting the cultural exception, has used the expressions "intellectual property creative industries"[13] and "copyright industries."[14] These concepts capture other aspects of the sector, but they still do not evoke the values, beliefs, and identities with which Europeans and Canadians see culture industries to be infused.

Canada and the EU sought to exclude culture industries from NAFTA and GATT because of the supposed contribution that they can make to identity formation. In both cases, officials repeatedly invoked the potential threat to identity and cultural particularity posed by American dominance of culture industries. In addition, the circumstances surrounding the Canadian and European industries and policy choices support this explanation rather than an interpretation in which the cultural explanation only cloaks a protectionist economic agenda. Nevertheless, despite evidence to the contrary, many American commentators persisted in embracing the latter explanation. Former governor Pete Wilson of California provides just one example of such a perspective with the following statement: "We are concerned with some of the areas we see remaining for California products in Canada. Canada's claim of cultural sovereignty frankly strikes me as little more than thinly disguised protectionism."[15]

The majority of Americans involved in the trade disputes seemed to be talking past the Canadian and European negotiators, never fully comprehending the rationale for the cultural exception strategy. I argue that this philosophical impasse stems from the fact that American, Canadian, and European policy makers are products of very different normative environments such that certain arguments literally do not "make sense" within the context of specific norms, rules, and beliefs embraced in the respective national communities. Periodically, the extent of the incomprehension reached ridiculous levels. For example, in 1991, the U.S. trade representative, Carla Hills, infuriated Canadians when she tried to soothe fears about NAFTA by assuring that Canada could still have "fairs . . . and that sort of thing" (quoted in Wilson 1996: 20). But, in general, the respective positions appear to be grounded in clear normative and ideological commitments that resonate with core principles upon which conceptions of the American identity have been constructed.

Prominent among the arguments American representatives used to protest exclusion of culture industries from the trade agreements is one grounded in a commitment to the principles of free enterprise. For example, during NAFTA negotiations, Hills argued:

Our consumers should not be deprived of the broadest range of choice and lowest possible price in important areas like books, films and documentaries. These choices should be left open to the market.[16]

During GATT talks, President and CEO of the Motion Pictures Arts Association, Jack Valenti, echoed Hills's sentiments.

The quotas are an artificial barrier in the market place which is authorised by governments. No government should be allowed to force an Englishman, or a Scot or a Frenchman or Spaniard, to watch something on television that he doesn't want to see.

Shortly after the conclusion of GATT talks, U.S. Trade Representative Mickey Kantor reported on GATT negotiations to the U.S. Congress.

There is nothing more pernicious than trying to tell people what to watch and what to hear. Nothing is more devastating to our entertainment industry, which is dominant, frankly, in the world, which has a major trade surplus, as you know, than this growing, I think, trade cancer, that in the guise of cultural—protection of cultural heritage or cultural—they call it specificity, these protective measures which would lock out our films, our television programming and our music.[17]

During 1989 debates over the proposed European "Television without Frontiers" quota arrangement, the president of Walt Disney Studios Richard Frank was quoted as saying:

He asked rhetorically why more American films were shown on Italian and German television than on French television; the answer, he said, is that the French have quotas. "It's simply that Italian and German television markets are essentially free and open, with decisions being based on what people *want* to see and not on what self-appointed 'guardians of culture' *think they should* see." (emphasis in original, quoted in Brown 1991: 3)

Former vice president of the Motion Picture Export Association, William Nix, testifying before the House of Representatives, invoked the same sort of ideological reproach of the Canadian position on culture industries during U.S.-Canada Free Trade talks.

[I]n too many countries there are governmental regulations which actually conspire against American films freely entering the marketplace. . . . Even Canada, our neighborly friend to the north, tries to frustrate both new market entry and existing footholds in their market. Trade barriers take the cloak of cultural sovereignty there and in too many other places as well . . . all the American film industry wants is the chance to compete fairly and freely with all other movies from all other nations.[18]

Hills, Valenti, and the others all protest the exclusion of culture industries in similar terms. Specifically, they object to the apparent interference with the market that accompanies such a policy. Underlying their remarks are beliefs in limited government, in the wisdom of consumer choice, and in commitment to the free flow of information and to a specific conception of authors' rights, as well as a belief that government involvement in the cultural sector smacks of censorship, all of which resonate with the dominant principles and narratives around which American identity has been constituted.

Ostensibly, the founding myths of American identity are unique because they do not emphasize shared ethnic heritage or ancestry. Instead, they are grounded in a set of political values that can transcend the ethnic, religious, and racial origins of the United States' immigrant population (Huntington 1981).

> Almost everyone agrees that the United States was conceived in terms of certain political ideals and inspired by the promise or dream of liberty and equality. These political ideals are central to the American national identity and have played a critical role in shaping American political evolution and development. . . . (Huntington 1981: 10)

Campbell (1993) arrives at similar conclusions about the American imaginary.

> If all states are imagined communities, then America is the imagined community par excellence. For there never has been a country called "America," nor a people known as "Americans" from whom a national identity is drawn. There is a United States of America, and there are many who declare themselves to be "Americans" (though the U.S. census form does not list "American" as an ethnic option), but "America" only exists by virtue of people coming to live in a particular place. The histories of Americans are located in places other than the one in which they live, such that "the flag and the Pledge are, as it were, all we have." (1993: 48)

Ruggie (1998), too, notes:

> [M]ost nations claim an 'organic' basis in either land or people, and these are the usual referents of a nation's foundational myths. The American form of nationalism, in contrast, has no such organic basis. . . . American

> nationalism, then, is a civic nationalism embodying a set of inclusive core values: intrinsic individual as opposed to group rights, equality of opportunity for all, anti-statism, the rule of law, and a revolutionary legacy which holds that human betterment can be achieved by means of deliberate human actions, especially when they are pursued in accordance with these foundational values. Being an American is defined as believing and doing these things. (1998: 218)

The manner in which the American identity is imagined, then, owes its political nature to the country's unique historical experience. It is unnecessary to rehearse the circumstances under which the United States was founded. The story of the colonists' flight from England to protest "taxation without representation" and constraints on religious practice, among other things, is well known. In addition, few would deny that American political institutions owe their nature to a desire on the part of the founders to avoid the abuses of the eighteenth-century English feudal monarchy. A strong central authority in England led American founders to embrace the democratic ideal of power residing with the people and to demonstrate a general antigovernment attitude that remains pervasive in the United States. The presence of a privileged aristocracy in England led Americans to extol the virtues of egalitarianism.

> In what was truly a novel event in world history, Americans did not assert their independence because their ethnicity, language, culture, or religion differentiated them from their British brethren. The United States came into existence at a particular moment in time—July 4, 1776—and it was the product of a conscious political act based on explicit political principles. "We hold these truths to be self-evident," says the Declaration. Who holds these truths? Americans hold these truths. Who are Americans? People who adhere to these truths. National identity and political principle were inseparable. (Huntington 1981: 24)

Inspired by Enlightenment thinkers like John Locke, the founders sought to honor the individual by limiting constraints on her behavior, while protecting basic rights. In one particularly famous formulation, Louis Hartz (1955) asserts that "the American community is a liberal community" (3), characterized by "national acceptance of the Lockean creed" (9). Many others have offered similar definitions of the "American Creed."[19]

> What are the values of the American Creed? Innumerable studies have itemized them in various ways, but the same core political values appear in virtually all analyses: liberty, equality, individualism, democracy, and the rule of law under a constitution. (Huntington 1981: 14)

Lipset (1986) expands on this definition:

> With respect to the United States, the emphases on individualism and achievement orientation by the American colonists were an important motivating force in the launching of the American Revolution, and were embodied in the Declaration of Independence. The manifestation of such attitudes in this historic event and their crystallization in an historic document provided a basis for the reinforcement and encouragement of these orientations throughout subsequent American history. Thus, the United States remained throughout the nineteenth and early twentieth centuries the extreme example of classically liberal or Lockean society which rejected the assumptions of the alliance of throne and altar, of ascriptive elitism, of mercantilism, of *noblesse oblige*, of communitarianism. (1986: 114)

In the 1970s and 1980s, McClosky and Zaller (1984) conducted a series of national surveys in order to learn about "traditional American values." They conclude that "[t]wo major traditions of belief, capitalism and democracy, have dominated the life of the American nation from its inception" (1984: 1).

> In part because of their common origins, the two traditions share many values, foremost among them a commitment to freedom and individualism, limited government, equality before the law, and rational—as opposed to feudal or merely traditional—modes of decision-making. (1984: 2)

The liberal strand of the American identity narrative has been specified with greater precision as the country has developed. The commitment to egalitarianism, for example, means equality of opportunity and not equality of outcome. In theory, all Americans start with the same rights and privileges, but self-made individuals may enjoy varying degrees of success.

> Like their forebears, contemporary Americans believe that a person's success in life should depend on his own efforts and abilities rather than on his social standing at birth. (McClosky and Zaller 1984: 94)

This identity narrative has both political and economic components. In the economic sphere, the core American values lead to a commitment to free enterprise and consumer choice.

> A passion for "choice" may, in fact, be the central thrust and value of the society. It is the active mode of freedom, and assumes not only an absence of political or economic restraint, but an opportunity to select from a rich

> menu of possibilities. At its most trivial, the culture indulges this value in
> the proliferation of an endless and often meaningless variety of consumer
> options. . . . At a deeper level there is, in the love of choice, a memory of
> the chance to escape the dead end of lives in ancestral cultures and to cre-
> ate in a New World the life one chooses to live. (Pachter 1995: 30)

The economic and political elements overlap and intermingle. As a result,
the American conception of democracy includes a notion not only of *political* leveling, but also of equal access to the free market. However, this access
does not presume socioeconomic equality as an outcome.

In the political sphere, a commitment to the free flow of information and
to the fierce protection of first amendment rights, as well as a fear that government involvement in the media might lead to censorship, all emerged
from the liberal strand of the American identity narrative. Indeed, McClosky
and Zaller (1984) argue that the values underpinning the American imagined
community establish a normative environment within which Americans operate and set the parameters for political activity.

> Thus capitalism and democracy have always commanded broad support as
> the authoritative values of the nation's political culture. They determine in
> large measure what kinds of arguments about public affairs Americans find
> fair, reasonable, and attractive, what kinds they do not, and hence what
> kinds of arguments one dares to make (or is better advised not to make).
> (1984: 4)

The liberal strand is not the only element of the American identity narrative. Indeed, debate continues over the degree to which it informs—or should
inform—the American foundational myth. In particular, communitarians have
provided one important response to and critique of the supposed pervasiveness of Lockean liberalism in the American imaginary. In choosing to focus
on the liberal strand in the American identity narrative, I am not suggesting it
forms the basis of a homogeneous notion of American-ness. I am suggesting, however, that it has been a dominant strand, and one that is particularly
resonant in official discussions and justifications of U.S. trade policy toward
culture industries. Insomuch as officials in this realm mobilize elements of
the American identity narrative to justify their position, they consistently
rely on the liberal strand to do so.

Perhaps surprisingly, there is some similarity between the American and
the Canadian identity narratives. In both countries, a commitment to certain
political practices is espoused, the Canadian more sociopolitical, the American politicoeconomic. Nonetheless, both move away from ethnicity. Canada
accepts ethnic diversity and encourages it, even in the public sphere. The

United States accepts ethnic diversity also, but mostly in the private sphere. In the public sphere, it encourages assimilation and the embrace of American core values.

Of course, the Canadian and American identity narratives are very different in the role that alterity plays in their construction. A Canadian identity would not exist without an "other"—the American—from which to distinguish itself. The Canadian "other" is the citizen of another country. The American is conceptualized as self-referential. It is defined not against citizens of other countries, but against the pure theoretical forms of the ideas on which American identity discourse is based. It is this element of the American narratives that allows "Communism" to be identified as the "other," and to sometimes find "the other" lurking *within* American borders. Campbell (1993) goes so far as to argue that American identity is not only ideological in nature, but even ethical, in some cases covering "all the conceivable filaments of the desired American nation: religion, family, sexuality, gender, law and order, civilization, morality, and economic relations" (1993: 55).

Although we can identify a set of core American values, they need not map neatly onto the everyday reality of life in the United States. They are a social construction of a mythological way of life. As Ruggie (1998) asserts, what is being described is "a dominant belief system—America's foundational myth—not an empirical reality that has held equally well for all Americans at all times" (268, fn 17). The mythological dimension need not diminish the importance of the set of beliefs. All identities are, in some way, mythological, conveniently forgetting some attributes and national historical events, while embellishing others. Still, as narratives that touch on such things as the "proper" relationship between business and the state or the "proper" role of the state in cultural life, they provide guidelines and benchmarks against which policy choices can be evaluated and precepts with which policy must resonate.

American entertainment industry trade policy is not the only realm of cultural policy that echoes the values and principles animating American identity narratives. Policy in two other areas—arts funding and broadcasting—are conceived in the same discursive terms.

Arts Funding in the United States

American cultural policy differs markedly from the European tradition.[20] Mankin (1982) characterizes the United States as "a climate where art appreciation is not a widespread social value" and goes on to say that "support for the arts does not seem to flow naturally from our people" (1982: 111). Schuster echoes this position, noting that the "United States . . . has no nationally articulated 'cultural policy.' The emphasis is, instead, on a policy *in support of* the arts" (Schuster 1985: 5). This does not mean that the arts go without support in the United States; they do not. But, a different perception of cultural policy has consequences for the nature and extent of that support.

Perhaps most striking in comparing the United States with Europe is the differing role of the state in arts funding.

> Public patronage and public arts agencies have played a highly circum-scribed role in the nation's culture. . . . The United States has eschewed the idea of establishing an official culture in which the state would act as the sole or even the most influential patron of the arts. The government has seen itself as a minority stockholder in the nation's culture. (Mulcahy 1987: 312)

In Europe and Canada, the state takes the lead to varying degrees and private actors play a much less substantial role.

Public support is a relatively recent phenomenon in the United States. Many point to the Works Projects Administration (WPA, later renamed Works *Progress* Administration)[21] of the New Deal era as the first federal experiment with direct involvement in the arts. This initiative included programs in writing, theater, painting, and music. For example, the Writer's Project commissioned authors to write state travel guides. Other aspects of the WPA, like the Music and Theater Projects, contributed more to the development of the arts at the time by subsidizing artistic works. But analysts of this program are quick to point out that, despite its successes, "[t]he President and Harry Hopkins (the Administrator of the WPA) envisioned the program to be primarily one of economic relief with secondary emphasis on artistic competence and achievement" (Mankin 1982: 121). Therefore, the National Endowment for the Arts (NEA), established in 1965, is the first permanent federal body intended to support cultural programs.

The NEA differs from its counterparts in other Western countries in many ways.

> The NEA has not functioned as a national "ministry of culture"—that is, a Cabinet-level department responsible for comprehensive cultural policy-making and for administering the nation's artistic activities—but has promoted arts in strictly limited ways. (Mulcahy 1987: 312)

The NEA funds fewer areas than similar federal bodies (Schuster 1985: 7) and the type of funding it provides reflects an inclination for short-term commitments.

> The predominant form of support in all the countries [in the study], except the United States, is the direct budget allocation for ongoing support to institutions. . . . The predominant mode of subsidy in the United States, on the other hand, is still the project grant. . . . (Schuster 1985: 36–37)[22]

Alternative forms of direct government support commonly found outside the United States include subsidies for operating expenses, capital investments in facilities, advances against receipts, and loans.

In addition to funds awarded by the NEA, the federal government in the United States provides tax incentives for private contributions. In fact, indirect support in the form of foregone taxes provides more than three times the level of direct public support (Schuster 1985: 44).

> "Tax expenditures," taxes foregone by governments through various tax provisions—particularly those that provide incentives for charitable contributions, are the most important source of public support for the arts in the United States. . . . Tax expenditures are of only marginal financial importance in the other countries [in the study]. [T]his difference seems to have less to do with the existence of tax incentives for charitable contributions (the most important tax expenditure for the arts) than with the historic evolution of the relationship between the public and private sectors in each country. (Schuster 1985: 9 and 44)

Tax expenditures are present in the British and Canadian systems, but, in general, tax incentives play a relatively marginal role (compared to public contribution) outside of the United States. Indeed, the "American model" of arts funding has come to be identified with a "heavy reliance on and encouragement of private sources of funding" (Schuster 1985: 48), including individual, corporate, and foundation giving. While the dollar values may no longer be representative, Schuster's calculation of the proportion of direct versus indirect support in the United States, France, and Canada is instructive. He presents data showing a per capita public expenditure of thirty-two dollars in both Canada and France in the early 1980s. At the same time, the per capita public contribution in the United States, *including tax expenditure*, was thirteen dollars, and only three dollars if forgone taxes are removed leaving only direct government support. Yet addition of private support in the United States brings the per capita expenditure to twenty-three dollars, while the figures for France and Canada do not change appreciably (Schuster 1985: 45–47).

Various scholars of cultural policy have noted that the system of arts patronage in the United States is a product of its historical experience and of the normative environment that has arisen from it. For example, Levy (1997) asserts that "French *Academie*-type centralization of cultural standards appears to have been *too much beyond the norms* for American leaders" (Levy 1997: 55). Mulcahy (1987) argues that anything beyond the limited and indirect role of the NEA would be "at odds with the American pluralist tradition" (1987: 313). He continues:

> [I]t cannot be overemphasized that the policies and programs of the National Endowment for the Arts are not simply an administrative convenience. *These arrangements reflect the realities of American politics. In particular, the history of cultural politics in the United States* strongly suggested the advisability of a grant-making agency with limited authority and indirect responsibility rather than a comprehensive cultural department with direct responsibility for artistic production. (Mulcahy 1987: 316, emphasis mine)

Swaim (1982) maintains that "high culture [is not] meritorious by definition alone" due, in part, to "a strong American tradition that public culture should serve a useful purpose" (1982: 2–3).

The contention that, in general, it is not an American value to accept art as intrinsically valuable may be attributable to a strong pluralist or antielitist strain in the American identity narrative. In the highly class-stratified societies of Europe, the aristocracy (and the clergy) has historically taken the lead in arts cultivation. An aristocracy of this sort is not only absent in the United States, but generally viewed negatively by the citizens of what is ostensibly a meritocracy.

These sentiments are closely related to the individualistic and liberal democratic assumption that government should limit its role in *all* sectors. With respect to the arts and culture, this is especially important because direct government involvement can potentially threaten the free market of ideas— free expression may be constrained, and censorship can ensue. Therefore, temporary, renewable support on a project basis, as is favored by the NEA, may protect against these sorts of abuses. The American arts funding strategy is also grounded on economic assumptions that are in line with the country's identity discourse. In particular, tax incentives allow private entities in a free market to influence outcomes in a way that public subsidies could not. A similar argument can be made about American broadcasting policy.

Public Broadcasting in the United States

During NAFTA negotiations, Canadian and American negotiators disagreed over regulation of a broad range of culture industries. During GATT, however, representatives of the European Union and the United States concentrated their discussion on audiovisual industries, with the "Television without Frontiers" directive providing a major sticking point. Underlying these controversies are indeed differing conceptions of the relationship between culture, identity, and the state, but also varying notions of the sociological role of broadcasting.

The public service role of broadcasting is deeply engrained in Europe and Canada.

> Emphasis has been placed on a regulatory framework that would encourage broadcasters to inform, educate and entertain (and very much in that rank order); sustain high standards of programming; ensure a universality of access and appeal; establish a very special relationship of broadcasters to the sense of national identity and community; distance broadcasting from vested interests, whether government of the day or agglomerations of commercial power; and cater for minority interests. (Dyson and Humphreys 1990: 21)

The same cannot be said for the United States. Instead, American broadcasting settled into a commercial pattern several decades ago. Referring to the debates between advocates and opponents of commercial broadcasting, leading to the passage of the Communications Act of 1934, McChesney (1993) asserts:

> This episode is immediately remarkable in two respects. First, it arguably constitutes the sole instance in which the structure and control of a major mass medium were subject to anything close to legitimate political debate in U.S. history. Since the middle 1930s, the topic has been decidedly "off-limits" in public discourse. . . . Moreover, the subject of how best to organize and support the mass media has been and is a legitimate issue, in varying degrees, in most other nations on earth. In this sense, this is a clear case of American exceptionalism. (1993: 3)

McChesney (1993) goes on to note that "[b]y 1935 the system was entrenched economically, politically, and ideologically" (1993: 3) as a commercial, for-profit, advertiser-supported broadcasting system into which television would be born in the 1940s and 1950s. Schwoch (1990), too, contends that "[t]he value of private enterprise as the leader of policy formation in the communications sphere was discovered, protected, and promoted by American policymakers" (1990: 5) during the first four decades of this century. He goes on to note that debate indeed occurred as to whether public or private entities should direct the growth and development of the American radio industry. Nevertheless, once "American private enterprise successfully convinced the public sector that industry should lead the state in both domestic and global radio matters" (1990: 6), public and private forces "put the past behind them" and formed a united front to promote the "American style" of broadcasting. "That style was based on private ownership of stations, popular entertainment for broadcast programming, and advertising support as a method of financing operations" (1990: 8).

The Corporation for Public Broadcasting (CPB) does play a role in American broadcasting, but it is certainly not as predominant as public service broadcasters found in Europe and Canada. Furthermore, the mandate of the CPB is largely educational. Therefore, there is an effort in the United States to provide programming that might not be available if only market forces dictated program supply. But the motives, goals, and relative importance of the CPB are different and are grounded in the American historical experience.

For nearly six decades, there has been no debate about whether the American broadcasting system should incorporate public service elements. The fact that this is a settled issue in the United States is in stark contrast both to the loud and public opposition to recent Canadian government attempts to cut funding to the Canadian Broadcasting Corporation (CBC) and to the deeply reflective debates over privatization of the TF1 television channel in France just over a decade ago. Even Great Britain, traditionally most closely aligned with the United States in terms of economic ideology, boasts the flagship public broadcasting system in the British Broadcasting Corporation (BBC).

For their part, American commercial broadcasters argued that it would be unpatriotic to embrace something other than for-profit, advertiser-supported broadcasting. By 1935, "there was little opposition to the widely disseminated promotional claims of the commercial broadcasters that their control of the ether was innately democratic and American; indeed, that no other system could even be conceivable to a freedom-loving people" (McChesney 1993: 226).

Much of the debate over the regulation of culture industries during the 1980s and 1990s revisits many of the themes dealt with in discussions over other areas of cultural policy. Although U.S. government officials do not explicitly connect identity and culture industry trade policy formulation, I would argue that the consistency of American cultural policy across its various subsectors tells another story. This consistency arises not only from material interest calculations, but also from the normative parameter dimension of identity functioning in the American context.

While the normative parameter dimension seems most prominent, the instrumental dimension is also of great importance with regard to American culture industry trade policy formation. Its influence, however, has perhaps been most pronounced in wartime or in countries not considered to be close allies of the United States. The existence of the Voice of America and the use of propaganda films during World War II, for example, are just two reminders that American officials are well aware of the instrumental power of culture industries.

The pluralist dimension of identity also influences U.S. trade policy in the cultural sector, although the focus is different. Representatives of the American government and culture industry sector, like the Canadians and Europeans, often voice a desire to ensure that a variety of voices are heard. However, Canadians and Europeans are generally referring to their own domestic markets when they make these statements, while Americans generally refer to the global market for these goods and services.

There is no doubt that identity is contingent. Nonetheless, we do see patterns over time in how the American government approaches the cultural sector. This consistency suggests that the three dimensions of identity that I identified above are intervening in culture industry trade policy formation in the United States to varying degrees. Unless the United States shows a willingness to acknowledge this, we are likely to see further conflicts in future trade talks over whether identity is an acceptable justification for practices currently construed as protectionist.

Conclusion

I have argued that aspects of identity influence trade policy formation with regard to culture industries, both inside and outside the United States. In other words, identity contributes to trade policy formation not as an alternative to the pursuit of economic interests, but as a complement. Judith Goldstein (1993) has demonstrated convincingly that economic ideas influence trade policy formation. I take this one step further to include ideas not only about favored economic policy, but about such things as the kind of society one hopes to build and the importance accorded to cultural institutions and their mode of operation. I am not necessarily saying that identity *creates* interests. I am much more inclined to accept Bukovansky's (1997) assertion that there is a dialectical relationship between identity and interests. Nor am I attributing primacy to either identity or interests as an "explanatory variable." I am asserting that looking at both gives us a richer picture.

Showing that identity influences culture industry trade policy formation in the Canadian and EU cases has implications for our understanding of protectionism and what motivates it. Showing that identity plays a similar role in the American case, where we might be tempted to stop once we have delineated an explanation founded on economic interests, has other implications, some of which I believe go beyond the theoretical to the ethical. The explanation we find for American policy based solely on economic interest calculations has the effect of marginalizing noncommercial considerations. In addition, such a limited explanation privileges a certain discourse and the categories and meanings attendant to it. For example, conducting a discussion of the cultural exception solely in terms of economic interests leaves a circumscribed range of benchmarks against which we can assess actor's policies. Governments are either protectionist or free/fair traders. Accompanying these labels are, of course, underlying judgments that protectionism is bad and free/fair trade is good, as well as fairly narrow notions of what counts as protectionism. Confining ourselves to this reductionist narrative immediately impoverishes the debate by foreclosing a more sophisticated discussion wherein commercial pursuits cannot be so easily isolated from political and cultural ones, a discussion that leaves room for the much more complex reality of each actor's situation.

For example, France, Canada, and the EU are defined as protectionist with regard to culture industries. This has the effect of portraying their policy measures as nefarious because they are anticompetitive. In this discourse, it is the fair-trading United States that is victimized and limited in what its culture industries can do. The reality, however, is that Canadians, Europeans, and Americans are all committed to free trade, yet often protect domestic industries. They do this in different ways and these different ways may be linked to identity. The French and the Americans both value their film industries and would like to see them succeed in domestic and foreign markets. The French government offers assistance in the form of domestic subsidy arrangements, while the American government aids in the opening of foreign export markets. The Europeans and Americans are both leaders in commercial aircraft manufacture. The Europeans protect their industry through direct subsidies to the Airbus consortium. The American government assists Boeing-McDonnell Douglas through favorable tax provisions and government contracts.

Lost in the reductionist either-protectionist-or-free-trader dichotomy are details about how each government assists its respective industries and why some forms of assistance count as protection while others do not. Furthermore, there is no room for any nonmaterial justification of measures that move outside the narrow parameters of permissible economic activity. But speaking as if only economic interests are determinative sets a potentially far-reaching precedent as we expand the reach of the WTO to include goods and services previously outside the purview of the international trading regime.

In May 2000, a Burmese official attending a meeting of ASEAN economic ministers in Myanmar was asked about his country's human rights record. He answered, "we are not here to talk about human rights; we are here to talk about trade."[23] A similar sentiment can be read into the U.S. stance on culture industries. We are not here to talk about identity and culture; we are here to talk about trade. For Canadians and Europeans, it is almost impossible to separate the two when it comes to culture industries. It is also difficult to separate them in many sectors that either do, or soon will, fall under the jurisdiction of the WTO. These include genetically modified foods, intellectual property, and health care provision services. I would argue that Americans do not separate dimensions of identity from interests in the cultural sector either, making it inappropriate to carry on trade negotiations as if noncommercial concerns are irrelevant. Indeed, even a value as seemingly innocuous as advocating private or public broadcasting or viewing direct government involvement in the cultural sector as positive or negative manifests itself in important ways at the international level.

The cultural exception will be reopened in the next round of WTO negotiations, with American officials threatening to dismantle it. If rules that give primacy to the commercial aspects of tradable goods and services, while denying noncommercial concerns, are institutionalized in industries where culture and commerce are so clearly intertwined, will future rounds of WTO negotiations find American officials arguing, for example, that comprehensive health care in Canada is an unfair trading practice rather than the manifestation of a certain set of social democratic priorities that Canadians claim to value? This is indeed likely if the WTO continues to sanction discussion of the regulation of new categories of goods and services in terms whose relevance may be waning. However, a constructivist approach to the analysis of the respective national government positions may illuminate the degree to which objective interests combine with identity narratives and legacies of national practices to produce competing policy preferences. In providing a richer understanding of policy sources, such an analysis may, in turn, enhance opportunities for greater cooperation in sectors such as culture industries.

Notes

1. Streeter, (1996), p.7.
2. See Sikkink and Finnemore (1998) on this point as it pertains to international norms in IR. See also Bates, de Figueiredo, and Weingast (1998) on the complementarity of rational choice and interpretivist approaches.
3. For a related argument about the early development of American neutral rights

policy, see Bukovansky (1997). See also Ruggie (1998) for an analysis of the influence of identity factors in shaping U.S. foreign policy.

4. The term is Theodor Adorno's. See Horkheimer and Adorno (1972) and Adorno (1975). I choose it rather than using one of the three terms favored by the key actors in the cases under consideration: cultural industries in Canada, audiovisual industries in the European Union, and entertainment industries in the United States.

5. Talks between Canada and the United States took place from May 1986, to December, 1987. The Canada-U.S. Free Trade Agreement officially took effect on January 1, 1989.

6. Negotiations between Canada, the United States, and Mexico began in June 1991. NAFTA officially went into effect on January 1, 1994.

7. The Uruguay Round of GATT negotiations spanned the seven-year period from 1986 to 1994, officially taking effect in January 1995.

8. At the Seattle WTO meeting in November 1999 that failed to launch the Millennium Round of negotiations, Canada and the EU made it clear that they will endeavor to retain the protections existing for the cultural sector. In recent months, countries including South Korea and Japan have joined the chorus.

9. I borrow this formulation from Doty (1993), inspired by her analysis of American policy toward the Philippines.

10. The original quote is as follows:

> Si l'instruction a pour but d'éclairer le peuple et de le préparer à exercer un métier, l'éducation a aussi une fonction directement politique: instituer en nation une foule d'individus. . . . De Condorcet à Jules Ferry, de Mirabeau à Ferdinand Buisson, un même fil guide ainsi toutes les réformes successives en matière d'éducation: l'obsession de former des citoyens, c'est-à-dire des individus préparés à la vie collective, conscients de leur communauté de destin. . . . On peut également comprendre dans cette perspective l'origine de l'attachement au principe du monopole public de l'éducation.

11. For more on this as it pertains to national cinema, see Higson (1989).

12. French "New Wave" film makers claim a debt to American "B" movies of the 1950s, "British Invasion" rock and roll was influenced by blues musicians from the American South, and so forth.

13. "Testimony of Jack Valenti," *Hearings before the Subcommittee on Oversight and Investigation of the Committee on Energy and Commerce*, U.S. House of Representatives, 101st Congress, 1st session, March 1 and 2, 1989, on "Unfair Foreign Trade Practices." Serial no. 101–28, p. 73.

14. "Statement of Jack Valenti, President and Chief Executive Officer, Motion Picture Association of America," *Hearings before the Committee on Ways and Means and its Subcommittee on Trade*, U.S. House of Representatives, 102nd Congress, 2nd session, Sept. 9, 15, 17, and 22, 1992, on "North American Free Trade Agreement." Serial no. 102–135, p. 177.

15. "California targets our cultural protection," *Financial Post* (Toronto), August 22, 1991, p. 3.

16. "Culture should be a dead issue," *Financial Post* (Toronto), August 29, 1991, p. 10.

17. Testimony of Michael Kantor, U.S. trade representative, before the House of

Representatives Committee on Energy/Commerce, Consumer Protection and Competitiveness, March 23, 1994.

18. Statement of William Nix, senior vice president and worldwide director for Antipiracy, Motion Picture Export Association, *Hearings before the Subcommittee on Commerce, Consumer Protection, and Competitiveness of the Committee on Energy and Commerce.* U.S. House of Representatives, 100th Congress, 2nd Session, February 23, March 22, and April 26, 1988, on "U.S.–Canada Free Trade Agreement." Serial no. 100–125, pp. 359–61.

19. The term "American Creed" was coined by Gunnar Myrdal.

20. I consider Canadian cultural policy to be within the European tradition, grounded as it is in British practice.

21. For more on the WPA, see Larson (1983) and Levy (1997).

22. Compared to any other countries in the study—Canada, West Germany, France, Great Britain, Italy, the Netherlands, and Sweden.

23. National Public Radio Morning News (KCRW Los Angeles), May 1, 2000.

Bibliography

Adorno, Theodor. 1975. "Culture Industry Reconsidered." *New German Critique* 6: 12–19.

Anderson, Benedict. 1991. *Imagined Communities.* New York: Verso.

Bates, Robert H., Rui J.P. de Figueiredo, and Barry R. Weingast. 1998. "The Politics of Interpretation: Rationality, Culture, and Transition." *Politics and Society* 26 (4): 603–642.

Brown, Duncan. 1991. "Citizens or Consumers: U.S. Reactions to the European Community's Directive on Television." *Critical Studies in Mass Communications* 8: 1–12.

Brubaker, Rogers, and Frederick Cooper. 2000. "Beyond 'Identity.'" *Theory and Society* 29: 1–47.

Bukovansky, Mlada. 1997. "American Identity and Neutral Rights from Independence to the War of 1812." *International Organization* 51: 209–243.

Campbell, David. 1998. *Writing Security: United States Foreign Policy and the Politics of Identity.* Minneapolis: University of Minnesota Press.

———. 1993. "Cold Wars: Securing Identity, Identifying Danger." In *Rhetorical Republic: Governing Representations in American Politics*, ed. Frederick M. Dolan and Thomas L. Dumm, 39–60. Amherst: University of Massachusetts Press.

Doty, Roxanne. 1993. "Foreign Policy as Social Construction: A Post-Positivist Analysis of U.S. Counterinsurgency Policy in the Philippines." *International Studies Quarterly* 37: 297–320.

———. 1996. *Imperial Encounters.* Minneapolis: University of Minnesota Press.

Dyson, Kenneth and Peter Humphreys, eds. 1990. *The Political Economy of Communication: International and European Dimensions.* London: Routledge.

———. 2000. "Accepting the Cultural Exception: A No-Cost Policy for Cultural Diversity." Paper prepared for the Center for Arts and Culture, Washington, DC.

Foucault, Michel. 1978. *The History of Sexuality, Volume I: An Introduction.* New York: Vintage Books.

Goff, Patricia. 2000. "Invisible Borders: Economic Liberalization and National Identity." *International Studies Quarterly* 44: 533–562.

Goldstein, Judith. 1993. *Ideas, Interests, and American Trade Policy.* Ithaca: Cornell University Press.

Hartz, Louis. 1955. *The Liberal Tradition in America.* New York: Harcourt, Brace and World.

Higson, Andrew. 1989. "The Concept of National Cinema." *Screen* 30(4): 36–46.

Hopf, Ted. 1998. "The Promise of Constructivism in International Relations Theory." *International Security* 23: 171–200.

Horkheimer, Max, and Theodor Adorno. 1972. "The Culture Industry: Enlightenment as Mass Deception." In *The Dialectic of Enlightenment, 120–167.* New York: Continnum.

Huntington, Samuel. 1981. *American Politics: The Promise of Disharmony.* Cambridge, MA: Harvard University Press.

Katzenstein, Peter J., ed. 1996. *The Culture of National Security: Norms and Identity in World Politics.* New York: Columbia University Press.

Klotz, Audie. 1995. *Norms in International Relations: The Struggle Against Apartheid.* Ithaca: Cornell University Press.

Lapid, Yosef, and Friedrich Kratochwil, eds. 1996. *The Return of Culture and Identity in IR Theory.* Boulder: Lynne Rienner.

Larson, Gary O. 1983. *The Reluctant Patron: The United States Government and the Arts.* Philadelphia: University of Pennsylvania Press.

Levy, Alan H. 1997. *Government and the Arts: Debates over Federal Support of the Arts in America from George Washington to Jesse Helms.* Lanham, MD: University Press of America.

Lipset, Seymour Martin. 1986. "Historical Traditions and National Characteristics: A Comparative Analysis of Canada and the United States." *Canadian Journal of Sociology* 11: 113–155.

Loriaux, Michael. 1999. "The French Developmental State as Myth and Moral Ambition." In *The Developmental State*, ed. Meredith Woo-Cumings, 235–275. Ithaca: Cornell University Press.

Mankin, Lawrence. 1982. "Government Patronage: An Historical Overview." In *Public Policy and the Arts*, ed. Kevin V. Mulcahy and C. Richard Swaim, 111–140. Boulder: Westview Press.

McChesney, Robert W. 1993. *Telecommunications, Mass Media and Democracy.* New York: Oxford University Press.

McClosky, Herbert and John Zaller. 1984. *The American Ethos.* Cambridge, MA: Harvard University Press.

Morley, Dave. 1980. "Texts, Readers, Subjects." In *Culture, Media and Language*, ed. Stuart Hall. London: Hutchison.

Mulcahy, Kevin V. 1987. "Government and the Arts in the United States." In *The Patron State: Government and the Arts in Europe, North America, and Japan*, ed. Milton C. Cummings, Jr. and Richard S. Katz, 311–332. New York: Oxford University Press.

Pachter, Marc. 1995. "American Identity: A Political Compact." In *Identities in North America*, ed. Robert L. Earle and John D. Wirth, 29–39. Stanford: Stanford University Press.

Rosanvallon, Pierre. 1990. *L'etat en France: de 1789 a nos jours.* Paris: Seuil.

Ruggie, John Gerard. 1998. *Constructing the World Polity.* New York: Routledge.

Schwoch, James. 1990. *The American Radio Industry and Its Latin American Activities, 1900–1939.* Urbana: University of Illinois Press.

Schuster, J. Mark Davidson. 1985. *Supporting the Arts: An International Comparative Study.* Washington, DC: Policy Planning Division, National Endowment for the Arts.

Shapiro, Michael. 2000. "Genres of Nationhood: The 'Musico-Literary' Aesthetics of Attachment and Resistance." *Strategies* (Forthcoming).

Sikkink, Kathryn, and Martha Finnemore. 1998. "International Norm Dynamics and Political Change." *International Organization* 54: 887–917.

Streeter, Thomas. 1996. *Selling the Air: A Critique of the Policy of Commercial Broadcasting in the United States.* Chicago: University of Chicago Press.

Swaim, C. Richard. 1982. "Public Culture and Policy Analysis: An Introduction." In *Public Policy and the Arts*, ed. Kevin V. Mulcahy and C. Richard Swaim, 1–9. Boulder: Westview.

"Truth and Power: Interview with Michel Foucault." 1984. In *The Foucault Reader*, ed. Paul Rabinow, 51–75. New York: Pantheon Books.

Waever, Ole, Barry Buzan, Morten Kelstcup, and Pierre LeMaitre. 1993. *Identity, Migration and the New Security Agenda in Europe.* New York: St. Martin's.

Weber, Eugen. 1976. *Peasants into Frenchmen.* Stanford: Stanford University Press.

Wendt, Alexander. 1992. "Anarchy Is What States Make of It: The Social Construction of State Politics." *International Organization* 46: 391–425.

———. 1994. "Collective Identity Formation and the International State." *American Political Science Review* 88: 384–396.

8

The West Is the Best: Occidentalism and Postwar German Reconstruction

Patrick Thaddeus Jackson

> *The West is the best*
> *The West is the best*
> *Get here and we'll do the rest*
> —Jim Morrison[1]

What might the preceding quotation, by the controversial rock artist Jim Morrison, possibly have to do with the postwar reconstruction of Germany? Obviously the quote cannot enjoy a conventional *causal* relationship with German reconstruction, as reconstruction took place between 1945 and 1955, and the date of Morrison's lyric is 1967; German reconstruction might conceivably have caused Morrison's lyric, but that would be a matter for a very different kind of inquiry. Nor am I arguing that any such linear, neopositivist causal relationship exists. However, there is an important connection between Morrison's lyric and German reconstruction, in that both deploy the same *rhetorical commonplace*, a commonplace that I have named "occidentalism." According to occidentalist rhetoric, there exists a historical and cultural community called "the West" or "Western civilization," which lies somehow behind or underneath the divisions between states and nations which belong to it; in addition, the values of this community are superior to those of other cultural communities, enjoying some kind of special relationship with History or God or Truth (and sometimes all three). Just as Morrison deploys the notion of the West in his lyric to represent the endpoint of a journey of consciousness, prominent political and social elites, and the "organic intellectuals" important to these elites, deployed the notion of the West to help justify the political and social arrangements of the postwar world order, including Germany's participation in those arrangements as a near-equal.

There is another facet of occidentalism which Morrison's lyric helps to illustrate: As is well known, Morrison was deeply influenced by the German philosopher Friedrich Nietzsche, from whom he absorbed a reverence for things Greek and Dionysian. The intellectual matrix in which Morrison worked when crafting his lyrics was in important respects a German creation, somewhat modified by conditions obtaining in the United States, but owing much to the thinking of nineteenth-century German intellectuals. In a similar fashion, the occidentalism that helped to legitimate postwar reconstruction derives from German intellectual sources, and in particular from social theorists who combined older cultural notions to produce an analytically usable West that could generate explanations and policy prescriptions alike. This conceptual groundwork had to be laid both in Germany and in the United States *before* German reconstruction could become a possibility—or before Jim Morrison could deploy the notion in a song and have a chance of being understood.

This chapter will be an exercise in conceptual archaeology, similar in approach to what Reinhart Koselleck has called *Begriffsgeschichte* (Koselleck 1985) or Michel Foucault has called the analysis of discursive formations (Foucault 1972). What is being sought are the identity-related underpinnings of the various policies making up the process of German reconstruction, which I believe revolve around the notion of the West. The causal argument—for there *is* a causal argument here, albeit not a *neopositivist* causal argument—is simple: no West, no German reconstruction, at least no German reconstruction in the way it happened historically. That there were other possibilities, which the rhetorical commonplace of the West was instrumental in delegitimating, is part of what I will need to show in order to substantiate my argument.[2] But before I can get to the empirical narrative, it is necessary to take a brief detour through the philosophy of social inquiry, because the object I wish to analyze—the rhetorical commonplace of the West and its participation in processes of legitimation—is not the kind of object easily apprehended by the neopositivist methods prominent in the discipline, and requires a somewhat different approach. So that my claims are not misunderstood, I need to make their status (ontological, epistemological, and methodological) clearer.

Clearing the Ground

I am sure that there will be some readers who are impatient to "get on with it," and jump right into the empirical matter: facts first, theory afterwards. I am also sure that there will be some readers who do not feel that yet another critical treatment of neopositivism is required, and that either those issues have been settled by such programmatic treatises as King, Keohane, and Verba's (KKV) recent methodological manual (King, Keohane, and Verba 1994), or that the debate about social inquiry should constitute a wholly different endeavor from empirical research. I do not agree with either of these positions: at its root, the word "theory" means "way of seeing," and hence there is no such thing as atheoretical inquiry. It makes more sense to me to know a few things about *how we are seeing* before trying to look at something. Treatises like KKV are certainly not the last word in designing social inquiry, and contain a number of assumptions which make them unsuited for the kind of investigation which I am undertaking here. Hence the need for this excursus.

Ontology

"Ontology lies at the beginning of any enquiry," argues Robert Cox. "We cannot define a problem in global politics without presupposing a certain basic structure consisting of the significant kinds of entities involved and the form of significant relationships among them" (Cox 1996: 141). In addition, we cannot begin inquiring about a problem until we have (at least implicitly) located our own investigation in relation to the phenomenon in question. Both of these kinds of presuppositions constitute the *ontological* component of a theory, since they define what it means for something to "exist" and hence what kinds of things exist in the world. Much of the contemporary analysis of global politics shares three linked ontological assumptions: the "solidity" of the (sovereign, territorial) state; the primacy of material factors, or "interests"; and the "exteriority" of the observer to the process under observation. These three assumptions help to define a conceptual space which Ole Wæver has termed the "neo-neo synthesis" (Wæver 1996), which much contemporary work in international relations (IR) and comparative politics (CP) inhabits.

The "solidity" of the state, also known as "state-centrism," is a persistent feature of IR research. The primary actors are thought to be more or less unitary states, which look out on an anarchical world characterized by dangerous potential security threats, and seek to preserve the sanctity of their domestic realms by adhering to the dictates of a "self-help" system. Alexander Wendt argues that such theories are "agentic" inasmuch as they derive the character of interstate interaction from assumed characteristics of the units themselves (Wendt 1987); hence there is no room in such approaches for nonstate actors, or even for causal factors that cannot be clearly linked to one state or another. Unfortunately, Wendt's later work (Wendt 1992, 1999) ends up repeating this state-centrism, concentrating almost exclusively on how state actions at one point in time can structure action at a later point in time.[3] A primary implication of this ontological presumption is that "identity" must be a unit-level attribute, in the sense that a state's "identity" must be a property

of the state in the same way that its borders and form of government are—
even if a state gains an identity by "internalizing" a role which is given to it
by the social system in which it participates.

Along with this assumption of "solidity,"[4] we find a privileging of material factors, usually under the heading of "interests." The idea is that actors
(states, in most cases) have a set of interests determined by the intersection
of the environment in which they find themselves and the preferences they
have developed concerning which goals they ought to pursue. What is specifically material about these approaches is that interests are thought to flow
directly from the material environment, so that choices made by actors are
held to be pure reactions to an objectively existing realm of constraints and
opportunities which circumscribes action. The interest most often cited by
IR scholars is that of "security," which is thought to be a supreme interest in
an anarchical system: a state must do whatever it can to preserve its own
independent existence. Stephen Krasner has argued that a state might pursue
"ideological" goals *after* having secured its physical security, but these are
clearly secondary matters: "Ideological goals can be pursued only by the
very powerful and perhaps also the very weak, by those who can make things
happen and those who cannot change what happens. For most states it must
be interests, and not visions, that count" (Krasner 1978: 340). Similarly, Robert
Gilpin has argued that the truest causal factor in world politics is the distribution of material capabilities, which is essentially a measure of a state's
relative war-making potential; although he accords the "hierarchy of prestige" some independent influence, this hierarchy is firmly circumscribed by
material factors (Gilpin 1981).

Security approaches understand American involvement in Europe after
World War II as stemming from the changed geopolitical environment. The
United States, now a superpower, was essentially *forced* to "balance" with
the Soviet Union; the choice of Europe as the major terrain was dictated by
strategic and technological factors. It was inevitable that Germany would
become the front line of the emerging power struggle, and hence it was in the
United States' best interests to build up a strong Germany which could serve
as the first line of its own defense. Similarly, the threat posed by the Soviet
Union gave European states, including (most of all) Germany, an incentive
to court United States involvement, seeking alliance commitments and economic ties. While there are some variations on this theme,[5] security arguments remain convinced that objective security imperatives straightforwardly
drew the United States into Europe in general and Germany in particular.

Another type of interest-based argument is based on economics. Simply
put, these scholars argue that the United States wanted a rebuilt Western
Europe so that it could have a ready market for its goods, a set of "peripheral"

dependents that could function as a sort of informal empire.[6] It was to the advantage of the European states, including the nascent Federal Republic of Germany, to assent to this arrangement because of the benefits they derived from it; with the United States agreeing to act as the stabilizer, a relatively open economic order could be constructed, and the logic of comparative advantage would allow all to benefit (even if the United States benefited more than others).[7] In the most sophisticated form of this thesis, the informal empire becomes an "empire by invitation," in which the European states effectively request the United States to take over (Lundestad 1990). The basic logic of the argument is not dissimilar to that of the security argument, in that objective imperatives (market conditions, in this case) drive policy in an unmediated manner.

These interest-based approaches suffer from empirical inaccuracy and theoretical incompleteness. Empirically, security arguments cannot account for the fact that Germany was being reconstructed almost from the day the war ended, which is to say, *before* a clear Soviet threat had emerged (Backer 1971; Eisenberg 1996). This does not fit well with the causal impact assigned to "balancing" by these arguments. While the presence of Soviet troops in Eastern Europe were an important factor motivating U.S. actions, the presence of these troops is not sufficient to explain German reconstruction; more crucial was the way in which the presence of these troops was understood, because a different understanding would almost certainly have led to a different policy response. In addition, security arguments have trouble explaining why a neutralized and permanently disarmed Germany—perhaps occupied by Allied troops—would not have served U.S. (and German) security equally well, especially given strong French resistance to the idea of a reconstituted German military. Economic arguments have similar empirical problems, such as the fact that German reconstruction was part of the *transformative* project of "embedded liberalism," explicitly intended to alter state/market relations in a way which would provide governments with more tools for managing their own domestic economies (Ruggie 1983). If the United States was merely looking for a captive market, it makes little sense that it would seek to provide other governments with the means by which they could direct their domestic economies in ways perhaps contrary to the wishes of the United States. The net result of these empirical problems is that an analyst drawing only on interest-based arguments would be unable to explain key facets of German reconstruction, particularly its scope and timing.

These empirical failings derive from the theoretical incompleteness of interest-based approaches. Because these approaches try to derive behavior from the material context in an unmediated fashion, they run into problems in those cases where the material environment does not unambiguously point in a single direction. In such situations, where interests are indeterminate and a variety of courses of action appear to be possible, interest-based approaches need to be supplemented by additional theoretical equipment. However, even if interest-based approaches are able to claim that interests are not indeterminate, they are still unable to say much about the *means* by which a particular goal (such as the reconstruction of Germany) is pursued, since they assume that any actor in a comparable material position would have done exactly the same thing. Unless we are willing to imagine that any other victorious state would have reconstructed its former enemy in exactly the same way, the interest-based approach will still have to be supplemented.

The emphasis placed on material interests by most analyses of the problem of German reconstruction is bolstered, if not actually produced, by the third ontological assumption: the "exteriority" of the analyst to the phenomenon under study. Stressing material factors, which are thought to be independent of what any particular actor might think about them, allows the analyst to effectively ignore the way in which any particular actor relates to those material factors, "black-boxing" the actor and transforming her into a link between input and outputs. The actor can be discounted because an analyst is able to concentrate on more and more accurate measurements of various material factors (troop strength, geographic proximity, economic potential) and link them to various outcomes, establishing a causal relationship by demonstrating a (Humean) "conjunction" of events. To borrow Jon Elster's distinction, "exteriority" and the stress on material "interests" combine to create a "push-causal" theory of political behavior, in which actors are compelled to certain courses of action by factors essentially beyond their control. (Elster 1989) Elster calls for a different kind of analysis, one which takes causal mechanisms much more seriously and is not content to "black-box" actors; it is my belief that such an alternative approach is capable of solving some of the problems I have identified with other accounts of German reconstruction.

Epistemology

The first step in constructing an alternative account is to get away from the assumption of "exteriority." Contemporary social science has a tendency to see itself as engaged in a process of formulating lawlike generalizations about groups of phenomena; according to this conception, theories are guesses about the character of the world which are held up to Nature for her approval. Nature can prove one of our guesses wrong, but can never definitively prove any of our (limited, human) guesses right. Thus there can be, by assumption, no contact between the phenomenon and the researcher *except* through the mechanisms of hypothesis testing, and thus it would be nonsensical to compare the *theoretical* assumptions made by researchers with the *actual* way in which the phenomenon unfolds. Indeed, "the actual way in which the phenomenon unfolds" is a nonsensical concept for a neopositivist, for whom knowledge is nothing more than our best guess about how two distinct observable states of the world are linked.

Whatever the utility of this conception when dealing with the inert and mute objects of the natural sciences,[8] it is surely inappropriate when dealing with human beings. A crucial difference between studying human beings and, say, planets orbiting a star is that the human beings have a language and a culture upon which they draw in making sense out of the world around them. If planets (or molecules, or ant colonies) have such a social and intersubjective component to their existence, we are only dimly aware of it: In a very real sense, we cannot "speak their language." By contrast, we *can* learn the language of other human beings and enter into their worlds in important ways; indeed, the very identification of the specific behaviors we wish to explain *requires* that we engage in at least some amount of world entry. Activities like "war" or "worship" (or "reconstruction") are *social*, and attempts to describe or understand them necessarily involves the use of some of the terms and notions which are actually operative in the process under consideration. Along these lines, Donald Moon (1975) has noted that social-scientific theories necessarily contain a "model of man" at their core; if one does not get the model right, one will end up getting the story wrong.

According to this argument, all social theories are essentially *interpretive* rather than positivistic. And since such social scientific theories *always* have to engage in world-entry, they might as well do it *openly* and *rigorously*, taking the theories-in-use of historical actors as their point of entry into the hermeneutic circle. Our first priority must be with the particular actors involved, and in particular with the worlds in which they live, but this does *not* mean that we are concerned with what goes on inside of an actor's head (even an actor like "the state" which only has a metaphorical head). It is entirely possible to incorporate "perceptual variables" into an account of social action without stepping outside of a neopositivist epistemology, but nuancing a materialist account by adding some "intervening" factors does not answer the more pressing causal question of *why actors perceive situations in a particular way*. In addition, even if "perceptions" could explain one policy maker's beliefs, unless we are willing to assume that cognitive theory can be applied to collective actors such as "the state," we will need to confront a pair of (perhaps insurmountable) aggregation problems: how one policy maker's beliefs become accepted by others, and how the beliefs of those policy makers and other social elites relate to the beliefs of the populace as a whole.

I do not think that "perceptions" are the appropriate way to incorporate the "world" of actors into an analysis. Rather, I believe that analysts have to move "beyond belief" and outside of actors' heads if they are going to try to take the causal mechanisms of social action seriously (Laffey and Weldes 1997). Where analysts need to move is towards what Clifford Geertz called culture, which he defined as "socially established structures of meaning in terms of which people do such things as signal conspiracies and join them or perceive insults and answer them"—or determine that Germany is part of "Western Civilization" and enact policies which accord with this position (Geertz 1973: 12–13). A focus on culture understood in this way allows the analyst to sidestep any aggregation problems involved in relating two people's beliefs to one another, since examining the fundamentally public documents of culture is a wholly different endeavor from the measurement of opinion codified in (for example) the techniques of opinion polling; "individual thought" is *not* the object of analysis here. Rather, emphasis is placed on the "community of knowing" which provides the particular individual with a language in which to order her experiences, and the "social rules" which make behavior meaningful in a particular situation (Mannheim 1936; Winch 1990).

To make this clearer, I will differentiate "motivations" from "intentions," on the grounds that motivations take place inside of an actor's head and are basically *private*, while intentions take place in conversation and social interaction and are therefore basically *public* (by which I mean *intersubjective*).[9] I am *not* claiming that policy makers were motivated by a common belief in Western Civilization. It is entirely consistent with my approach to argue that a particular policy maker was motivated by a desire to get elected or to retain her official position; evidence of the cynical deployment of particular phrases or appeals does not invalidate my claims. This is because human beings are knowing participants in their world rather than simply empirical components of it; hence the kinds of reasons given by an actor for her action—even reasons given only to herself—are *essential* parts of the causal complex which brings about the result in question. This is particularly the case when we are analyzing the actions of public officials and policy makers, who are forced by the nature of their positions to offer *public* reasons for the courses of action they desire to undertake.[10] The discursive frameworks which permit a public official to give reasons that are taken to be valid are therefore an important element in the causation of policy, even if the personal motivations of the official are altogether different. This is not to say that motives do not exist, or to deny that meaningful research into motives could not be carried out; it is, however, to deny that an account of motivations is *required* for a causal account of how a policy comes to be enacted. For this purpose, a focus on the intersubjective cultural environment is sufficient.

We must also be careful to avoid a premature emphasis on homogeneity, as if culture consisted of only one unambiguous set of precepts and publicly acceptable reasons for action. Rather, the intersubjective realm of culture consists of multiple *symbolic technologies*, which are "intersubjective systems of representations and representation-producing practices." Symbolic technologies are "fundamentally *social and intersubjective* rather than . . . *collective or shared*" and therefore "make possible the articulation and circulation of more or less coherent sets of meanings about a particular subject matter"(Laffey and Weldes 1997: 209). These symbolic technologies participate in social action by providing a "vocabulary" common to speakers and audiences, and thus shaping the debates about policy by defining the terms of discourse and giving rise to historically situated, particular actors with concrete interests. Hence symbolic technologies are also "rhetorical commonplaces," *literally* held in common by multiple actors and social entities. But there is no logical need for each participant in such a conversation to *agree* on the precise meaning of these commonplaces; participants in a conversation must merely be conversant with the different commonplaces and how they may be pieced together so as to make a point. Much of the analysis of these symbolic technologies involves an examination of how they are mobilized differently for different purposes, as various actors struggle to control the discursive environment (Shotter 1993: 65–69; Kratochwil 1989: 40–42). Culture in this conceptualization is *not* the same thing as what once went under the name "political culture," as that older notion stressed homogeneity and stability. Instead, the relational approach outlined here preserves contingency and creativity, and participates in the "culturalist" turn discussed by Dan Green in the first chapter of this volume: not merely a "return" to culture, but a new approach to culture which places social construction at the center of the analysis.

A clearer view of the causal role played by rhetorical commonplaces can be gained from a consideration of "identity," a term that has become increasingly popular in the social sciences in recent years. As deployed by many scholars of nationalism, "identity" has been analyzed as a focal point around which self-interested rational actors can coordinate their behavior (Hardin 1995; Hechter 1987), as an irrational emotional attachment that affects individual calculations (Smith 1986), and as a tool that cynical elites can use to increase their power and influence, sometimes with disastrous consequences (Snyder 1991; Snyder and Ballentine 1996; Laitin 1986). A number of scholars critical of this "instrumental" notion of identity and more sympathetic to notions of social construction (see, e.g., Anderson 1991, Brubaker 1996) have proposed that "identity" be reconceived as a permissive condition, a kind of level of social life which necessarily mediates between individuals and the environments in which they find themselves. Thus, identity *precedes* interests in a very real sense, because "to ask someone to make a careful deliberation of a preference is to ask that person to figure out what he or she 'really wants,' but in order to answer that question he or she will first have to figure out who he or she 'really is.' Only as that *real* person can he or she have *real* interests" (Ringmar 1996: 52). As the permissive conditions for these kinds of considerations, identity components—which I have called rhetorical commonplaces—should be considered when giving an account of policy outcomes.

It should be clear that the way in which rhetorical commonplaces are causal is somewhat different from the way in which variable attributes are thought to be causal in neopositivist analyses. I *am* arguing that "reasons" can be "causes," but in a way somewhat different than that upheld by others who put forth this claim (e.g., Davidson 1963). I am *not* arguing that reasons can be causes because the reasons offered have *anything whatsoever* to do with any "internal" (motivational) processes that produce behavior; rather, I am arguing that reasons can be causes because they participate in a socially significant process of negotiating and (re)drawing boundaries, simultaneously giving rise to both actions *and* the actors that carry them out. John Shotter suggests that an appropriate metaphor to use in thinking about this issue is that of a "living tradition" which consists not of "fully predetermined, already decided distinctions" but of "a certain set of historically developed . . . 'topological' *resources*" that can be "expressed or formulated in different ways in different, concrete circumstances" (Shotter 1993: 170–171). Without the particular constellation of rhetorical commonplaces that was actually deployed, the events in question would not have unfolded in the way in which they did; "the vocalized expectation of an act, its 'reason,' is not only a mediating condition of the act but it is a proximate and controlling condition for which the term 'cause' is not inappropriate" (Mills 1940: 907). In this way identity is indeed "in constant flux" (Green, chapter 1 of this volume), continually in need of restatement and reinforcement through concrete rhetorical deployments. The contours of these repeated deployments produce the conditions of possibility for action, and *in this sense* identity is "causal."

Concentrating on identity understood in this relational fashion also allows scholars a way to get beyond the state as a unit of analysis, and to focus on the components of world politics that do not fit neatly within state borders. There is nothing in the notion of symbolic technologies that precludes such technologies from spanning a number of states, and indeed the intersubjective nature of symbolic technologies makes it extremely likely that they will do so. A single symbolic technology might easily be incorporated into the legitimation strategies of more than one state, giving those states a basis on which to interact; if this incorporation is harmonious,[11] relations between the two states can be underpinned by their common adherence to cultural constructs, and the spread of institutional innovations from one state to another can be explained without having to resort to the empirically untenable assumption that one state presented a "blank slate" on which another state could draw whatever it wished. In addition, this analytical move is entirely congenial to the analysis of a historical situation in which the very unity of the state being reconstructed was often in question—such as in the case of postwar German reconstruction. Thus the adoption of the language and techniques of social constructionism[12] is entirely appropriate to the empirical situation at hand.

Methodology

It is my contention that best way to approach questions involving large-scale processes such as "reconstruction" is through an explicit consideration of *legitimacy*; and in this particular case the legitimacy of American[13] actions in Germany after the war. The importance of legitimacy flows directly from the concept of "reconstruction" itself, which might be defined as the process by which a new social order is built on the ashes of an old social order. In the case of German reconstruction, the process takes the form of a path back to sovereign statehood;[14] the form of the sovereign state directs reconstruction into at least three conceptually distinguishable areas, namely the establishment of governing institutions, a functioning political economy, and some armed forces.[15] Reconstruction can be said to have been completed when all three of these areas have been addressed, which in my estimation occurs by 1955 when the rearmed West German state becomes a member of NATO. Although there have been many attempts in recent years to analyze the creating and sustaining of social orders without deploying the concept of legitimacy[16]—and thus attempting to analyze social reality *without* adopting any of the social constructionist commitments which I am advocating here—Max Weber's classic statement still retains analytical utility:

> Experience shows that in no instance does domination voluntarily limit itself to the appeal to material or affectual or ideal motives as a basis for its continuance. In addition every such system attempts to establish and to cultivate the belief in its legitimacy. . . . What is important is the fact that in a given case the particular claim to legitimacy is to a significant degree and according to its type *treated as "valid"*; that this fact confirms the position of the persons claiming authority and that it helps to determine the choice of means of its exercise. (Weber 1978: 213–214, emphasis added)[17]

Legitimacy, as Weber makes clear, is fundamentally "a *belief*, a belief by virtue of which persons exercising authority are lent prestige," (Weber 1978: 263) and the process of establishing legitimacy is never simply reducible to the aggregation of pre-existing material interests.[18] A social order that existed without *any* appeal to legitimacy would be a situation of pure domination, and it is unlikely that any such social order has ever existed (or could exist, because even the most pure dictatorship needs soldiers with guns to enforce its order, and these soldiers need something to keep them from turning their guns back on the erstwhile authorities). Reconstruction necessarily involves the legitimation of the new institutions and practices among the subjects of the new regime. And this process always has something of a strategic element to it, as there is always room in a symbolic technology for a "diplomatic choice" of ways of characterizing a situation (Mills 1940: 907). The interesting question is *how* different deployments and usages of particular rhetorical commonplaces come together to produce outcomes, such as the construction of a new social order in the western zones of occupied Germany.

The concept of legitimacy can also shed some light on the American side of the story. Since it was by no means obvious that the United States should take a leading role in the reconstruction of Germany, it was necessary that this policy be justified to the American public. To be sure, part of this justification involved a direct appeal to "material or affectual or ideal motives," but these do not exhaust the scope of the justifications given by key policy makers for their actions. In fact, there is a striking similarity in the justifications advanced by American and German policy makers and political leaders: both groups of officials seek to ground the reconstruction of Germany by the United States in the notion of the West, arguing that their actions are in accord with (or even demanded by) the heritage of Western Civilization. It is my contention that these appeals to the West—the rhetorical commonplace which I term "Occidentalism"—are a causally important part of the process of German reconstruction.

Because of the nature of the issues I am examining, a research strategy based on independent and dependent variables is not appropriate; what is called for, rather, is a tracing of the rhetorical commonplace of the West as it progresses from German academia to American policy discourse and back to West German governmental actions. The primary point here is that rhetorical commonplaces are a *constitutive* part of the policies which they help to produce, and hence are not separable from those policies; instead, the focus should be on the way in which the particular commonplace, in conjunction with others commonplaces, *makes possible* the policy in question, by providing public officials with a discursive context in which the policy may be rendered acceptable. What is being investigated, then, is a *process*, and not merely an *outcome*; while this does not mean that the process of German reconstruction is completely *sui generis*, it does mean that it simply can not be compared to some other reconstructive process using a variant of one of Mill's Methods (Tilly 1997). In particular, a research design seeking to compare Germany and Japan would not be appropriate, both because no strictly comparable *case* exists when one is conducting research on constitutive elements of a situation,[19] and because the object of analysis is neither "Germany" nor "America," but rather the symbolic technology of the West which occupies a transnational "region" somewhere beyond state boundaries.[20] Instead of looking for cases to compare this account of reconstruction to, we should be looking for situations in which a rhetorical commonplace could be traced through a concrete process of legitimation which results in the (re)production of an actor with relatively stable boundaries. In the terms that Daniel Nexon and I deploy elsewhere in this volume (chapter 3), we should not be trying to construct (case) comparisons as much as we should be comparing constructions (of entities in social life). What is generalizable from an account such as this is not a specific set of nomothetic generalizations, but a "toolkit" of analytical devices which might be used to analyze similar situations.

A final methodological consideration concerns the appropriate places to look for evidence of the symbolic technology of occidentalism. These are somewhat different than the usual sources to which analysts turn when trying to make causal arguments. Since much of the traditional work on postwar reconstruction is interested in motivation, it makes sense for such research to concentrate on those documentary sources which have the best chance of revealing an actor's true motives: private records, personal letters, and similarly "hidden" sources that are less likely to have been corrupted by strategic deployment. As I am not interested in motivation, but in the intersubjective presentation of intentions, the relevant source material is almost wholly public: press conferences, speeches, legislative hearings. This reversal of the ordinary historian's rule of evidence is justified by the nature of the research and the ontological and epistemological status of the investigation (Ringmar 1996: 41–42). Intersubjective processes of social construction should be sought where they actually occur, which is *not* inside of individual heads.

Occidentalism in Practice

It is my contention that the rhetorical commonplace of occidentalism, when incorporated into the public legitimation of policies, exercised a causal (in the sense discussed above) impact on the course of German reconstruction, helping to shape the process at almost every step. In order to understand how appeals to the West produce this effect, it is necessary to examine the content of the commonplace in more detail; this will also provide an account of the proximate origins of the notion in nineteenth-century German social thought. I believe that it is useful to divide a rhetorical commonplace into two "levels" or "moments" for the purposes of explanation: first, a "mythological"[21] level, which contains the basic discursive materials which may be used to justify a number of actions and policies, and second, an "ideological"[22] level, which contains the specific articulations or projects linking the more general myths to specific courses of action.[23] This two-part division is analogous to the common distinction between underlying and proximate causes: both components exercise causal powers, but in somewhat different ways.[24] Since the myths come before the ideological projects both logically and empirically, I will discuss them first.[25]

Mythology

A complete tracing of the mythology of the West would have to extend at least as far back as the fifth century BCE, when Herodotus and other Greek thinkers propounded a division of the world along "continental" lines (Lewis and Wigen 1997: 21–23); comparison of these regions, and their ranking in a sequence from east to west, was accomplished by a few centuries later, when the Romans began to see themselves as the most recent bearers of the torch of civilization from east to west (Schulte Nordholt 1995: 2–4). However, it is not necessary to go back quite this far in order to understand the version of the commonplace which is relevant to postwar German reconstruction. There are two distinct lines of thought contributing to the notion of the West with which we are familiar, and it was the accomplishment of nineteenth-century German social thinkers to combine them and thus create the myth which is causally significant.[26] The first line of thought is the "heliotropic" notion that civilization follows the path of the sun, and continually increases and advances as one moves further to the west; it is linked to the theme of "imperial succession," and hence manifests itself in the discourse legitimating the various European colonial empires (Schulte Nordholt 1995; Baritz 1961). There is a strong component of historical destiny in this line; heliotropism provides the basis for the claim that the West is superior to all other cultures and civilizations. The other line of thought is a "metageography" that regards the West as a *destination* rather than merely a *direction*, and seeks to discover specific cultural attributes which can be linked to the particular territory of the West. As Christopher GoGwilt has argued, this metageographical notion of the West emerged in the debates between "Slavophiles" and "Westerners" in nineteenth-century Russia; it was then linked to the "heliotropic" notion of the West by German social theorists anxious to differentiate themselves and their country from Russia (GoGwilt 1995; cf. Neumann 1996). It is my contention that this composite West is the relevant symbolic technology for the purposes of this account.

In this form, the West was deployed by German intellectuals anxious to explain the events of the nineteenth century, most notably the rise of European countries to world dominance. A striking example of this usage can be found in Hegel's "philosophical history":

> In the geographical survey the general course of world history is given. The sun, the light, rises in the East [*Morgenlande*]. But the light is simple self-relation; that light which is general in itself is at the same time a subject, in the sun. . . . World history goes from East to West, for Europe is simply the end of world history, just as Asia is its beginning. For world history there is an East *par excellence*, as opposed to the merely geographical "East" which is merely relative; although the earth is a sphere, world history does not make a circle around it, but has a much more definite East, and that is Asia. This is where the external physical sun comes up, just as it goes down in the West. . . . (Hegel 1986: 133–134)

The myth of the West also provided a framework for understanding the societal shocks associated with rapid industrialization by situating present events within a broad world-historical course of cultural development; fertile ground was also provided for those wishing to critique these "modern" transformations on the grounds of a supposedly "ancient" tradition of cultural values. This is one of the functions of a myth: to order a series of disparate facts, and lend coherence to a flow of events. The acceptance of a myth therefore depends on its "plausibility," which is to say on its ability to account for facts; but we should not fall into the trap of assuming that people make individually rational choices about which myth to adopt based on explanatory power (which would be a subtle form of functionalism).[27] Instead, the process by which a new myth is introduced is a subtle and contingent affair, and the point of a conceptual investigation like this one must be "to identify the accidents, the minute deviations—or, conversely, the complete reversals—the errors, the false appraisals, and the faulty calculations that gave birth to" a notion like Western civilization (Foucault 1977: 146).

The place to begin is with the intellectual debates surrounding the notion. Two participants in these debates who are particularly important to the dissemination of the myth of the West beyond Germany are Max Weber, whose work helped to establish the West as a cultural unit worthy of analysis as such, and Oswald Spengler, whose depiction of "Western decline" helped to popularize the notion of a crisis of Western Civilization which demanded decisive political action. By singling these authors out, I do not mean to suggest that they are somehow responsible for inventing the West out of whole cloth and then somehow tricking the rest of the world into believing them; rather, they are exemplary of the discourse which shaped the scholarly debate. In addition, both Weber and Spengler acquired English-speaking advocates, who helped spread the myth of the West across the Atlantic to the United States. In addition to less well-known scholars, spokesmen for the West included Talcott Parsons (for Weber) and Arnold Toynbee (for Spengler).

Space limitations prevent me from doing justice to the occidentalist arguments advanced by Weber and Spengler.[28] I will confine myself to two examples, one from each author. For Weber, the most dramatic source is in the introduction to *The Protestant Ethic and the Spirit of Capitalism* ([1930] 1992), which contains a long catalogue of the distinctive elements of the West, including science, law, music, architecture, printing, and the state. It is not that these things have never been known elsewhere, he argues, but that the Western versions of them are qualitatively different. For example:

> The technical basis of our architecture came from the Orient. But the Orient lacked that solution of the problem of the dome and that type of classic rationalization of all art—in painting by the rational utilization of lines and spatial perspective—which the Renaissance created for us. There was printing in China. But a printed literature, designed *only* for print and only possible through it—and, above all, "the press" and "periodicals"—have appeared only in the Occident.

Above all, "[o]nly in the West does 'science' exist at a stage of development which we recognize to-day as 'valid'" (Weber 1992: 13–15). The West was therefore something *unique*, a civilizational community characterized by a plethora of common features, as well as by a common destiny: the "disenchantment of the world" through a process of "rationalization" which replaces spontaneous and organic happenstances with conscious, technical planning (Liebersohn 1988: 136–137).

Oswald Spengler shared this sense of a common Western destiny, although he was considerably less sanguine about it than Weber (not that Weber was exactly a *fan* of the disenchantment of the world).[29] Spengler's best-known book famously predicted—even in its title—*The Decline of the West*, a notion which (although seriously misunderstood) certainly pointed to an inexorable logic of destiny: What is different in each culture (Spengler identifies eight over the course of human history) is not the various stages and phases which it passes through, but how it manifests each stage as it proceeds from youth through maturity to old age. Every culture begins as a vital organism, developing its great works of art and distinctive religion, but eventually passes from the country to the city, from vital connection to the land to the rootless inhabiting of an artificial environment: "all art, all religion and science, become slowly intellectualized, alien to the land, incomprehensible to the peasant of the soil. . . . The immemorially old roots of Being are dried up in the stone-masses of its cities. And the free intellect—fateful word!—appears like a flame, mounts splendid into the air, and pitiably dies" (Spengler 1928: 90–92). At the present time, the culture undergoing this last phase of its life was the West, spanning both Western Europe and the United States. Indeed, he argued that "the word 'Europe' ought to be struck out of history. There is historically no 'European' type. . . . 'East' and 'West' are notions that contain real history, whereas 'Europe' is an empty sound" (Spengler 1926: 16).

What Weber and Spengler share is a sense that there exists a civilizational community encompassing both Western Europe and the United States, and the sense that that community was under threat from processes internal to it. The specifics of their diagnoses are less important to this story than these broad themes, particularly since the response of American intellectuals and politicians to such stories of stultification and decline was to argue that the West could be saved if the correct policies were enacted. In so arguing, American interlocutors *accepted* the occidentalist commonplace even as they *rejected* the pessimistic implications drawn by many of its initial formulators. The myth of the West was called into service around the time of World War I, when government-sponsored initiatives to educate Americans about the issues of the war picked up the myth and produced the "War Issues" course, a fixture at universities across the country in the interwar period (Allardyce 1982; Levine 1996). As part of a general attempt to place World War I in context, the myth of the West became firmly ensconced in the intellectual environment of the United States, helping to reorient (or, perhaps, reoccident?) the American view of Europe and making possible the consideration of alternatives other than traditional American isolationism. The myth of the West had not yet achieved dominant status, but it had become part of the backdrop against which an ideological project could be articulated.

Ideology

The "ideological" moment in the process occurs after World War II, when American policy makers were searching for a basis on which to place their postwar policies; uncertainty about Soviet intentions rendered the "antifascist alliance" somewhat questionable, and anticommunism made continued close cooperation with the Soviet Union difficult at best—even if it had proved cooperative with U.S. initiatives (Leffler 1994). Several options, including a return to isolation, emerged as possibilities for American policy; these options struggled for control of U.S. policy, until a project deploying the notion of the West emerged victorious and rendered isolationist policies illegitimate. As is well known, the victorious project committed the United States to the economic reconstruction of Europe through the Marshall Plan, and led to the establishment of the United States' first peacetime alliance in the North Atlantic Treaty. At the same time, postwar German leaders were searching for a viable policy to pursue in trying to put their country back together again; options included a communist Germany aligned with the Soviet Union, a socialist Germany which would remain neutral, and a capitalist Germany which would be a part of the West. The ensuing battle of projects led to a victory for the "Western" strategy, and underpinned the West German state's inclusion in the Marshall Plan and its rearmament under the auspices of NATO, the Western Alliance. The symbolic technology of the West also rendered the West German state *itself* legitimate, mainly through Konrad Adenauer's public diagnosis of Nazism as resulting from a "Prussian" authoritarian tendency which Germany would be better off without.

One way to see the impact of this rhetorical strategy is to briefly contrast the activities undertaken toward the reconstruction of Germany after the World War II with those undertaken after World War I. After both wars, the German economy[30] was in a shambles, and the existent currency was essentially worthless; shortages of key materials and the military occupation of industrial areas like the Ruhr combined to produce a situation in dire need of governmental action. After World War I, as is well known, the Allied governments imposed an impossible reparations burden on Germany, seeking both to recover some of their own expenses and to prevent Germany from threatening the peace again. This harshness indicates that the political leaders of the Allied countries were not viewing Germany as a country which belonged in a group with them; indeed, some even spoke of an "'iron curtain' between Germany and the West" (Craig 1978: 442), which effectively placed Germany outside of the community that included Britain and France (and the United States, although it had made clear its desire to withdraw from what were still understood as purely European affairs soon after the war, with its repudiation of the League of Nations). While it is surely the case that political leaders, especially those in France, were inspired by a desire to preserve their countries from a future German attack, their position was certainly encouraged by the availability of this rhetoric: The notion that Germany was somehow other than the West was extremely helpful in legitimating a firm anti-German stance.[31] In the United States, of course, the position of Germany was even more removed, as the United States sought a return to "normalcy" by wanting little to do with Europe in any official capacity; hence the United States, which could not yet conceive of itself as the leader of the West, did not put forth any kind of comprehensive plan to rebuild Germany. Americans (Dawes and Young) headed the two commissions which put forth more-or-less temporary fixes for Germany's difficulties in keeping up with reparations payments, but the United States as a whole was not officially involved.

It is important to note that the United States' refusal to become involved officially in European affairs was not simply generated by the victory of a homogenous "isolationist" position; the rhetorical coalition of firm opponents to the League revolved principally around the notion that the United States was ontologically distinct from Europe, a kind of "American exceptionalism" which suggested that the best course for the United States was to remain aloof from the power-political games of the Old World. The arguments about foreign affairs found in the works of the country's founders had a "prelapsarian" character, "intent upon preventing the original sin of a balance of power from being committed in North America" (Ninkovich 1994: 46). This appeal linked up with domestic anticommunism, which in this period was not directed *outward* at the Soviet Union as much as it was directed *inward* and aimed at internal purification: "Most Americans were more concerned with Bolshevism at home than with Bolshevism abroad" (Leffler 1994: 14–15). These formed the basis of powerful arguments against American involvement in Europe. Transcending them would require some kind of breaking down of American exceptionalism, so that anticommunism could be retargeted at *external* threats and thus legitimate the "foreign entanglements" warned against in such traditional American documents as George Washington's Farewell Address. Absent any such rhetorical linking mechanism, the United States stayed relatively uninvolved.

The results are well known: the New York stock market crash led to a cascading failure of all of the industrialized economies, but the German economy was perhaps the hardest hit. No international institutions were in place to help deal with the effects of this widespread depression; lacking the ideological underpinnings that would enable the conceptualization of the Western world as an economic unit, states pursued individual programs, and the confusion persisted until the alliance against Hitler came into being in the 1940s. It is interesting to note that this alliance was never "the West," as it included Russia; sometimes it was "the free world," but graphic depictions of this version of the alliance usually limited themselves to the United States and Britain.[32] Ironically, the only major political leader drawing on the notion of the West for legitimacy was Adolf Hitler, who sometimes claimed that Nazi Germany was the only possible border against Eastern Bolshevism;

Hitler's ideological package was extremely eclectic, however, and his appeals to the West had little effect.

U.S. inaction and the persistence of an ideological system which excluded Germany as a whole stands in direct contrast to the ideological project promulgated after World War II. During the interwar period, bolstered by the transformation of the older "war issues" course into the more elaborate "Western Civ" course as well as by the entry into political life of those who had served in World War I (or had been influenced by the rhetoric directed at those who had), a new ideological project took shape in the United States, one which held that the effective unit in terms of which policy had to be made was larger than one state (Fromkin 1996). That unit, not surprisingly, was the West, a cultural community to which such diverse minds as Walter Lippmann, T.S. Eliot, and George Kennan applied their analytical skills and public performances. A particularly clear statement of the new salience of the West is Carlton Hayes' Presidential Address to the American Historical Association on December 27, 1945:

> The principal threads of our historic Western culture, like those of the Chinese or Moslem cultures, have not suddenly been cut in A.D. 1945. . . . American history should, of course, be taught in our schools—more, rather than less, American history—but it should not be taught as beginning with the political independence of a new nation in 1776 or even with the discovery of a New World in 1492. To understand what America really is, of what actually it is a frontier, its history should be studied continuously from at least the ancient Greeks and the first Christians. (Hayes 1946: 215)

This project had two major implications for postwar reconstruction: new institutions, both domestic and international, had to be built to contain the social pressures that had given rise to the two world wars; and the United States, as leader of the West, needed to take the lead in this process.

In Germany, meanwhile, the end of the war saw the reemergence of those scholars who had been exploring the notion of the West, particularly those economic theorists and historians who were searching for a "third way" of organizing state/market relations which would be between strict laissez-faire and totalitarian command (Nicholls 1994). Bolstered both by the return of scholars who had fled Germany, and by the lifting of formal and informal restrictions on academic debate, a new school of "neoliberal" thought emerged, and sought to link the tradition of theorizing about the West with specific policy recommendations for a new Germany. This group, centered at Freiburg, articulated a detailed plan of socioeconomic organization, which they called the Social Market Economy (*Soziale Marktwirtschaft*); this plan was depicted as the result of a long historical evolution in Western civilization, and intentionally linked by several of the initial articulators of the project to the older German intellectual tradition of Weber and Spengler (Friedrich 1955).

But it was not only scholars who made such arguments. In his initial statement before joint House and Senate Committees on the foreign aid package which would eventually become the Marshall Plan, Secretary of State George Marshall argued:

> The automatic success of the program cannot be guaranteed. The imponderables are many. The risks are real. They are, however, risks which have been carefully calculated, and I believe that the chances of success are good. There is convincing evidence that the peoples of western Europe want to preserve their free society *and the heritage we share with them.* To make that choice conclusive they need our assistance. . . . In helping them we will be helping ourselves—because, in the larger sense, our national interests coincide with those of a free and prosperous Europe. (U.S. Congress 1947: 9)

I have added emphasis to the significant section of the argument, which grounds Marshall's evaluation of "our national interests" and serves as the basis for the policy as a whole. It is true that this is only one part of one sentence, but its role in framing the issue is crucial: it implies that if the European countries were no longer willing or able to preserve this heritage, aid would not be forthcoming. The program is cast not merely as an initiative for *economic* recovery, but for *civilizational* recovery as well. Similarly, when speaking before the House Foreign Affairs Committee a few months later, Marshall declared:

> [If the European countries are] left to their own resources there will be, I believe, no escape from economic distress so intense, social discontent so violent, political confusion so widespread, and hope of the future so shattered that the historic base of Western civilization, of which we are by belief and inheritance an integral part, will take on new form in the image of the tyranny we fought to destroy in Germany. (quoted in Pogue 1987: 240)

Two things are striking in this appeal: Marshall's deployment of the prominent reference to the West, and his implicit characterization of Nazism as outside of the West. The terms of debate had obviously shifted, so that an appeal like this could be found in such a public setting. Such an articulation struck against the rhetorical heart of the so-called isolationist position, decoupling the character of the United States from anticommunism by linking the United States to a broader cultural community; threats to this larger community can now be understood as issues for the United States, and in particular the threat of communism in western Europe can be understood as the kind of thing which the United States should legitimately expend resources to oppose. Opponents of American involvement in Europe now had to confront the charge of being "anti-Western" while still claiming to oppose communism, a task which proved beyond the rhetorical skill of most "isolationists."

A distinctive component of the postwar American vision involved the relationship between technical economic administration and the defense of the West from communism. Throughout this period the opposition to communism rested more on a characterization that communist doctrine was wrong about economic realities and represented the deluded response of deprived individuals to an unhealthy economic situation, than on the later McCarthyite notion that the real threat came from organized communist infiltrators. The opposition to communism thus adopted two forms: the "counter[ing] of the Kremlin's propaganda of the lie with its [America's] own propaganda of the truth," as Paul Hoffman, the Administrator of the Economic Cooperation Administration (ECA, the agency that carried out the Marshall Plan) expressed it, (Hoffman 1951: 134–136) and the strengthening of the rational functioning of the free market through the application of American technical knowledge, which would "eradicat[e] the social and political and economic conditions on which communism thrives." Hoffman's imagery is particularly striking when intertwining these two threads of anticommunism:

> In this respect the Marshall Plan has been and remains pilot plant and proving ground for an American foreign policy that is firm, constructive and far-reaching. . . . [T]he Marshall Plan's hydroelectric power plants and housing developments and tractors and seed have been set against Marxist dialectic; as the Marshall Plan's bread and butter are set in contrast to the hollow cake of the Big Lie. (Hoffman 1951: 33–34)

Because of this close tie between Western values and technical economic efficiency based on scientific facts, it was necessary for the administration of the European Recovery Plan (ERP) to adhere to sound business practices when allocating aid money; otherwise, the deviation from scientifically justified practice would mean the failure of the attempt to shore up the West.

One striking example of this feature of the ERP is the decision on "counterpart funds," which provided that the aid provided by the United States would not be mere charity. The counterpart funds mechanism had been a feature of the United Nations Relief and Rehabilitation Administration (UNRRA), a program which had failed to spark European recovery in the immediate postwar period and whose failure had led to the perception that a new, U.S.-led aid program was required. The counterpart fund mechanism provided that purchasers in a European country wishing to buy goods that were funded under the ERP would deposit the price of the goods in their local currency into a special account; the ECA would pay the American supplier in dollars, and the special account would then be administered jointly by the ECA and the local government to promote reconstruction projects or debt retirement (Arkes 1972: 157; Hogan 1987: 152–153). Besides the technical advantages of this kind of system (essentially, ERP money counted twice: once in dollars and once in local currency; also, the counterpart funds allowed the ECA some discretion over the uses to which aid money was put), the fact that the recipients of U.S. aid would be paying for the goods which they received was important to the moral position of American policy makers.

Alan Dulles, in a book that was intended as a propaganda device in favor of the Marshall Plan, makes a point of stressing that the United States "should not give away this nation's assets without obtaining in return what we can reasonably require from the receiving government"; "outright gifts are unwise," he argues, because "no self-respecting nation likes to be an object of charity" (Dulles 1993: 81). This kind of institutional configuration is in accord with what Dulles calls the "real issues" in world politics in 1947: "a struggle between the principles which underlie the Magna Carta, the Declaration of Independence, the French and American revolutions, on the one hand, and the materialism of Marx, Lenin, and Stalin, on the other—a struggle between the right of the individual and the claims of an all-powerful materialistic state." Two pages later, he comments that "the principles underlying the Declaration of Independence became common to the United States and to much of Western Europe," with the clear implication that it is the responsibility of the United States to defend those historic principles against communist encroachment wherever they are manifest (1993: 109–111).

The supposed congruence of the ERP with the psychological health and self-reliance of individuals—as well as the tenets of good business practice —also figures into ECA efforts to convince businesses to arrange sales with European purchasers under the ERP:

> The citizens in the Western European nations who receive American products under the Marshall Plan do not get them for *free*. Our aid is free to the nations but not to the individuals. They *pay* their own governments for the products in their own currencies. . . . The ECA serves as the *banker* for the buyers and sellers, making sure that the investments in the economic recovery of Western Europe are on the soundest possible basis to yield to greatest returns in world peace and prosperity. (ECA 1949: 1–2)

The scientific and technical justification for a businesslike ERP is thus linked to a moral imperative with its roots deep in Western Christianity; economic health requires individual thrift and the balancing of accounts. The emphasis in this kind of anticommunism, then, is not only on the *goal* of defending the West, but on the effect of the *means* used to combat communist initiatives; "[i]t was not just the United States" that policy makers "sought to serve but, in a broader sense, the culture and civilization of the West" (Isaacson and Thomas 1986: 406–407). The intertwining of moral, scientific/technical, and economic imperatives constitutes the American approach to the postwar world, and stems from a social order which had been legitimated by the process of recovering from the Great Depression; in elaborating the mechanisms and goals of the ERP, policy makers were engaged in working out tactics for the furthering of a strategy which is more about a politicized West than about the pursuit of a narrow American advantage.[33]

This project can also be seen in the German debates, especially in the person of Konrad Adenauer. As one historian has pointed out, Adenauer's "German Catholic condemnation of communism is made not only from a religious and moral basis, but also on the grounds of the supposed excellence of Western civilization, which permits the believer to close his mind to criticism from the other camp with a good conscience" (Grosser 1964: 97). At a speech given in 1946—just after he had been elected president of the Christian Democratic Union (CDU) in the British Zone—Adenauer defined Christian Democracy in this way:

> We name ourselves Christian democrats because we are of the deep conviction that only a democracy which is rooted in a western-Christian worldview, in Christian natural law, and in the basic principles of Christian ethics can accomplish the great task of educating the German people and bringing about their reascension [*Wiederaufstieg*].[34] (Adenauer 1975: 87)

Even more striking is Adenauer's analysis of the Nazi period, which diagnoses the failure of the German social order to prevent a totalitarian dictatorship as a weakness of the spirit. "National Socialism," he argues in his memoirs, "despite its suppression of individual liberty, had found so large a following because political awareness and responsibility were very poorly developed in a great many people." This lack of development results from a lack of attention to "[t]he proposition that the dignity of the individual must be the paramount consideration, even above the power of the state, . . . [which] derives naturally from occidental Christianity" (Adenauer 1966: 45). Therefore the turn towards Christian principles represented a solution to the problem of reestablishing a legitimate German social order in the wake of the

Nazi regime: the Nazi period was characterized as an aberration, a deroga-
tion from the basic principles of the Christian West, and the renewed stress
on the dignity of the individual was seen as a return to the proper course.

This new social order was manifested in a number of positions adopted
by the CDU (under Adenauer's considerable influence), including the support for European integration, the strongly religious and natural-law oriented language of the Preamble and first article of the *Grundgesetz*, and
the support for a federal German structure which removed the power to
centrally administer the economy from the central government. Significantly, the CDU also downplayed the anticapitalist dimensions of its program, and accepted the free market as one of the basic organizing principles
of a legitimate social order. Adenauer's opposition contributed to the rejection of the quasi-socialistic methods proposed by the CDU's more conservative Catholic components; he "was one of the first to employ the
formula distinguishing between political dictatorship—necessarily bound
to a planned economy—and a liberal market economy equated with political freedom" (Ambrosius 1977: 24–26). The effect of this formula was to
delegitimate the demands of those—both inside and outside of the CDU—
who would increase the role of the government in the market by linking
their position to both the Nazis and the communists, and strengthen
Adenauer's own position. Instead of the replacement of capitalism, the
CDU undertook to make capitalism work in accordance with Christian principles. The method that they adopted to achieve this goal was the *Soziale
Marktwirtschaft*, which sought to give the market as much leeway as possible while using the state to ensure that certain basic minimum standards
of living were met.

The postwar German economy can therefore be understood as resting on
three basic imperatives that were closely intertwined parts of the German
postwar strategy: the Christian stress on the dignity of the individual, the
support for the free market and the ownership structure of capitalism, and
the understanding of economic rationality as a technical matter best achieved
by scientific experts. Ludwig Erhard, nicknamed "the Professor," exempli-
fies these notions; firmly committed to defending the principle of individual
liberty through the application of economic science, Erhard was a powerful
member of the Adenauer government throughout the postwar period, and
helped to shore up the market economy through his influence. He successfully prevented the German government from becoming too involved in the
operations of the economy, and contributed greatly to the relegitimation of
the social order. Erhard also masterminded the currency reform of 1948 that
led to the "shop window miracle" as merchants brought previously hoarded
goods out to be sold for the new currency, and the evident success of the

reform reinforced his claim to be a custodian of objective knowledge which he could use on behalf of the ordinary citizen.

All three of these principles are explicitly tied to the symbolic technology of the West, which transforms these abstract principles into weapons which can be used in defense of Western Civilization. In particular, politicians are able to articulate their appeals using the language of the West, and render their policy prescriptions, such as the reincorporation of Germany into the U.S.-led international economic system as a full partner and the steady raising of the level of German domestic industry despite French resistance, justified. In fact, the use of a project based on Western civilization reduced the options available for the French to keep up their opposition to German reconstruction, as there was not enough discursive space for such claims to carry much weight. In the event, the French strategy for minimizing the chances of a renewed German attack involved the mutual binding of the French and German economies in the European Coal and Steel Community (later replaced by the EEC): driving Germany further into the West, rather than excluding it.

Implications

Two implications follow from this brief examination of postwar German reconstruction, one theoretical, the other empirical. Earlier, I claimed that what was likely to be "generalizable" from a relational account of legitimation was a set of analytical tools which might be used to parse different situations, and the theoretical result of this chapter is in fact to have begun the development of such a set of tools. In particular, the notion of a *rhetorical commonplace* can be applied to other situations, providing a way of linking the language used by policy makers with the language already present among their audience without descending into the misleading problem of the (neopositivist causal) "role of ideas." Is it not as if George Marshall and Konrad Adenauer shared particular *beliefs* with their audiences, or with one another; had they done so, there would have been no need for Adenauer and Marshall to *articulate* their positions in language, as the previously internalized beliefs would have simply done their causal work in the privacy of each person's head. Instead, if we regard public speech acts as deployments of rhetorical commonplaces which inhabit an *intersubjective* realm, we can account for "persuasiveness" and the like without having to penetrate people's skulls—which, given the probably insurmountable practical difficulties involved in doing so, is undoubtedly a good thing.

In addition to the concept of a rhetorical commonplace, the distinction between the "mythological" and "ideological" moments of a commonplace can be profitably utilized to analyze other commonplaces, as they are imagined and disseminated as myth and then deployed as ideology to legitimate particular courses of action. Keeping this dual character of rhetorical commonplaces in mind can help to protect us from the error of assuming that policy makers can simply offer any grounds they like in justifying a policy, and also from the error of assuming that the only influence which intellectuals might have on policy lies in the wholesale adoption of their positions by politicians (a presumption which seems to inform quite a bit of the literature on the "role of ideas"): myths permit *various* ideological deployments. Finally, the focus on legitimation *itself* can be applied elsewhere, to any situation in which courses of action are rendered acceptable or unacceptable by a process of drawing boundaries around the limits of what is permissible. Legitimation is a kind of *boundary-demarcation*, a process whereby rhetorical commonplaces are assembled so as to produce a social space in which action may be meaningfully carried out. A successful legitimation process produces an *actor* in the name of which action is performed, and thus establishes the limits of *agency* for that actor: Where after World War I the United States could not support a massive European recovery program, after World War II it could do so. Intersubjective process, not any essential attributes of some putative "agent," should be the focus of our analyses (Jackson and Nexon 1999).

This leads to the second, more empirical, implication of the investigation. The rhetorical commonplace of "occidentalism," and in particular the notion of the West as a civilizational community that it carries with it, is a key feature of the postwar world order, helping to legitimate forms of socioeconomic organization in several countries. One might say that the West helped to grease the wheels of American hegemony, transforming U.S. dominance from a threat requiring other states to balance against a potential world conqueror, into a benefit worthy of bandwagoning with. Or one might say that "occidentalism" decreased the likelihood of defection from the western alliance, and thus helped to determine its form. But these are only partial ways of expressing a more important conclusion: "occidentalism" helped to reconfigure the very identities of states involved, rendering certain actions permissible and others impermissible by "nesting" them inside of a larger community in whose name significant aspects of postwar reconstruction were carried out (Ferguson and Mansbach 1996: 47–51).

In a way, postwar reconstruction *created a new actor in world politics*: Western civilization. The character of the postwar order—embedded liberalism, multilateralism, democratic solidarity, what have you—cannot be correctly understood without accounting for the actual language used to legitimate the policies actually followed by state officials, and that language tends to invoke the larger civilizational community in which the particular states are thought to be embedded. It is only the state-centric prejudices of our implicit "map" of the world that demand that we attribute all action in world politics to *state* actors, even when those actions are themselves conceptualized and legitimated in radically different terms. We need to get past the notion that *either* "domestic politics" or "the international system" constitutes discrete, closed realms of interaction, and focus instead on the concrete transactional processes which serve to demarcate these two realms from one another at certain times, while not doing so at other times. Postwar reconstruction is best understood as a *mutation* in those (transnational) processes of boundary demarcation, and the emergence of a novel entity in whose name action could be carried out.

In important respects, postwar reconstruction policies are *not* "state policies" at all, but "civilizational" policies, demanding a rather different set of theoretical lenses through which to view them properly. We cannot do this as long as we persist in trying to impose an abstractly derived set of actors and identities on a mass of social relations, ignoring the manifest patterns formed *by those relations themselves.* "Don't think, but look!" Wittgenstein once urged (Wittgenstein 1953: §66); if we do so, we discover that world politics is a good deal more complex than traditional accounts privileging state action would have us believe. There are more actors in the world than merely states, more boundaries than those delimiting spheres of sovereign territorial authority, and more forms of influence than those which directly alter governmental policies. Agency consists of discursively produced social spaces, continually being renegotiated through a myriad of complex transactions; the contours of those social spaces *should* be the object of our investigations into the texture of world politics.

Studying the postwar settlement from this angle can also shed some light on the persistence of the notion of the West as a rallying cry for countries seeking admission to the EU and NATO. In addition, an awareness of the constructed nature and recent vintage of this civilizational actor may prompt us to start asking whether the West really *is* the best after all, instead of taking it for granted as we so often do.

Notes

1. From the song "The End," composed and performed by The Doors (although scholars agree that the lyrics were written by Morrison), from the album *The Doors* (Electra Records, 1968).

2. I do this at considerably greater length in my dissertation (Jackson 2001). What follows in this chapter is a much abbreviated account.

3. To be fair, Wendt makes this move in an effort to develop a theory of *the international system*; such a theory, he suggests, must be state-centric: "it makes no

more sense to criticize a theory of international politics as 'state-centric' than it does to criticize a theory of forests for being 'tree-centric'" (Wendt 1999: 9). As I argue below, I am not interested in developing such a theory, and it is from this perspective that Wendt's state-centrism appears "unfortunate."

4. Even theorists of "domestic politics" tend to keep this 'solidity' in place, usually by introducing domestic politics as an intervening variable between international ("outside") causes and foreign policy outcomes; state borders may drop into the background of the analysis, but as long as they are present as presumptive units, the analysis remains to some degree state-centric.

5. For instance, Robert Pollard (1985) points out that the United States had a variety of policy instruments from which to choose in balancing against the Soviet Union, and was initially reluctant to use military instruments; he understands the Marshall Plan as a sophisticated instrument for the pursuit of security instruments. At base, objective and material factors drive policy.

6. This was the contention of many Marxian "revisionist" scholars, who saw the postwar economic order as a way for the United States to stave off a crisis of overproduction by opening foreign markets.

7. This argument is consistent with the analysis of "hegemonic stability theory" advanced by such authors as Charles Kindleberger and Arthur Stein; other states have an incentive to assent to this hegemony so that they can "free ride" on the hegemon's activities.

8. And many philosophers of science feel that it has little use even there; see, e.g., Bhaskar (1975).

9. Intentions are "public" and motivations are "private" in precisely the same sense in which this distinction is utilized by Wittgenstein in his denial of the possibility of a "private language" (Wittgenstein 1953: 269–278).

10. An exception, of course, would be covert activity, which by definition is not publicly known and does not require public justification; however, public reasons usually have to be given for the existence of covert activities in the first place, and there is usually some *post facto* public oversight of covert activities (which sometimes results in actors being punished for not having good enough reasons for their actions). So reasons are merely delayed, not dispensed with, in covert activity.

11. This is an important qualification, because two states might use a symbolic technology which casts each of them in the world-historical role of global savior, and their relations might be highly conflictual after that.

12. I utilize this term rather than the more familiar "constructivism" in order to signal the fact that my inspiration is the sociological and social theoretical literatures—particularly that associated with "relational" sociology (Emirbayer 1997)—rather than what might be called "mainstream IR constructivism." Mainstream IR constructivism is largely concerned with the causal impact of roles and norms, and questions of whether "logics of consequences" or "logics of appropriateness" are better accounts of social behavior; relational sociological constructionism is more concerned with intersubjective negotiations of meaning and processes of social transaction.

13. I am focusing on American actions because the United States took a leading role in German reconstruction almost from the beginning of the occupation, and certainly from the point at which the fusion of the American and British zones began to become a reality (mid-1946). The French are important to these events primarily as the state which was most opposed to *any* reconstruction of Germany, but which even-

tually acquiesced after a long period of U.S. pressure. Legitimacy is not unimportant to this part of the story either, as I shall discuss below.

14. Legal sovereignty for Germany was assumed by the four allied powers by the Declaration of Berlin, June 5, 1945; from this point, the Allies were the legitimate government of Germany and would remain so until sovereignty was formally transferred to a new German government. See the discussion in Kelsen (1945).

15. Many scholars have established the links between the form of the sovereign state and these three specific areas; for sophisticated recent treatments, see Giddens (1985), Thomson (1994), and Spruyt (1994).

16. Indeed, several of these efforts are quite explicit about trying to eliminate the concept of legitimacy from their theoretical repertoire, and replacing it with a rational-choice model of human behavior in which social orders can be accounted for by examining the utility-maximizing calculations of individuals. For examples of this kind of work, see Przeworski (1985) and Levi (1988).

17. While Weber initially deployed legitimacy as a typological category useful for distinguishing between rational, traditional, and charismatic types of domination, I believe that the concept can be used in general to refer to the grounds on which any given ruling organization makes its claim to rule, and so the fact that the postwar German government relied primarily on rational authority (as do most modern states) does not preclude further analysis. On this extension of the concept of "legitimacy," see Habermas (1975) and Lyotard (1984).

18. Note that Weber's use of the word "belief" in this context is not charged with the same resonance as is the usage of the word "belief" I have criticized above; in my reading, Weber grants intersubjective factors far more autonomy than most contemporary analysts of the "role of ideas."

19. James Fearon stresses the importance of "counterfactuals" in conducting neopositivist causal analyses (1991). In the case of constitutive factors, however, *there is no possible or cotenable counterfactual*, because removing a constitutive factor does not leave the rest of the situation untouched, but instead eliminates it entirely. Think of trying to remove "Irish national sentiment" from the IRA; what would be left to compare to other cases?

20. It would be correct to say that I am using "German reconstruction" as a case in which to view the effects of the symbolic technology of the West; an appropriate parallel would therefore be with something like the symbolic technology of "China" as it appears in the Han empire, or the symbolic technology of "Europe" as it appears in European colonialism or European integration. Again, Tilly's (1997) argument is relevant here: the purpose of social research is to trace causal processes in historically specific circumstances.

21. This mythological level is comparable to what John Ruggie (1993) has called the "social episteme," which contains the raw interpretive material out of which actors generate functional stories about their everyday experiences. My use of the term "mythological" is drawn from Joseph Campbell's work on the role played by myth in everyday life (1968).

22. I am not using the term "ideological" in a pejorative sense here, but more after the fashion of Mannheim's (1936) notion of a "total" or "nonevaluative" ideology which is simply a condition of social life as such: more specific and concrete than myth, but still fully a part of the identity-level which mediates between actors and their material reality.

23. This two-level distinction is widespread in post-Marxist thought on the ques-

tions of legitimacy and (Gramscian) hegemony, although each author has a slightly different way of expressing the distinction: Bob Jessop (1990) speaks of "islands of discourse" which are knitted together to form a "hegemonic project," while Laclau and Mouffe (1985) prefer to conceptualize "fragments" being reassembled by an "articulatory practice." Although there are debates about the precise ontological status of these various elements, there is general agreement that there are two different components of any given project or articulation.

24. To be extremely precise, neither myths nor ideologies are "proximate causes" of action, since proximate causes are usually understood to be *necessary* causes as well; by definition, no intersubjective or discursive factor can be a necessary cause, since the very concept of "necessity" is tied up with the notion of counterfactuality and the refusal to consider constitutive factors in a way that "sufficiency" is not.

25. Myths have to be disseminated throughout the relevant target audience before projects based on them have a chance of controlling policy; as Gramsci put it, a "war of position" must precede any possible "war of movement."

26. What is being investigated here has the character of what Foucault (1972) has called a "discursive formation," which is less a particular word or phrase than a habit of thought and action (especially interpretive action). Hence it is not enough to look for uses of the term "the West" or "Western civilization," since the context in which this term is rendered meaningful is not static, but changes in observable (if not predictable) ways over time.

27. This kind of functionalism is widespread among mainstream IR constructivist arguments; see Jackson and Nexon (2001) for a more detailed exposition of this argument.

28. Interested readers are referred to chapters 3 and 4 of my dissertation (Jackson 2001).

29. Weber's fundamental discomfort with rationalization and the disenchantment of the world can easily be seen in his choice of terms like "the iron cage" to describe the contemporary impact of innerworldly asceticism (Weber 1930 [1992]: 181–183).

30. I will concentrate on the economic aspects of German reconstruction for the remainder of this paper; it should be kept in mind that this economic component is only one of the three parts of reconstruction, which are only separable analytically. In practice, powerful individuals like Lucius Clay or Konrad Adenauer were simultaneously engaging in all three dimensions of reconstruction.

31. There is a certain ambiguity about the precise boundaries of the West, as with any mythology; myths shape thought and perception in a fairly broad sense, and specifics are left to the ideological projects erected "on top" of those myths which have previously diffused throughout the populace. Thus the fact that Germany was thought *not* to be in the West after World War I is not a blow against my argument, as I have never argued that the specific boundaries of the West as conceived by some particular ideological project continue to have causal relevance for later history, but only that the presence of the myth of the West makes possible projects which include (or exclude) Germany in the West, changing the terms of debate in a way which is necessarily causally relevant *for that particular situation*. Besides which, it was more the politicians of France and Britain who drew upon the notion that Germany was not the West, and even after World War II they needed some (American) convincing in order to accept the notion.

32. Frank Capra's *Why We Fight*, a U.S. army training film, which was also released for public viewing as the war went on, is a notable example of this iconography.

33. This does not deny that the United States—and even more importantly, particular corporations and social groups/classes within the United States—enjoyed great material benefits from the postwar settlement. The point is that these benefits cannot be reduced to a generic or objective notion of "interest," because the collective social understanding in terms of which "interest" was calculated shifted during this period. One cannot account for the content of the structures of the post-war world without explicit consideration of this cultural strategy.

34. The word *Wiederaufstieg* is etymologically related to *Wiederauferstehung* (resurrection), and the religious resonance is most probably fully intentional.

Bibliography

Adenauer, Konrad. 1966. *Memoirs 1945–53*, trans. Beate Ruhm von Oppen. Chicago: Henry Regnery.

———. 1975. *Reden 1917–1967*, ed. Hans-Peter Schwarz. Stuttgart: Deutsche Verlags-Anstalt.

Allardyce, Gilbert. 1982. "The Rise and Fall of the Western Civilization Course." *American Historical Review* 87: 695–725.

Ambrosius, Gerold. 1977. *Die Durchsetzung der Sozialen Marktwirtschaft in Westdeutschland, 1945–1949*. Stuttgart: Deutsche Verlags-Anstalt.

Anderson, Benedict. 1991. *Imagined Communities*. London: Verso.

Arkes, Hadley. 1972. *Bureaucracy, The Marshall Plan, and the National Interest*. Princeton: Princeton University Press.

Backer, John. 1971. *Priming the German Economy* Durham: Duke University Press.

Baritz, Loren. 1961. "The Idea of the West." *American Historical Review* 66: 618–640.

Bhaskar, Roy. 1975. *A Realist Theory of Science*. London: Verso.

Brubaker, Rogers. 1996. *Nationalism Reframed*. Cambridge: Cambridge University Press.

Campbell, Joseph. 1968. *The Hero With A Thousand Faces*. Princeton: Princeton University Press.

Cox, Robert. 1996. "Towards a Posthegemonic Conceptualization of World Order." In *Approaches to World Order*. Robert Cox and Tim Sinclair, eds., 144–173. Cambridge: Cambridge University Press.

Craig, Gordon A. 1978. *Germany 1866–1945*. Oxford: Oxford University Press.

Davidson, Donald. 1963. "Actions, Reasons, and Causes." *The Journal of Philosophy* 60: 685–700.

Dulles, Alan. 1993. *The Marshall Plan*. Providence, RI: Berg.

Economic Cooperation Administration (ECA). 1949. "Information for American Businessmen on the Marshall Plan." Washington, DC: Office of Marshall Plan Information.

Eisenberg, Carolyn Woods. 1996. *Drawing the Line: The American Decision to Divide Germany*. Cambridge, UK: Cambridge University Press.

Elster, Jon. 1989. *Nuts and Bolts for the Social Sciences*. Cambridge, UK: Cambridge University Press.

Emirbayer, Mustafa. 1997. "Manifesto for a Relational Sociology." *American Journal of Sociology* 103: 281–317.

Fearon, James. 1991. "Counterfactuals and Hypothesis Testing in Political Science." *World Politics* 43: 169–195.

Ferguson, Yale, and Richard Mansbach. 1996. *Polities: Authority, Identities, and Change*. Columbia: University of South Carolina Press.

Foucault, Michel. 1972. *The Archaeology of Knowledge*, trans. A.M. Sheridan Smith. New York: Pantheon.

———. 1977. "Nietzsche, Genealogy, History." In *Language, Counter-Memory, Practice*, trans. Donald F. Bouchard, 139–164. Ithaca: Cornell University Press.

Friedrich, Carl. 1955. "The Political Thought of Neo-Liberalism." *American Political Science Review* 49: 509–525.

Fromkin, David. 1996. *In the Time of the Americans*. New York: Knopf.

Geertz, Clifford. 1973. *The Interpretation of Cultures*. New York: Basic Books.

Giddens, Anthony. 1985. *The Nation-State and Violence*. Berkeley: University of California Press.

Gilpin, Robert. 1981. *War and Change in World Politics*. Cambridge, UK: Cambridge University Press.

GoGwilt, Christopher. 1995. *The Invention of the West*. Stanford: Stanford University Press.

Grosser, Alfred. 1964. *The Federal Republic of Germany*. New York: Frederick A. Praeger.

Habermas, Jürgen. 1975. *Legitimation Crisis*. Boston: Beacon Press.

Hardin, Russell. 1995. *One For All*. Princeton: Princeton University Press.

Hayes, Carlton J. H. 1946. "The American Frontier: Frontier of What?" *American Historical Review* 51: 199–216.

Hechter, Michael. 1987. "Nationalism as Group Solidarity." *Ethnic and Racial Studies* 10, 415–426.

Hegel, G. W. F. 1986. *Vorlesungen über die Philosophie der Geschichte*. Frankfurt am Main: Suhrkamp Taschenbuch Verlag.

Hoffman, Paul G. 1951. *Peace Can Be Won*. Garden City, NY: Doubleday.

Hogan, Michael. 1987. *The Marshall Plan*. Cambridge, UK: Cambridge University Press.

Isaacson, Walter, and Evan Thomas. 1986. *The Wise Men*. New York: Simon and Schuster.

Jackson, Patrick Thaddeus. 2001. "Occidentalism: Rhetoric, Process, and Postwar German Reconstruction." Ph.D. Dissertation, Columbia University, New York.

Jackson, Patrick Thaddeus, and Daniel H. Nexon. 1999. "Relations Before States: Substance, Process, and the Study of World Politics." *European Journal of International Relations* 5: 291–332.

———. 2001. "Whence Causal Mechanisms?" *Dialogue-IO* (available at http://mitpress.mit.edu).

Jessop, Bob. 1990. *State Theory*. University Park: Pennsylvania State University Press.

Kelsen, Hans. 1945. "The Legal Status of Germany According to the Declaration of Berlin." *American Journal of International Law* 39: 518–526.

King, Gary, Robert Keohane, and Sidney Verba. 1994. *Designing Social Inquiry*. Princeton: Princeton University Press.

Koselleck, Reinhart. 1985. "Begriffsgeschichte and Social History." In *Futures Past: On the Semantics of Historical Time*, trans. Keith Tribe, 73–91. Cambridge, MA: MIT Press.

Krasner, Stephen. 1978. *Defending the National Interest*. Princeton: Princeton University Press.

Kratochwil, Friedrich. 1989. *Rules, Norms, and Decisions*. Cambridge, UK: Cambridge University Press.

Laclau, Ernesto, and Chantal Mouffe. 1985. *Hegemony and Socialist Strategy*. London: Verso.

Laffey, Mark, and Jutta Weldes. 1997. "Beyond Belief: Ideas and Symbolic Technologies in the Study of International Relations." *European Journal of International Relations* 3: 193–237.

Laitin, David. 1986. *Hegemony and Culture*. Chicago: University of Chicago Press.

Leffler, Melvyn. 1994. *The Specter of Communism*. New York: Hill and Wang.

Levi, Margaret. 1988. *Of Rule and Revenue*. Berkeley: University of California Press.

Levine, Lawrence. 1996. *The Opening of the American Mind: Canons, Culture and History*. Boston: Beacon Press.

Lewis, Martin, and Kären Wigen. 1997. *The Myth of Continents*. Berkeley: University of California Press.

Liebersohn, Harry. 1988. *Fate and Utopia in German Sociology, 1870–1923*. Cambridge, MA: MIT Press.

Lundestad, Geir. 1990. *The American 'Empire.'* Oslo: Universitetsforlaget.

Lyotard, Jean-François. 1984. *The Postmodern Condition: A Report on Knowledge*, trans. Geoff Bennington and Brian Massumi. Minneapolis: University of Minnestota Press.

Mannheim, Karl. 1936. *Ideology and Utopia*. New York: Harvest Books.

Mills, C. Wright. 1940. "Situated Actions and Vocabularies of Motive," *American Sociological Review* 5(6): 904–913.

Moon, Donald. 1975. "The Logic of Political Inquiry." In *Handbook of Political Science*, vol. 1, ed. Nelson Polsby and Fred I. Greenstein. Reading, MA: Addison-Wesley.

Neumann, Iver. 1996. *Russia and the Idea of Europe*. London: Routledge.

Nicholls, A. J. 1994. *Freedom With Responsibility*. Oxford: Clarendon Press.

Ninkovich, Frank. 1994. *Modernity and Power: A History of the Domino Theory in the Twentieth Century*. Chicago: University of Chicago Press.

Pogue, Forrest. 1987. *George C. Marshall: Statesman, 1945–1959*. New York: Penguin.

Pollard, Robert. 1985. *Economic Security and the Origins of the Cold War*. New York: Columbia University Press.

Przeworski, Adam. 1985. *Capitalism and Social Democracy*. Cambridge, UK: Cambridge University Press.

Ringmar, Erik. 1996. *Identity, Interests, and Action*. Cambridge, UK: Cambridge University Press.

Ruggie, John Gerard. 1983. "International Regimes, Transactions, and Change: Embedded Liberalism in the Postwar Economic Order." In *International Regimes*, ed. Stephen Krasner, 195–231. Ithaca: Cornell University Press.

———. 1993. "Territoriality and Beyond." *International Organization* 47: 139–174.

Schulte Nordholt, Jan Willem. 1995. *The Myth of the West*. Grand Rapids, MI: Eerdmans.

Shotter, John. 1993. *Cultural Politics of Everyday Life*. Toronto: University of Toronto Press.

Smith, Anthony. 1986. *The Ethnic Origins of Nations*. Oxford: Oxford University Press.

Snyder, Jack. 1991. *Myths of Empire*. Ithaca: Cornell University Press.

Snyder, Jack, and Karen Ballentine. 1996. "Nationalism and the Marketplace of Ideas." *International Security* 21: 5–40.

Spengler, Oswald. 1926. *The Decline of the West, Vol. 1: Form and Actuality*, trans. Charles Francis Atkinson. New York: Knopf.

———. 1928. *The Decline of the West, Vol. 2: Perspectives of World-History*, trans. Charles Francis Atkinson. New York: Knopf.

Spruyt, Hendrik. 1994. *The Sovereign State and its Competitors*. Princeton: Princeton University Press.

Thomson, Janice. 1994. *Mercenaries, Pirates, and Sovereigns*. Princeton: Princeton University Press.

Tilly, Charles. 1997. "Means and Ends of Comparison in Macrosociology." *Comparative Social Research* 16: 43–53.

U. S. Congress, House of Representatives, Committee on Foreign Affairs. 1947. *Hearings, Emergency Foreign Aid*.

Wæver, Ole. 1996. "The Rise and Fall of the Inter-paradigm Debate." In *International Theory: Positivism and Beyond*, ed. Steve Smith, Ken Booth, and Marysia Zalewski, 149–185. Cambridge, UK: Cambridge University Press.

Weber, Max. 1978. *Economy and Society*, ed. Guenther Roth and Claus Wittich. Berkeley: University of California Press.

———. [1930] 1992. *The Protestant Ethic and the Spirit of Capitalism*, trans. Talcott Parsons. London: Routledge.

Wendt, Alexander. 1987. "The Agent-Structure Problem in International Relations Theory." *International Organization* 41: 335–370

———. 1992. "Anarchy Is What States Make of It." *International Organization* 46: 391–425.

———. 1999. *Social Theory of International Politics*. Cambridge, UK: Cambridge University Press.

Winch, Peter. 1990. *The Idea of a Social Science*, 2nd ed. London: Routledge.

Wittgenstein, Ludwig. 1953. *Philosophical Investigations*, trans. G. E. M. Anscombe. Oxford: Blackwell.

Index